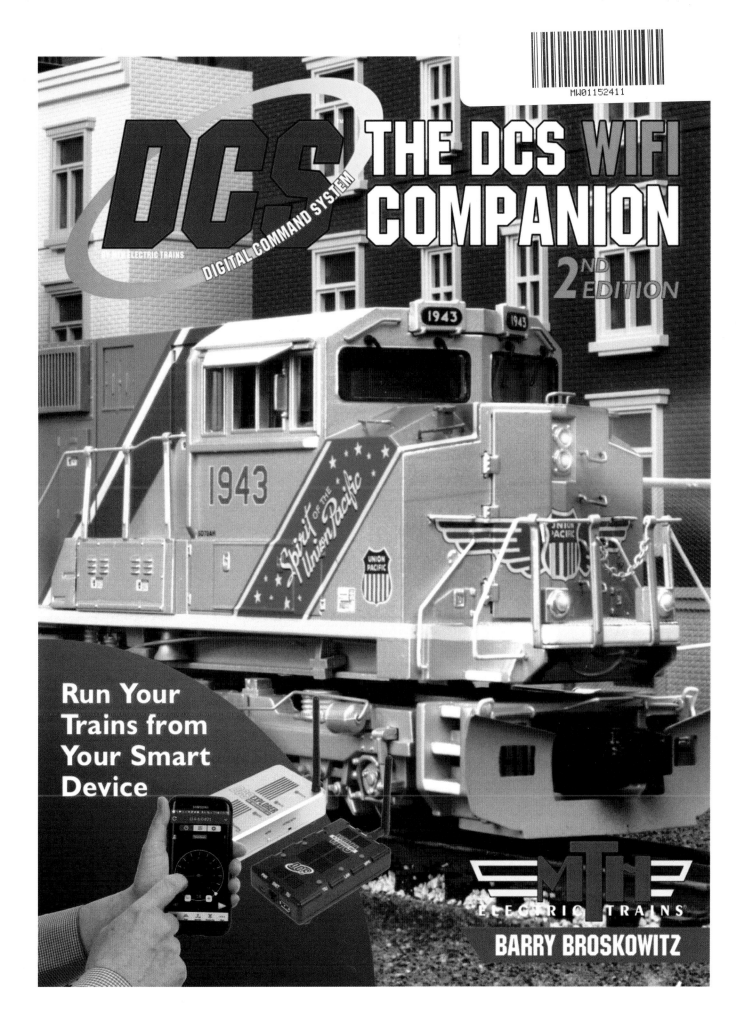

DCS
BY MTH ELECTRIC TRAINS
DIGITAL COMMAND SYSTEM

THE DCS WIFI COMPANION

2ND EDITION

Run Your Trains from Your Smart Device

MTH ELECTRIC TRAINS

BARRY BROSKOWITZ

The DCS WIFI Companion

**Published by
M.T.H. Electric Trains
7020 Columbia Gateway Drive
Columbia, MD 21046
mthtrains.com**

Acknowledgements

This book benefited from the efforts of several individuals who contributed to make it a better book than I ever could have by myself. I would like to thank those whose efforts made a real difference.

Jim Barrett provided constant moral support during the entire process and provided special assistance in a time of personal need.

Jason Wenzel has, from the very beginning of my endeavours to intelligently explain the inner workings of DCS, been my go-to guy for information regarding how DCS works, "under the hood."

Andy Edleman put up with my continuous nagging and provided much-needed insight into MTH's product road map.

Jessica Zwirble took my thoughts and ideas, and put them into a format that presented them both clearly and with style.

Marty Fitzhenry and Jim Osborne ensured that the book's content was technically sound and made suggestions that provided additional technical detail.

My daughter Stacey MacMillan taught her father how to improve upon his writing skills by painstakingly proofing the book and providing numerous improvements to its readability.

My son Allan Broskowitz was the first person to suggest to me that someone should develop a WiFi application to operate DCS trains from a smart device, and that I should write a book about it.

My grandkids Libby, Ella and Olivia, provided input from the next generation of potential model railroading enthusiasts.

The MTH R&D department designed and developed the DCS Application that brought DCS enthusiasts a whole new way to operate their model railroads.

The O Gauge Railroading Forum whose members, singly and collectively, provided a basis for discussion of a wide variety of DCS topics.

Last and most certainly not least, my wife Cora provided encouragement and support for me and this project in more ways than can ever be put down on paper.

Thank you all for helping this odyssey come to a successful completion!

Foreword - How To Use This Book

Thank you purchasing the DCS WiFi Companion. This book is not a discussion of DCS using the DCS Remote. Instead, it is an alternative to The DCS Companion 3rd Edition and discusses, in equivalent detail, using the WiFi-based DCS Application, rather than the DCS Remote.

If you're interested in learning how to operate DCS using the DCS Remote, you can do so by reading the DCS User Guide or, even better, the DCS Companion 3rd Edition.

The subject of this book is the implementation of WiFi operation of DCS that allows all of the many features and functions of DCS to be utilized via an iOS or Android smartphone or tablet that has WiFi capability. Specifically, the book discusses, in detail:

- Introduction to command control for model trains
- Implementation of DCS on a new or existing layout
- Installation of MTH's WiFi Interface Unit (WIU)
- Installation of MTH's DCS Application on Apple iOS, or Android devices
- Upgrading the DCS Application from the free version to the Standard or Premium versions
- Operation of all of the DCS Application's (Premium version) features and functions
- Troubleshooting issues on DCS layouts
- Upgrading the firmware in the WIU and other DCS components
- Discussion of the installation, operation and firmware upgrading of the DCS Explorer.

This book does not presume any existing knowledge of DCS.

Each section of the book builds on previous sections so that when a new topic is introduced, the foundation on which it stands has already been built. This allows the book to be used as a learning tool that guides you through all of the aspects of obtaining, installing, upgrading, and operating the DCS Application, starting with the most basic and easiest to grasp topics, all the way through the use of the app's most complex and sophisticated features.

It's also important to note that the PDF eBook version of The DCS WiFi Companion is a fully searchable document. Any word or phrase may be quickly located in the document by using the search feature of Adobe's Acrobat Reader. Acrobat Reader is included with many PCs, and is also a free download from Adobe's website. There's also a version for iOS and Android smart phones and tablets.

The flow of the book, combined with the easy access to specific topics, allows the book to serve as both a tutorial for learning about DCS' WiFi capability and also as reference text for more experienced DCS operators.

It would be best to read the entire book at least once to gain an understanding of what's covered. Then, depending upon the individual topic, various sections of the book should be read again, perhaps with closer attention to detail, to apply the information herein according to specific needs.

I hope you find this book to be a welcome addition to your DCS layout, and that you enjoy reading it as much as I enjoyed writing it!

Table of Contents

Table of Figures

Part I - Introduction to DCS

1. What is Command Control?

Conventional vs. Command Control

DCS is a command control system for your O gauge trains. Command control systems control O gauge trains differently from the way trains were controlled before command control was invented. Prior to the advent of command control, O gauge engines were controlled by increasing or decreasing track voltage to make the engine go faster or slower. Pressing the horn/whistle or bell buttons on the transformer caused a DC pulse to be inserted into the AC voltage to sound the horn or whistle, or ring the bell. Operating O gauge trains in this manner is generally referred to today as conventional control.

Conventional control of O gauge trains was simple and straightforward. All that was necessary to do was to connect two wires from the tracks to a transformer and then plug the transformer into an AC wall outlet. Turning up the transformer throttle increased the voltage to the tracks and made the trains go faster. Turning down the throttle decreased the voltage and slowed the trains down. Pressing a direction button caused the engine to cycle through forward, neutral, reverse, neutral, and back to forward.

In effect, the transformer did not really control the trains, rather, the tracks themselves were controlled. The trains simply reacted to changes in the track voltage. This made it extremely difficult to control two or more trains running on the same track. Every time the direction button on the transformer was pressed, all the trains on the track went into neutral or changed direction. Every time the horn/whistle or bell button was pressed, all the trains on the track would sound their horns or whistles or ring their bells. Operators went to great lengths to construct elaborate relay-controlled track block systems, using multiple transformer outputs, to build large layouts where multiple trains could be controlled somewhat independently. When command control was introduced to O gauge railroading, that all changed forever.

Command control looks at controlling engines in a very different way. Command control engines each have a small computer board inside them that can receive commands for that engine only. This allows the layout operator to issue commands from a handheld remote control that cause one particular engine to respond. All other engines receive the command, determine that it's not intended for them, and ignore it. Only the engine for which the command is intended will actually perform the command.

Command control systems always have voltage flowing through the tracks, however, command control engines don't react to voltage changes. Rather, track voltage is used only to power engines. Engines execute the commands that they receive from the remote control. For the first time, it is possible to actually control the trains themselves.

At the present time, several command control systems are available for O and other gauge train operators from several model train manufacturers. In this book, we will discuss in considerable detail what is arguably the most powerful and feature-rich of the command control systems available for O gauge trains - MTH's Digital Command System, DCS.

The DCS Command Control System

DCS is different from other command control systems. Other systems provide one-way communication from the remote control to the engines where engines cannot communicate back to the remote control. DCS, however, provides two-way communication that allows engines to talk back to the remote control. This allows DCS to provide a number of functions and features that are unavailable in any other command control system. There are three areas where DCS utilizes 2-way communication.

The first is to provide confirmation and feedback from engines that commands were received.

The second is to allow information regarding the status of the engine to be displayed on the remote control. This includes:

- Displaying the total time that the engine has been operated.
- Displaying the scale miles that the engine has been driven to date.
- Displaying the scale miles that the engine has driven over a distance. This allows measuring of scale miles of track on a layout.
- Displaying the status of the battery in the engine.
- Feedback and confirmation when programming an engine's special features.
- Displaying the engine name and allowing use of custom engine names.
- Displaying DCS signal strength over a section of track.
- Displaying track voltage.
- Allowing engines to have software updates to incorporate new or different sound effects.

The third is the ability to have 2-way communication between engines and operating cars through the rails. The first example of this is MTH's Coors Silver Bullet train, where the engine commands the cars to open doors, turn on strobe lights and release "dry ice" vapour.

DCS allows control of virtually any O gauge engine ever made. MTH's Protosound 2 (PS2) and Protosound 3 (PS3) engines are controlled by DCS in command mode. Lionel's Trainmaster command Control (TMCC) and Legacy engines (with the addition of a Lionel TMCC or Legacy command base, other Lionel cables and devices if required, and an MTH cable) are controlled in their respective TMCC or Legacy command mode, and all other engines are controlled in conventional mode. These other engines would include all other MTH engines, Lionel current production and postwar engines, and O gauge engines from other manufacturers. In addition to controlling engines, DCS can also control switch tracks and accessories from just about any O gauge train manufacturer.

Although there are some differences between MTH's PS2 and PS3 engines, they may all be referred to collectively as DCS engines, and may be operated in exactly the same way under DCS.

Differences Between PS2 and PS3 Engines

Although all PS2 and PS3 engines are DCS engines and can be operated on a mix-and-match basis with each other under DCS (or even conventionally), the two types of engines are different in several ways.

PS2 engines were first available from MTH starting in the year 2000, and PS3 engines were an evolution of the PS2 design that followed several years later. As a result of that evolution, there are several important differences between PS2 and PS3 engines.

PS3 engines contain a PS3 board, rather than a PS2 board. This technologically more advanced board, in addition to being smaller and requiring less power than a PS2 board, provides a number of differences between PS2 and PS3 engines:

- The most important difference between PS2 and PS3 engines is the type of computer chip used as a Digital Signal Processor (DSP). The DSP is the sender and receiver of DCS data packet commands, and the nature of the computer chip that is used to send and receive these commands has a direct effect on DCS signal strength. PS2 engines use an Application Specific Integrated Circuit (ASIC) chip, while PS3 engines use a much faster Field Programmable Gate Array (FPGA) chip. The nature of the FPGA allows PS3 engines to, "listen better", for DCS commands, allowing for much improved DCS signal strength.
- One feature of the PS3 board is that in addition to PS3 engines being capable of operating under DCS or conventionally, just as are MTH's PS2 engines, they also contain an on-board Digital Command Control (DCC) receiver that allows them to be controlled by DCC, a very popular command control system. This capability allows a DCC operator to purchase a PS3 engine for initially on a DCC layout and then add DCS capability at a later date.

- Under DCC, PS3 engines have the ability to execute 29 (0-28) different DCS functions from a DCC controller's function keys. Although at present there are few, if any, DCC controllers available that actually have 29 different function keys, when such controllers become available MTH PS3 engines will immediately be able to utilize the additional function keys. For a detailed explanation of how to operate a PS3 engine under DCC, or conventional, control, refer to the instruction manual that accompanied the particular PS3 engine.

- Another feature of the PS3 board is that PS3 engines do not require a battery for operation, regardless of whether they are being operated under DCS or DCC, or conventionally. Where PS2 engines are dependent upon a battery to retain changed settings on the PS2 board, including their actual DCS ID#, PS3 engines are not. They use a "super capacitor" type of device instead of a battery. This eliminates many of the most common problems encountered by DCS operators that are caused by a weak or dead battery within a PS2 engine.

- Newer O gauge PS2 engines are available with a 2 rail/3 rail switch, accessible from the outside of the engine, that allows the DCS operator to select whether the PS2 engine is to be run on 2 rail or 3 rail track. However, when operating such a PS2 engine on 2-rail track, the DCS operator must ensure that the engine is properly oriented, such that it knows which of the two rails carries the DCS commands from the TIU, DCS Remote Commander or DCS Commander, and which rail carries the acknowledgement signal back from the PS2 engine. PS3 engines, however, are able to sense which rail carries the DCS signal and which rail carries the acknowledgement from the engine, and can automatically adjust the engine's electronics for proper DCS operation.

- Revised firmware allows newer PS3 engines to be started up in DCS mode by simply rolling the thumbwheel up 1 click to 1 SMPH or via the Quickset Speed Command. This will also cause the engine to move forward.

- Revised firmware allows newer PS3 engines, manufactured starting in 2014, to have the capability to be reset to factory default settings through a combination of button presses using the DCS Remote Commander (SND, DIR, -). The engine will issue a double horn/whistle sound and start up under DCS.

- Revised firmware allows newer PS3 engines, while operating in conventional mode, to turn marker lights on and off with one Whistle button press, followed by one Bell button press.

- PS3 steam engines adhere to prototypical Rule 17 lighting, while PS2 steam engines do not. This means that when a PS3 steam engine is in neutral or its direction is reversed, the engine's rear headlight, if present, will illuminate. However, instead of the front headlight turning off, it will, instead, become dim as per Rule 17.

- All PS2 engines with ditch lights have the capability to flash their ditch lights whenever the engine is moving forward or sitting still and ready to move forward, and the engine's horn is activated by pressing the W/H key on the DCS Remote, DCS Remote Commander handheld control, or the DCS Commander. PS3 engines, however, must be moving in order to flash the ditch lights when the horn is sounded. Further, a PS3 engine may have functional rear ditch lights, as well as front ditch lights.

- A PS2 engine with an interior light will, when that light is turned on, have that light on all of the time. A PS3 engine's interior light is only on when the engine is stopped.

- If a PS2 engine's direction is reversed while the engine is moving and the thumbwheel (or the Quickset Speed function) is then used to increase the engine's speed from zero, the PS2 engine will slow to match the set speed and continue in the same direction. However, if the same operations are performed with a PS3 engine, the engine will, instead, slow to a halt, reverse direction, and speed up to match the set speed.

DCS Hardware Components

Although DCS currently has seven different hardware components, for the purposes of this book only five of these components will be discussed. The first three DCS components are:

- The DCS Remote which allows the operator to send commands to engines, switch tracks and accessories.
- The Track Interface Unit (TIU) which relays commands received from the DCS Remote to DCS, Legacy and TMCC engines, and to switch tracks and accessories.
- The Accessory Interface Unit (AIU) that connects switch tracks and accessories to DCS.

The next two DCS components, the WiFi Interface Unit (WIU) and the DCS Explorer, are discussed in detail later in this book.

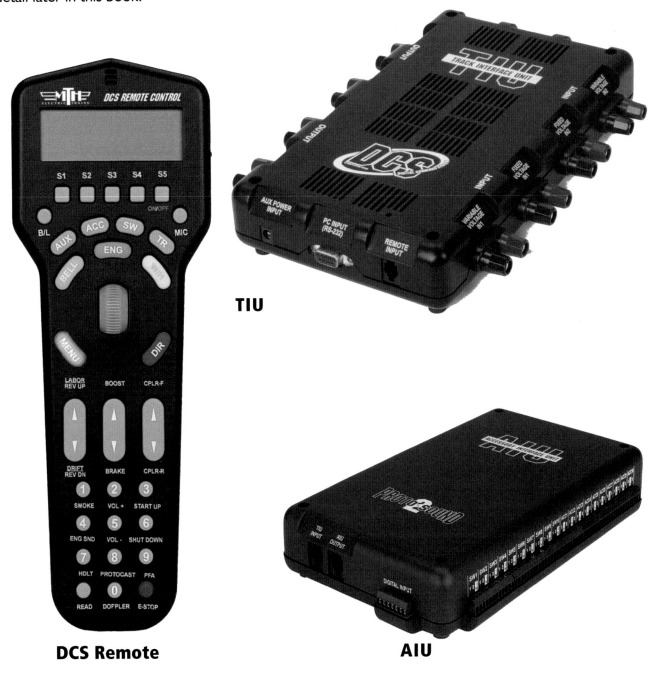

TIU

DCS Remote

AIU

Figure 1 - DCS Components

The DCS Remote has an LCD screen that provides a variety of information depending upon which DCS function or feature is being used at the time. Keypad buttons allow input of the various DCS commands and access to the DCS Menus. At the base of the DCS Remote is a port that allows the DCS Remote to be directly connected to a TIU (tethered) when necessary. The back of the DCS Remote has the battery compartment containing four AAA batteries. Either rechargeable or alkaline batteries may be used. The items displayed on the LCD screen and the keypad button functions are discussed later in this book. As many as 16 DCS Remotes may be used on a single layout. Each DCS Remote should be uniquely numbered, 0 through 15. Numbering remotes reduces the chances of communications errors since each remote ignores command responses sent to other remotes with different numbers.

Up to 5 TIUs may be used on any layout and must each be numbered uniquely from 1 through 5. Each TIU has a red LED that serves two purposes. First, it is a power-on indicator for the TIU. Second, when the TIU is first powered-on, the LED will blink one or more times to indicate the TIU's ID number. One blink is for ID number 1, 2 for ID number 2 and up to 5 for ID number 5. The TIU contains a number of input/output ports:

- Fixed Channels Input: these two ports connect the TIU's Fixed Channels to transformer power sources.
- Fixed Channels Output: these two ports connect the TIU's Fixed Channels to layout tracks.
- Variable Channels Input: these two ports connect the TIU's Variable Channels to transformer power sources.
- Variable Channels Output: these two ports connect the TIU's Variable Channels to layout tracks.
- ProtoCast: this port allows a sound source to be connected to the TIU so that music may be played through the speaker in DCS engines.
- ProtoDispatch: this port allows a microphone to be connected to the TIU so that the operator may speak through the speaker in DCS engines.
- AIU Input: allows connection of up to five AIUs to each TIU.
- Remote Input: allows the DCS Remote to be directly connected (tethered) to the TIU.
- Aux. Power: allows connection of a separate power source to power only the TIU. If a separate power source is not connected to this port, transformer power from Fixed Channel #1 Input is used to power the TIU. Any power supply that provides between 12 and 22 volts AC at 1.5 amps or greater, equipped with a compatible barrel plug, may be used.
- Serial Port: this port is used to connect the TIU to a personal computer for purposes of upgrading the DCS Remote, TIU or DCS engine firmware, or to connect to a Lionel command base to allow operation of TMCC or Legacy engines from the DCS Remote.

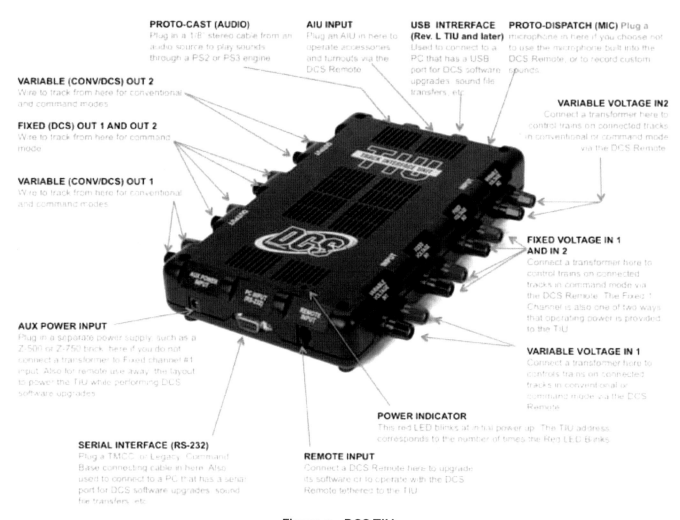

PROTO-CAST (AUDIO)
Plug in a 1/8" stereo cable from an audio source to play sounds through a PS2 or PS3 engine

AIU INPUT
Plug an AIU in here to operate accessories and turnouts via the DCS Remote

USB INTRERFACE (Rev. L TIU and later)
Used to connect to a PC that has a USB port for DCS software upgrades, sound file transfers, etc.

PROTO-DISPATCH (MIC) Plug a microphone in here if you choose not to use the microphone built into the DCS Remote, or to record custom sounds

VARIABLE (CONV/DCS) OUT 2
Wire to track from here for conventional and command modes

FIXED (DCS) OUT 1 AND OUT 2
Wire to track from here for command mode

VARIABLE (CONV/DCS) OUT 1
Wire to track from here for conventional and command modes

VARIABLE VOLTAGE IN2
Connect a transformer here to control trains on connected tracks in conventional or command mode via the DCS Remote

FIXED VOLTAGE IN 1 AND IN 2
Connect a transformer here to control trains on connected tracks in command mode via the DCS Remote. The Fixed 1 Channel is also one of two ways that operating power is provided to the TIU

AUX POWER INPUT
Plug in a separate power supply, such as a Z-500 or Z-750 brick, here if you do not connect a transformer to Fixed channel #1 input. Also for remote use away, the layout to power the TIU while performing DCS software upgrades

VARIABLE VOLTAGE IN 1
Connect a transformer here to controls trains on connected tracks in conventional or command mode via the DCS Remote

POWER INDICATOR
This red LED blinks at initial power up. The TIU address corresponds to the number of times the Red LED Blinks

SERIAL INTERFACE (RS-232)
Plug a TMCC or Legacy Command Base connecting cable in here. Also used to connect to a PC that has a serial port for DCS software upgrades, sound file transfers, etc.

REMOTE INPUT
Connect a DCS Remote here to upgrade its software or to operate with the DCS Remote tethered to the TIU

Figure 2 - DCS TIU

Each AIU allows connection of up to 10 switch tracks and 10 accessories for control via the DCS Remote and as many as 5 AIUs may be connected to each TIU. With up to 5 TIUs on a layout, as many as 250 switch tracks and 250 accessories may be controlled by DCS. Each AIU consists of 20 relays that are actuated by the TIU, based on switch track and accessory commands issued by the DCS Remote. The AIU contains two input/output ports:

- TIU Input: this port is used to connect the AIU to the TIU.
- AIU Output: this port is used to connect the AIU to other AIUs that are all connected to the same TIU.

It is important to note that if the incorrect port is used when AIUs are connected to TIUs, serious damage to the AIU may result.

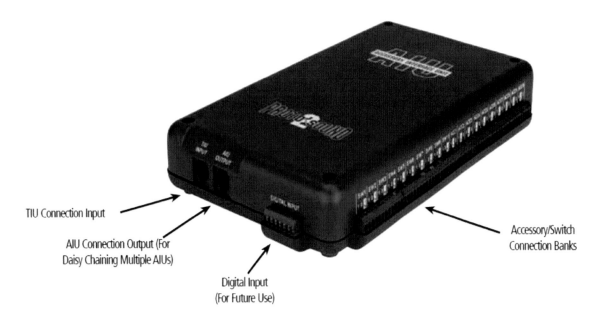

TIU Connection Input

AIU Connection Output (For
Daisy Chaining Multiple AIUs)

Digital Input
(For Future Use)

Accessory/Switch
Connection Banks

Figure 3 - DCS AIU

DCS Information Resources

There are several excellent sources of information regarding DCS available for DCS operators and those interested in learning more about the system. The author has found the following resources to be extremely informative.

DCS Users Guide

This is the manual that is included with each set of DCS Remote and TIU. It is intended to get the new DCS user up and running quickly and provides all the basic information regarding the DCS Remote and TIU, and the various control screens and DCS menu system. The function of each key on the DCS Remote's keypad and the use of each port on the TIU is described. The latest copy of the DCS Users Guide is always available for download from MTH's Protosound 2 website, www.protosound2.com.

MTH's Websites

MTH maintains several websites that will benefit the DCS operator. The MTH Electric Trains website, www.mthtrains.com, provides a great many resources, including a product locator that allows access to information about all MTH engines and other products, sound files and chain files for DCS engines, warranty information, basic troubleshooting, product descriptions, shipping schedules, downloadable catalogs, product documentation (instruction manuals and parts lists), dealer locator, and a wealth of other technical information. Additionally, the website provides access to the MTH Railroader Club (MTHRRC).

The Protosound 2.0 Official Website, www.protosound2.com, contains a wide selection of information that includes the most recent version of the DCS Users Guide, a number of DCS technical articles, DCS patent information, an explanation of DCS engine features and functions, the latest versions of the DCS Loader program and associated DCS component software files, DCS demonstration videos, DCS engine upgrade manuals (diesel/electric and steam), and much more.

O Gauge Railroading (OGR) DCS Video

The OGR DCS Video is available for purchase from either the OGR or MTH websites in either DVD or VHS format. It presents DCS setup and operation in an easy to understand format that can be paused and re-watched at the viewer's own pace. The video contains many examples and "how to do it" information that can make setting up DCS an easy to do, enjoyable experience.

O Gauge Railroading Internet Forum

The OGR Forum (http://ogrforum.ogaugerr.com/forums) is an outstanding source of information about all aspects of the O gauge model railroading hobby. Additionally, it has a specific MTH DCS and PS2/PS3 forum that is dedicated to PS2/PS3 engine and DCS discussions. It's a great way to exchange ideas and opinions with other DCS operators and enthusiasts, and to get answers to questions and assistance when encountering problems.

Part II - DCS Is An Operating System for Your Trains!

1. What is an Operating System and Why Do I Want One?

By definition, an operating system for a computer is, "the essential program in a computer that maintains disk files, runs applications, and handles devices such as the keyboard, mouse, monitor, and printer." Every modern computer uses an operating system as a framework within which commands are executed and work is done.

In the past, model train layouts were operated without the benefit of any such framework. There were no files, applications or hardware devices that needed to be managed. One simply put electricity to the tracks to make engines move forward or to reverse. Although the argument can be made that this conventional control of O gauge trains was easy to set up and simple to operate, it was also very difficult to run multiple trains on a single track and very limiting in terms of how prototypically the trains could be run. Sound effects were limited, operation at slow speed was extremely difficult, and the trains lacked the ability to perform more complicated tasks.

Command control provided the solution to these problems and DCS takes command control to a new level. In much the same way that a computer has an operating system, DCS is an operating system for train layouts that maintains files (lists of engines, accessories, switch tracks, and other things), runs engines, and handles devices such as AIUs, accessories, and switch tracks.

Advantages of an Operating System for Trains

Having an operating system for your trains allows prototypical, realistic operation, including: programming of complicated operating scenarios involving engines, accessories, and switch tracks; combinations of sound effects; and slow speed engine operation as low as 2 scale miles per hour (SMPH). Under an operating system such as DCS, rules of operation are well-defined, which makes adding new engines, accessories, and switch tracks completely standardized.

Since an operating system defines a standard way that commands are given to and received by various components of the layout (engines, accessories, switch tracks, and others), it makes managing and operating any size layout easier and more fun.

DCS is an Upgradeable Operating System

In the personal computer world, operating systems are improved regularly through software upgrades. Typically, new features and functions are added when the manufacturer of the operating system releases software upgrade packages that are then installed by the personal computer user.

Prior to the introduction of DCS, such software upgrades were impossible for O gauge model railroading command control systems. These systems were hardware-based, meaning that the only way that new system features or functions could be added was by the operator purchasing improved or additional system components. This could be very expensive.

On the other hand, DCS is software-based rather than hardware-based. This allows the DCS operator to take advantage of new DCS features and functions by downloading from MTH's website at no charge, system upgrades in the form of software update files. These files can then be used to update features and functions in the DCS Remote, TIU and WIU. Once these components are updated with the new software, they immediately have all the new features and functions. It's not necessary to buy new devices to incorporate new DCS features and functions into an existing DCS-based layout. At the present time, MTH has provided DCS operators with 10 DCS system upgrades at no charge.

Additionally, DCS engines can also be upgraded to incorporate new features or functions, or to change the engine's sound effects, by downloading new software files from MTH's website, also at no charge. In many cases, an older model of a DCS engine can be updated to include the sound effects found in the newest models of the same engine.

Every DCS layout can always be upgraded to include the newest DCS system features, functions and improvements.

2. How DCS and DCS Engines Communicate

As previously discussed, DCS commands are issued by the DCS Application to the TIU, and are then sent from the TIU to DCS engines. The engines acknowledge receipt of the command by sending a message back to the TIU and the TIU forwards the acknowledgement back to the DCS Application. The following discussion further explains this two-way communication process in more detail.

DCS Engine/TIU Association

Every DCS engine that is entered into a DCS Application is associated with one and only one TIU. The association takes place at the time the engine was last added to a DCS Application, and the associated TIU is the one that is connected to the track where the engine was when it was added. If an engine is added to more than one DCS Application, the association is based on the last time the engine was added. Under normal DCS operation, only the TIU that is associated with a DCS engine will actually send commands to that engine as described below. The only exception is when DCS is being operated in Super mode, which is discussed later in this book.

Data Packet Communication Process

Communication of information between the DCS Application and the TIU, and between the TIU and DCS engines, is accomplished using data packets. These data packets are digital packages of information that contain two items, an address and data.

When one or more data packets are sent from the DCS Application to the TIU, they contain the address of the TIU for which the packets are intended. Only the TIU that is addressed in a packet will actually process the packet. All other TIUs will ignore packets that are addressed to other TIUs. Each packet also contains a data item that has the DCS ID number of the engine for which the command is intended, as well as an actual command itself.

When the TIU receives the data packet it determines which DCS engine is supposed to execute the command based on the DCS engine DCS ID number in the data portion of the packet. The TIU then reconstructs the packet so that it is addressed to the DCS engine and sends the reconstructed packet to the DCS engine through the center rail.

When one or more data packets are sent from the TIU to a DCS engine, they contain the address of the DCS engine for which the packets are intended. Only the DCS engine that is addressed in a packet will actually process the packet. All other DCS engines will ignore packets that are addressed to other DCS engines. When the DCS engine receives the command packet, it acknowledges receipt of the packet by creating a new packet addressed back to the TIU. This packet contains a data portion that is an acknowledgement that the command was received. This packet is transmitted back to the TIU using the outside rails. The DCS engine then executes the command.

When the TIU receives the data packet back from the DCS engine, it re-addresses the data packet to the DCS Application that originally issued the DCS engine command, and wirelessly sends the reconstructed packet back to the DCS Application.

The DCS Application receives the acknowledgement packet and considers the process of sending the command to the DCS engine to be completed. Depending upon the command, an indication will be displayed on the DCS Application's Screen to indicate to the operator that the command has been successfully executed.

The Watchdog Signal

When a DCS engine is initially powered up, it needs to know whether to come up in DCS stealth mode (dark and silent, waiting for a Start Up command) or in conventional mode, in neutral. The watchdog signal is DCS' way to tell a DCS engine that it should switch into DCS mode rather than conventional mode when it powers up.

The TIU sends out a watchdog signal on a TIU channel whenever the output of that TIU channel changes from zero to any higher voltage. This signal only lasts for a brief period of time (the lesser of 44 seconds or until a DCS command is issued in DCS 5.0 and later releases), however, this is generally long enough for a DCS engine's electronics to recognize the watchdog signal and cause the engine to come up in DCS stealth mode, dark and silent.

There are, however, times when the engine will come up in conventional mode in neutral with sounds and lights. This occurs because transformer power is increased too slowly and the watchdog signal is gone before the engine's electronics are powered up enough to sense it. When this happens, the engine will come up in conventional mode. There are a couple of reasons why this may occur.

One reason is that the transformer handle is raised too slowly and the DCS engine's electronics are not sufficiently powered up enough that they can sense the watchdog signal. By the time the DCS engine's electronics have sufficient voltage to sense the watchdog signal (approximately 10 volts), the watchdog signal has already come and gone. The solution is to simply raise the transformer handle more rapidly.

A second reason is if track voltage is being raised using the DCS Application's Track Control Screen rather than a transformer handle. This would be the case when track power is controlled using a Variable Channel, as described in section Track Control Screen later in this book. In this case, it's sometimes difficult to scroll the DCS Application's slider from 0 volts to 10 volts in the short time that the watchdog signal is present. The solution in this case is to set the starting voltage for the Variable Channel to 10 volts or higher so that the first increment of the slider provides a high enough voltage for the DCS engine's electronics to sense the watchdog signal before it's gone.

If a DCS engine misses the watchdog signal, it can be forced into DCS mode by pressing either Start Up or Shut Down while the engine is displayed in the DCS Application's Engine Control Screen. If Start Up is selected, the engine will come up in DCS mode ready for operation, making sounds and displaying lights. If Shut Down is selected, the engine will become dark and silent in DCS stealth mode, waiting for a future Start Up command.

Part III - DCS Implementation

In the following section, we'll discuss all the things to consider when implementing DCS for the first time. We'll look at this from two perspectives. One is planning a new layout with DCS, and the other is adding DCS to an existing layout.

1. Planning For a New DCS Layout

When building a new layout that will incorporate DCS, planning for DCS before layout construction begins can make DCS operation on the completed layout more effective and enjoyable. This section looks at several key aspects of layout construction from a DCS point of view:

- TIU channel usage
- Wiring considerations
- TIU channel assignment and placement
- AIU connection and placement
- Transformer considerations

This section is not intended to discuss track planning, physical benchwork construction, scenery, or anything else unrelated to actual DCS operation. Those topics, while very important, are completely outside of the scope of this book.

TIU Channel Usage

Every TIU has four channels for control and operation of engines. Two of these channels are designated as Fixed Channels. Whatever voltage is applied to the TIU's input of each Fixed Channel is always present at the output of that Fixed Channel. These channels are ideal for operation of command control engines, such as MTH's DCS engines or Lionel's TMCC engines, because command control engines operate based upon commands sent to individual engines rather than changes in track voltage. Command control operation is based on the premise that there is always voltage sufficient to operate command control engines (typically 18 volts) present in the tracks.

The other two channels on every TIU are Variable Channels. Variable Channels allow the voltage input to the channel to be regulated such that the voltage present at the output of each Variable Channel may be different from the voltage present at the TIU's input for that Variable Channel. These channels are ideal for control of conventional, non-command control engines because conventional engines operate based upon changes in voltage in the tracks. Lower track voltage causes conventional engines to run slower while higher track voltage causes conventional engines to run faster, and interrupting the voltage to the track activates the reversing unit in conventional engines. Variable channels may not be used with DC voltage and are therefore unsuitable for use with MTH PS3 HO engines that require DC voltage.

While tracks connected to Variable Channels can be used to run either command control or conventional engines, tracks connected to Fixed Channels are really only suitable for operation of command control engines.

Although Variable Channels can be made to operate as Fixed Channels, Fixed Channels cannot be made to operate as Variable Channels. When planning a new DCS-based layout, it's a good idea to have a plan regarding which loops of mainline and which sidings will operate command control engines, which will operate conventional engines and which, if any, may operate both at one time or another. Once a determination is made regarding which layout loops or sidings will be dedicated to command control engines, conventional engines or both, the operator can begin to determine how to assign TIU channels to the various sections of the layout.

Wiring Considerations

An often asked question in regards to DCS is, "How many feet of track will one TIU support?" The answer is a definite, "That depends." In order to properly answer this question, it's important to first understand DCS signal strength.

DCS Signal Strength

DCS signal strength is a number, from 1-10, that's calculated based on the number of data packets that the TIU sends and receives back from a DCS engine that's performing a DCS signal strength test.

During the test, the TIU sends a continuous series of data packets to the DCS engine. The DCS engine is expected to reply to every packet that it receives, however, some packets are either not received by the engine or the response is not received by the TIU. Regardless, the TIU calculates DCS signal strength by counting how many response packets the TIU receives from the DCS engine out of each hundred data packets the TIU sent, and then looks at a sliding scale to determine the signal strength that should be reported. The scale is not linear, rather, it is such that 87-100 packets equates to a DCS signal strength of 10, 80-86 equates to a 9, and so on.

When using a DCS engine to measure the DCS signal strength on a particular section of track, the engine will report some value from 1 to 10. If DCS signal strength is exceptionally low, an error message may be displayed instead of a value. A value between 8 and 10 is generally described as strong, between 6 and 7 is generally described as adequate, and from 1 to 5 is described as low. While many operators strive for a consistent DCS signal strength of 10, it's a proven fact that nearly all DCS commands will operate just fine when DCS signal strength is 7 or higher.

The DCS signal becomes weaker if it is either split too many times or if it is spread over too many linear feet of track. It is also subject to degradation if the wire that carries the DCS signal and transformer voltage is of insufficient quality or size, or if the recommended wiring method, described below, is not used. It quickly becomes obvious that the DCS signal strength will vary based upon several major factors:

- The number of times the signal from a single TIU channel is split to feed track blocks and sidings
- The total number of feet of track upon which the DCS signal from a single TIU channel is spread
- The size and quality of the wire used between the TIU and the tracks
- The wiring scheme used, e.g., buss wiring vs. home run or star type wiring (more on that a little later)
- The conductivity of the tracks themselves

In general, the highest DCS signal strength will be obtained by adhering to the following guidelines as closely as possible:

- Attempt to limit the number of track blocks or sidings from a single TIU channel to no more than 12-15. If using a Rev. L or later TIU, that may be increased to 20-24.
- Limit track blocks to no more than 11 or 12 track sections where sections, long or short, all count. If sections are all short, consider soldering connections between sections to make longer ones. Regardless, track blocks should not exceed 100 feet in length.
- Use 16 gauge or higher stranded wire from the TIU to the tracks. Generally, 16 gauge stranded wire is sufficient for any wire run that is 30 feet or less and is often good for longer distances. Above 50 feet, 14' gauge stranded wire is recommended.
- Use only high-quality, paired wire.
- Use home run or star-type wiring.
- Ensure that track segments are tightly connected, and that the rails are clean and free of rust.

Practical experience has shown that stranded wire applications tend to perform better than solid core ones. Although this is not necessarily scientific, if one were to compare the surface area of stranded and solid wire of the same gauge the stranded wire would have a slightly greater overall surface area due to the "bumps" in the outer surface of the wire stands. This could provide a marginally greater surface area for carrying the DCS signal. Regardless, stranded wire is much easier with which to work, having greater flexibility than a solid wire of the same gauge.

If all of the above guidelines are closely followed, a single Rev. L or later TIU can provide sufficient DCS signal strength for as much as 3,000 feet of track, depending upon a number of factors. These include the length of wire runs, the gauge of wire used, and the number of times the DCS signal is split through terminal blocks.

Home Run/Star Wiring Methods

While the 2-way communication between the DCS Application and the TIU is done wirelessly, DCS provides 2-way communication between the TIU and DCS engines through the rails. Although DCS has been proven to work very well using a number of different wiring schemes, it works best when there is a clear path for command and acknowledgement between the TIU and DCS engines.

This clear path is best obtained when the wires for the center and outside rails are run as pairs. DCS uses a transmission method known as differential signaling to provide improved data communications through the rails between the TIU and DCS engines. Differential signaling transmits information electrically with two complementary signals sent on two separate wires. In the case of DCS, these wires are the Hot and Common wires between the TIU and the tracks. These two wires provide "mirroring" of data packets which serves to make commands more easily identified by DCS engines.

While DCS engines primarily receive commands through the center rail and respond to, or acknowledge, commands using the outside rails, in both instances the other rails not used provide the mirroring effect of differential signaling. To take best advantage of differential signaling, whenever possible home run or star wiring should be implemented as described below using transformers, TIU channels, and terminal blocks. A terminal block is any device that will one accept of pair of wires as input and then splits that pair into several pairs of wires for output. It's a good idea to use only one terminal block for each TIU channel.

A pair of wires is connected between the output of a transformer and the input to a TIU channel. The wire from the Hot transformer post is connected to the red TIU input terminal, and the wire from the transformer Common post is connected to the associated black TIU input terminal.

It's very important to make these connections correctly. If you're at all unsure about which terminal post on your transformer is Hot and which is Common, consult the instructions that accompanied your transformer or review the Transformer Compatibility information in Appendix D of the DCS Users Guide that is included in DCS kits containing the DCS Remote and TIU. This guide is also available for download from MTH's Protosound 2 website (refer to DCS Information Resources in Part I of this book).

Another pair of wires is connected between a TIU channel output and the input to a terminal block. The wire from the red TIU output post is connected to the input terminal of the terminal block designated as Hot and the wire from the black TIU output post is connected to the input terminal of the terminal block designated as Common.

Pairs of wires are connected from the terminal block to each track block or siding, ensuring that the Hot wire goes to the middle rail and that the Common wire connects to one or both of the outside rails. Either use a track lockon or solder the wires to the rails. Regardless, ensure that connections are tight.

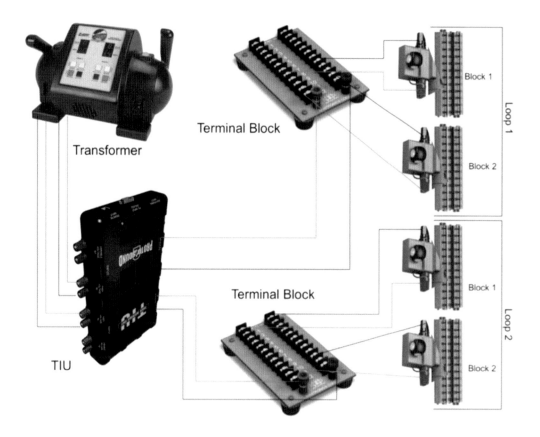

Figure 4 - Star/Home Run Wiring

Length of Wire Runs

As a general rule, it is best to keep the length of wire runs as short as possible after the DCS signal has been split, as when one channel of the TIU is input to a terminal block and the terminal block then is split to feed several track loop and sidings. This is most easily accomplished when terminal blocks are placed in such a way that each one is as equidistant as is practical from each of the track blocks to which it is connected.

It would then follow that TIUs should be placed in such a way that each one is as equidistant as is practical from each of the terminal blocks to which it is connected. This would tend to reduce the length of wire paths, giving first priority to the wires connecting the terminal blocks to the tracks with second priority to the wires connecting the TIUs to the terminal blocks. Last priority would be given to the wires connecting the transformers to the TIUs. This makes sense since the weakest (after the splits) DCS signals would have the shortest path to follow and the paths between the transformers and the TIUs, which have no DCS signal at all, would be the longest.

One caveat, however, is that some blocks may be toggle-switched, causing the wire path to go from a terminal block to a control panel before going on to the tracks. This only goes to point out that wiring schemes will rarely, if ever, be perfect. Wiring trade-offs and compromises are generally part of designing a layout.

Using the Proper Wire Size

As mentioned previously, the vast majority of layouts will perform just fine if 16 gauge, stranded wire is used for wiring from the transformers, through TIUs and terminal blocks, and to the tracks for runs of up to 30 or 40 feet. If a particular wire run is 50 feet or longer, 14 gauge stranded wire is recommended.

Switch track wiring can be 20-22 gauge, stranded wire, with 20 gauge recommended if wire runs are very long. Further, ensure that, whenever possible, switch tracks are not powered by voltage that passes through a TIU channel.

Accessory wiring should be based on how much current the accessory is expected to draw. In general, accessory wiring is recommended to be 18 gauge, stranded. However, accessories that draw very low amperages can be connected with smaller gauge wires and accessories that draw larger amperages can, if necessary, be wired with 16 gauge wire. Rarely, if ever, will accessories require larger than 16 gauge wire.

Regardless, the smallest wire that can easily be accommodated by the AIU SW and ACC port terminals is 18 gauge. If it's necessary to use 16 gauge wire with an accessory controlled by an AIU, the wire end that goes into the AIU terminals should be solder tinned.

Track Blocks

A track block is a section of track that is electrically isolated from other sections of track by insulating the center rail of the track section from the center rails on either side of it. There are good reasons for wiring layouts using track blocks.

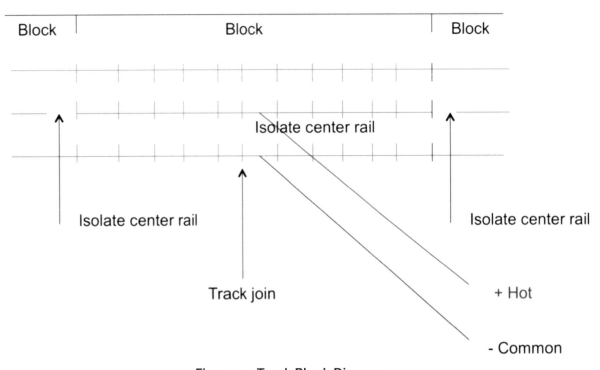

Figure 5 - Track Block Diagram

Isolating track sections into blocks makes electrical troubleshooting easier both during and after layout construction. It becomes easier to locate and correct wiring anomalies when a problem occurs. Isolating blocks makes good sense even for non-DCS layouts.

In a DCS-based layout, using track blocks with only one DCS/power feed to each block has other advantages, as well:

- Using track blocks allows isolation of DCS signal feeds from each other. If a DCS engine receives multiple occurrences of a DCS command, possible errors can result. Isolating track blocks prevents these problems.
- Using track blocks allows limiting the number of linear feet of track on which a DCS signal must propagate.

- Using track blocks allows DCS engines to reside on sidings that are unpowered. Otherwise, when a DCS engine resides on a powered siding, even when not started up under DCS, the engine's chronometer accumulates time and the engine's DCS board is functioning.

The length of a track block should be calculated based on the number of individual track sections that make up the block. A track block should be no longer than 5 or 6 sections of track on each side of the DCS/power connection to the track. Regardless of its length, each track section counts as one section. If sections are all short, consider soldering connections between sections to make longer ones. Regardless, track blocks should not exceed 100 feet in length.

Power Districts

A power district is a group of track blocks that are all provided power by the same power source. There are good reasons for wiring layouts using power districts.

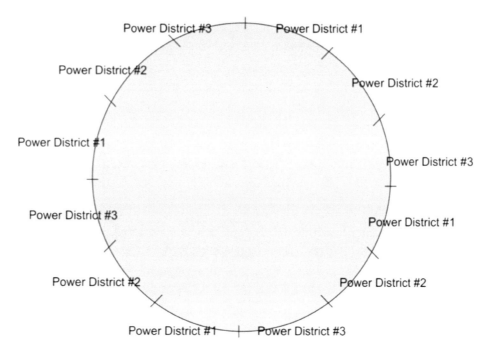

Figure 6 - Power District Diagram

Power districts may be implemented in such a way as to allow more power to be applied to a loop of track than could normally be obtained from one transformer handle. Consider the following example.

A single transformer handle can only generate 10 amps at 18 volts, however, the loop in question often has three trains with engines, lighted passenger cars, and cabooses that may require as much as 15 amps total to operate. Using power districts, there is a solution to this problem:

- First, the loop is broken into 12 blocks with one DCS/power feed at the center of each block.
- Three transformer handles are connected to three different TIU channels.
- The three TIU channels are each connected to their own terminal blocks.
- Each terminal block is connected to 4 blocks of the loop.
- Transformer handle #1 provides power to blocks 1, 4, 7, and 10.
- Transformer handle #2 provides power to blocks 2, 5, 8, and 11.
- Transformer handle #3 provides power to blocks 3, 6, 9, and 12.

Now, as trains run around the layout, the operator has 3 different power sources providing a total of 30 amps to the loop. Assuming that the loops are each long enough to accommodate an entire train and that the trains are equally spaced around the loop, the draw from each transformer handle should be less than 10 amps.

Practical experience has shown that stranded wire applications tend to perform better than solid core ones. Although this is not necessarily scientific, if one were to compare the surface area of stranded and solid wire of the same gauge the stranded wire would have a slightly greater overall surface area due to the "bumps" in the outer surface of the wire stands. This could provide a marginally greater surface area for carrying the DCS signal. Regardless, stranded wire is much easier with which to work, having greater flexibility than a solid wire of the same gauge.

If all of the above guidelines are closely followed, a single Rev. L or later TIU can provide sufficient DCS signal strength for as much as 3,000 feet of track, depending upon a number of factors. These include the length of wire runs, the gauge of wire used, and the number of times the DCS signal is split through terminal blocks.

Toggle Switches

Appropriate use of toggle switches can provide several benefits:

- DCS engines may be kept on toggle-switched sidings when not in use. This limits time on the engine's chronometer to actual time when the engine is in use and also reduces wear use of the electronics in the engine.
- Passenger cars with many lights and cabooses may be kept turned off to preserve bulb life and reduce current draw when not in use.
- Cabooses, other cars and conventional locomotives with smoke units will not have their smoke units run unnecessarily.
- Conventional locomotives that either start up in forward, or that would go into forward if power was momentarily interrupted, may be kept turned off until it is desired to operate them.

There are several considerations when using toggle switches:

- Toggle switches need not switch both the Hot and Common wires of the wire pair. Only the Hot wire needs to be switched. This allows use of toggle switches that are single pole, single throw (SPST).
- Only high quality toggle switches that are rated for 10 amps at 18 volts should be used.
- Toggle switches increase wire paths by adding wire runs from terminal blocks to control panels and then to tracks, rather than directly from terminal blocks to the tracks. This needs to be taken into consideration when selecting wire gauge based on wire run length.
- It may be more advantageous to have a toggle switch control a relay that turns power on and off to a track block if use of the toggle switch would greatly increase the wire run length between the terminal block and the tracks.

The "Magic Lightbulb"

Marty Fitzhenry was the first to note that placing an 18 volt light bulb across either the input to a terminal block or the output of a TIU channel can provide a great improvement in DCS signal strength. Why this works is much less important than the fact that it simply does. The author has seen improvements where DCS signal strength went from 4's and 5's to solid 10's simply by using the 18 volt light bulb across the input to a terminal block.

Additional light bulbs placed at the ends of sidings nearly guarantee that the siding will have a signal strength of 10. The author's practice is to place lighted bumpers on all sidings.

An alternative to using a light bulb is to use what is referred to as an, "engineered filter." The engineered filter's inventor notes that, "The filter consists of a resistor and capacitor of a specific values wired in series. The filters work best in pairs, one across TIU outputs and the other at the 'farthest' point from the TIU output."

As regards use of light bulbs or engineered filters to improve DCS signal strength:

- These devices should only be used if the DCS signal strength is lower than the operator desires.
- There is no guarantee that these devices will improve instances of low DCS signal strength although they tend to improve DCS signal strength when used with revisions of the TIU earlier than the Rev. L.
- To use these devices with the Rev. L TIU, first remove them all, install the Rev. L TIU, and then selectively add them back if and only if the DCS signal strength needs to be improved.
- While there are reports (by the author and others) that these devices adversely affect Rev. L TIU DCS signal strength, experiences of different operators, with different layout track topologies, may vary.

Summary of DCS Wiring Tips and Techniques

The following summarizes the various DCS wiring guidelines for use when constructing a new layout that will utilize DCS:

- DCS engines may be kept on toggle-switched sidings when not in use. This limits time on the engine's chronometer to actual time when the engine is in use and also reduces wear use of the electronics in the engine.
- Passenger cars with many lights and cabooses may be kept turned off to preserve bulb life and reduce current draw when not in use.
- Cabooses, other cars, and conventional locomotives with smoke units will not have their smoke units run unnecessarily.
- Conventional locomotives that either start up in forward, or that would go into forward if power was momentarily interrupted, may be kept turned off until it is desired to operate them.

There are several considerations when using toggle switches:

- Locate the TIUs centrally on the layout to all terminal blocks to which they will be connected (refer to TIU Channel Assignment and Placement below).
- Run 14 or 16 gauge wires from the transformers to each of the TIU's inputs.
- Run 14 or 16 gauge wires directly from the TIU outputs to the center of each of the areas of the layout that each channel supports.
- Place a terminal block at each of these locations. Use only one terminal block for any TIU channel.
- Run 16 gauge wire to each track block directly from the associated terminal block. If the track block is controlled by a toggle switch, run wires from the terminal block to the toggle switch and then on to the track block. DO NOT connect an output from a terminal block as the input to another terminal block.
- Attempt to limit the number of track blocks or sidings connected to a terminal block channel to no more than 12-15 or 20-24 if using a Rev. L or later TIU.
- Limit one TIU channel to no more than approximately 250 feet of track.
- If DCS signal strength across a channel is low, place an 18 volt bulb across that channel's terminal block's inputs. Alternatively, instead place the bulb across the output terminals of the TIU channel.
- Additionally, consider placing bumpers with lighted bulbs (not LEDs) at the end of each siding where DCS Signal strength is an issue. Alternatively, connect an 18 volt bulb across the end of such sidings.
- If possible, use a separate transformer for switch motor power rather than using track power.
- All wire should be either paired (like speaker wire) or, even better, twisted pair, to reduce signal loss on the longer runs. O Gauge Railroading Magazine sells 14 and 16 gauge wire that is excellent for wiring DCS (and other) layouts.
- Use lockons specifically made for your tracks or solder all connections to the rails.

- Crimp spade connectors to the end of every wire that gets screwed into a terminal block, unless you use terminal blocks that place the wire in a hole or slot and then screw down on top of it. Regardless, the intention is to get a very tight connection.
- Isolate all track blocks from all other track blocks by ensuring that the center rails of each block are isolated from adjacent blocks. It's NOT necessary to isolate the outside rails from block to block.

TIU Channel Assignment and Placement

There are two schools of thought as regards TIU placement and, depending upon which one you use during layout construction, there will be an impact on the length of the wire runs from the transformers to the TIUs, from the TIUs to the terminal blocks, and from the terminal blocks to the tracks. Regardless of which method of TIU placement is used, it's a good idea to locate TIUs so that there is a direct line of sight between the WIUs and the DCS Application whenever possible. This is best accomplished by physically placing TIUs so that they are at, or above, the height of the tracks whenever possible.

Loop Assignment of TIU Channels

This is the most straightforward method for assigning TIU channels to tracks. TIU channels are simply assigned to individual loops of track and are powered by one transformer handle for each TIU channel. If loops are small, one TIU channel may be connected to more than one loop by using one terminal block for all loops serviced by this channel. However, it still remains a good idea to limit the number of track blocks or sidings connected to a single TIU channel to 12-15, or 20-24 if using a Rev. L TIU.

If power requirements for loops are low, multiple TIU channels for multiple loops can be fed from a single transformer handle by splitting the output of the transformer handle into two or more TIU channel inputs.

If power requirements for a single loop are more than can be accommodated by a single transformer handle, more than one transformer can be used with more than one TIU channel to set up power districts as discussed previously in Initial Wiring Considerations.

The advantages of loop assignment of TIU channels is that wiring is straightforward and uncomplicated, and that if Variable Channels are used, operation of conventional engines is facilitated over multiple loops because a single power source is used for these loops.

The only real disadvantage to loop assignment of TIU channels is that wire runs may be longer in order to reach all blocks on a loop from the terminal block connected to a TIU channel.

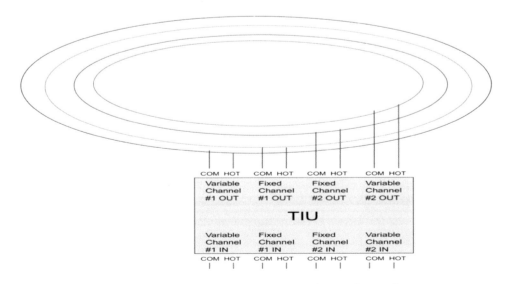

Figure 7 - Loop Assignment of TIU Channels

Geographic Assignment of TIU Channels

In this type of channel assignment, one TIU channel is connected to blocks on different loops rather than blocks on only one loop. This method is well suited for very large layouts. TIUs are located so that they are equidistant from a group of track blocks in the same geographic area of the layout without any concern as to which loop or loops the track blocks may be connected. This allows a terminal block for each geographic group of track blocks to be situated close to the TIU. The advantage is that wire runs are optimum, i.e., as short as possible, both from the terminal blocks to the tracks and from the TIUs to the terminal blocks. The disadvantage is that there is no individual control of the voltage for any one loop.

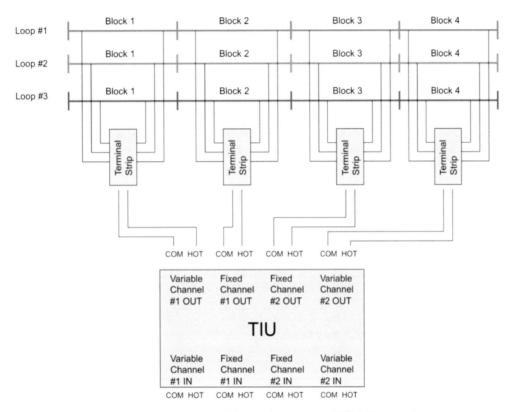

Figure 8 - Geographic Assignment of TIU Channels

All loops must be at the same voltage and conventional operation becomes exceedingly difficult, if not impossible, unless ALL TIU Tracks is selected in the DCS Application Track Control Screen.

Regardless of which method of assigning TIU channels is selected, there are a few simple rules for how to place TIUs physically:

- TIUs should never be stacked directly on top of one another, or on top of or beneath AIUs. Doing so can cause TIUs to be unable to vent heat properly.
- If it is necessary to stack TIUs then there should be adequate clearance between devices (approx. 2" or more) to allow heat dissipation and limit interference.
- Whenever possible, place TIUs vertically rather than horizontally. This provides better reception for the TIU's antenna in the event that a DCS Remote is used.
- Whenever possible, place TIUs such that the layout isn't between the WIU and the DCS Application's smart device during operating sessions. If engines, rolling stock, tracks, structures, and benchwork are in the path of communications between the WIU and DCS Applications, there can be interference issues.

Sometimes, TIU placement makes it inconvenient to remove a TIU from the layout to upgrade the TIU's DCS software, particularly if the TIUs are placed under the layout, as are mine. To get around this inconvenience, I connected extension cables to each TIU's serial, ProtoCast and ProtoDispatch ports to bring them out from under the table. I also have a long serial ribbon cable that goes from the PC in the train room work area, around the layout to where the TIUs are located.

When it's DCS upgrade time, I connect the serial cable from the train room to the serial port jumper cable connected to the TIU. I also jumper together the extension cables connected to the ProtoCast and ProtoDispatch ports. Then I can upgrade the TIUs in place, since a little known fact is that it's not necessary to unhook anything other than the serial, ProtoCast and ProtoDispatch ports when upgrading a TIU's DCS software.

AIU Connection and Placement

First, it's important to be aware of one caveat as regards AIU placement and connection. MTH strongly recommends that only the cables supplied with the AIU be used to connect AIUs to TIUs and advises against longer cables that could possibly cause the wrong device to activate. The experiences of the author and others would seem to indicate that judicious use of somewhat longer cables is practical when the overall cable length, from the TIU to the furthest AIU connected to the TIU, is not excessively long and when quality cables are used. AIU to TIU cables are standard 6-conductor crossover telephone cables and may be purchased in any number of electronics stores.

The AIU to TIU cable carries both DCS commands to control the relays and the electrical current to energize them. If only switch terminals are being used, the total AIU cable length can be well over 100 feet, because only one relay is energized at a time. When using accessory terminals, however, many relays may be energized simultaneously causing a greater voltage drop over a long wire run. If so, it's safest to stay under 25 feet of total length between all the AIUs on a chain.

It is extremely important that the correct ports on AIUs are used when connecting them to TIUs and other AIUs or serious damage to the AIU may result.

Whenever practical, AIUs should be placed in close proximity to TIUs. It's more important to have AIUs close to TIUs than it is to have AIUs close accessories and switch tracks. AIUs do not require their own power since they get power from the TIU to which they are connected so proximity to AC electrical outlets is not a factor.

The first AIU is connected to the TIU using the TIU INPUT port on the AIU and the AIU INPUT port of the TIU. The next AIU is connected to the previous AIU using the TIU INPUT port on next AIU and the AIU OUTPUT port of the previous AIU. This is repeated for the remaining AIUs, making a chain-like connection from the TIU to the last AIU that is connected. Up to 5 AIUs may be connected to a single TIU.

There are two simple rules for how to place AIUs physically:

- AIUs should never be stacked directly on top of one another, or on top of or beneath TIUs. Doing so can create heat dissipation problems and also make it difficult to access the wires connected to SW and ACC ports of AIUs that are lower in the stack.
- If it is necessary to stack AIUs then there should be adequate clearance between devices (approx. 2" or more) to allow heat dissipation.

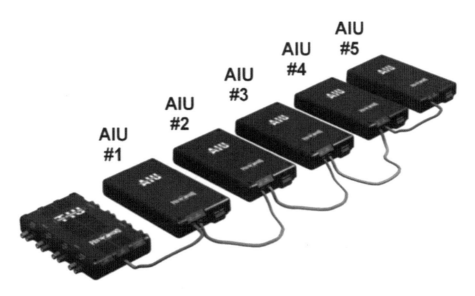

Figure 9 - AIU Connection Diagram

Transformer Considerations

Modern vs. Postwar Transformers

Although DCS was designed to work with most toy train transformers, modern transformers are preferred since they generally have built-in short circuit protection where postwar transformers are notorious for their lack of any effective short circuit protection. However, some modern transformers vary voltage by altering the AC sine wave. This is generally not a problem unless these transformers are used as input to a TIU's Variable Channel. The Variable Channels also control voltage by altering the AC sine wave and the combination of doing this twice can be upsetting to the electronics in DCS and other modern engines.

MTH Transformers

The ideal transformer for use with DCS is the MTH Z4000. In addition to excellent circuit breaker protection (for itself, the TIU and engine electronics) and readouts for voltage and amperage, its handles provide a maximum voltage of 22 volts which is what the TIU's Variable Channels expect as input.

MTH brick-type transformers, such as the Z500, Z750 and Z1000 also have excellent built-in circuit breakers. When used with the TIU, however, the bricks should be directly connected to TIU channels without using the included Z-Controller, since the Z-Controller alters the AC sine wave.

Other Modern Transformers

Modern transformers from other manufacturers will generally interoperate effectively with DCS, however, the design of some transformers can cause problems with DCS engines and are to be avoided.

Postwar Transformers

Many postwar transformers are good sources of power for DCS. They all vary current using large transformer coils rather than by altering the AC sine wave and will not cause problems with DCS engines or other engines that contain electronic components. However, there is one important disadvantage to using these transformers. They do not incorporate any effective short circuit protection at all. If postwar transformers are to be used with DCS, it is imperative that additional short circuit protection be included in the form of circuit breakers or fuses.

Fuses and Circuit Breakers

Although the later revision TIUs (Rev. H and newer) have built-in fuses to protect the TIU and trains from short circuits, it's still strongly recommended that the DCS operator use modern transformers that have their own built-in circuit breakers for protection against short circuits or, if using postwar transformers, take steps to ensure that adequate short circuit protection is included. It's less than convenient to have to open a TIU to replace a blown fuse. It's much easier to either reset a circuit breaker or replace an external fuse.

Modern transformers generally have built-in short circuit protection in the form of quick-acting current sensing or thermal circuit breakers. Postwar transformers were manufactured with older technology circuit breakers such as bimetallic strips that, after many years, become nearly or completely nonfunctional. Even when these transformers were new, these crude (by today's standards) circuit breakers took much too long to trip to protect modern electronics. If transformers such as these are used, it is essential that either circuit breakers or fast-acting fuses be inserted in the Hot wire between each transformer output and the TIU channel input.

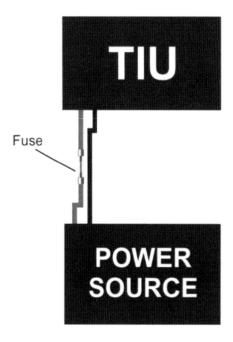

Figure 10 - Inline Fuses

If circuit breakers are used, they should be rated such that they will open immediately when current exceeds 15 amps for more than a few seconds. Fuses should be rated at no higher than 15 amps, with 10 amps being a recommended, conservative rating.

Phasing Transformers

All transformers are plugged into AC electrical outlets that have either two or three prongs. The vertical slit openings are for AC Hot and Common while the round opening, if present, is for earth ground. The following discussion relates to the Hot and Common openings.

Modern transformers have AC plugs where one blade is slightly broader than the other. This allows the AC plug to be inserted into the outlet in only one way. However, not all transformers were manufactured with the blades in the correct orientation. Postwar transformers generally lack this blade orientation altogether, allowing them to be plugged into an AC outlet in two ways. Regardless of which transformers you use with your layout, if you use more than one transformer it's important that they all be in phase with each other to eliminate the possibility of inadvertently creating dangerously high voltages. This can occur when locomotives or passenger cars with dual pickup rollers bridge two sections of track powered by different transformers, or when a transformer other than a track power transformer is used to power switch motors wired for non-derailing operation.

To ensure that multiple transformers are in phase:

- Start by plugging any two transformers into AC outlets of the same power strip or the same wall outlet.
- Turn on both transformers and set the output of each transformer to zero.
- Connect a wire from any Common terminal of one transformer to any Common terminal of the other transformer.
- Connect two wires, one to a Hot terminal of one transformer and the other to a Hot terminal of the other transformer.
- Set both transformers to as close to the same voltage as possible, at or above 10 volts.
- Select one of the following three ways to now test to see if the two transformers are in phase or not: briefly touch the wires connected to the two Hot terminals to each other. If a spark results the transformers are not in phase. If there is no spark, they are in phase; using a voltmeter, measure the AC voltage between the two wires connected to the Hot terminals. If it is approximately twice the value of the voltage to which the transformers are set, they are not in phase. If it's less than a few volts, they are in phase; connect an 18 volt light bulb between the two wires connected to the Hot terminals of the two transformers. If the bulb glows brightly the transformers are not in phase. If the bulb is dim or does not light at all, the transformers are in phase.
- If the transformers are not in phase, reverse the AC plug of one of them in the outlet and repeat the test. This may be difficult if the transformer has a plug where one blade is broader than the other.
- Now, repeat the above procedure using one of the two transformers that are now in phase (either one is fine) and the next transformer that will be used on the layout. In step 7, if the two transformers are not in phase, reverse the plug of the transformer just added to the test, not the one that was previously tested.
- Continue the above process until all transformers to be used on the layout are in phase.

Once the transformers are in phase, mark the AC plugs of all tested transformers so that you'll always know the correct orientation for plugging them into AC outlets.

Connecting Transformer Common Terminals

It's important to connect together one Common terminal from each of the transformers to be used on the layout, regardless of whether they are used to power the tracks, switch track motors, or accessories. There are several reasons to do this:

- This will ensure that the DCS signal always has a return path to the TIU.
- This will ensure that any out-of-phase transformers are quickly identified.
- This will ensure that switch track motors using non-track power (preferred in a DCS environment) that are wired for automatic non-derailing operation will always work correctly.
- If TMCC is present on the layout, this will ensure that the TMCC signal is present over the entire layout.

2. Adding DCS to an Existing Layout

Although there's been quite a bit of discussion about all the guidelines to follow when implementing DCS as part of building a new layout, many DCS operators have found that adding DCS to their existing layouts was much easier than they anticipated. While it would be unrealistic to expect that DCS would work perfectly when added to any existing layout, the author's experiences and the experiences of others has been that adding DCS to an existing layout is quite a bit less difficult than one might believe.

The best approach when adding DCS to an existing layout is to simply hook it up by inserting a TIU between the tracks and the transformers and determine how well DCS performs. A quick DCS setup is accomplished as follows:

- Disconnect the wires to track power from the transformer output terminals and connect them to the output terminals of the TIU channels instead.
- Connect the input terminals of the TIU channels to the output terminals of the track power transformers.
- Set any Variable Channels connected to Fixed mode of operation.
- Power up each transformer, one at a time, and use a DCS engine to test the DCS signal over the layout.
- If the DCS signal is weak on any channel, place an 18 volt light bulb across the output terminals of that TIU channel and re-test the DCS signal strength.
- Analyze any areas where the DCS signal is still weak and use the Troubleshooting Problems section later in this book to resolve any problems encountered.
- Once the transformers are in phase, mark the AC plugs of all tested transformers so that you'll always know the correct orientation for plugging them into AC outlets.

Remember that DCS will generally operate effectively with DCS signal strength as low as 7. Once DCS is operating as well as possible, determine which areas of the layout are candidates for rewiring and which can be left as-is. Analyze any areas where the DCS signal is still weak in terms of the information presented earlier in the section Planning for a New DCS layout.

3. Large and Modular Layout Considerations

Large and modular layouts can be challenging candidates for the addition of DCS. The following discussion builds on the previous discussions regarding implementing DCS in a new layout and adding it to an existing one. Many of the items discussed previously are also applicable to large and modular layouts.

Additional Considerations for Large DCS Layouts

One way to approach adding DCS to large layouts is to consider a large DCS layout to be a combination of smaller DCS layouts. A large layout can generally be broken down into a collection of loops and sidings. These loops and sidings can then be grouped in such a way that the same rules for implementing DCS in more modest layouts can be applied for the large layout, as well.

Often, it will be advantageous to assign TIU channels geographically rather than to finite loops and sidings. A determination should be made as regards which track blocks and sidings should be assigned to which TIU channels in order to get the maximum coverage from each TIU channel, and to keep wire runs from the TIU through terminal blocks and to the tracks as short as possible.

For a large layout, top priority is to maximize the use of each TIU channel. This would include making track blocks as long as possible and having as many blocks connected to each TIU channel as is possible without degrading the DCS signal. In general, all of the wiring guidelines previously discussed should be followed as closely as possible.

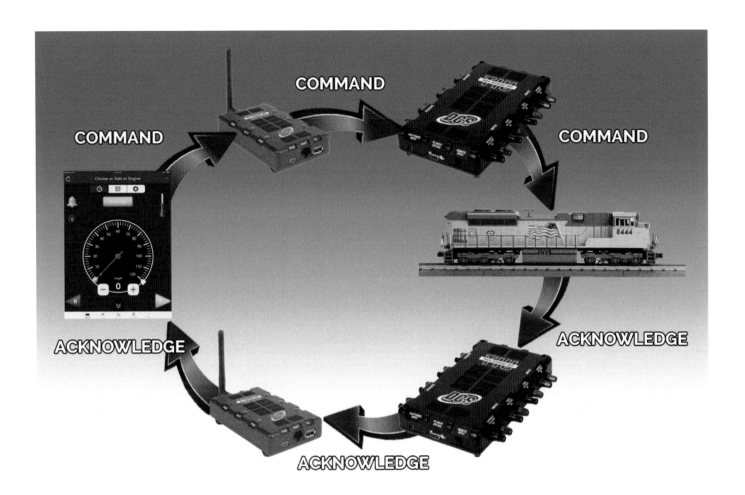

Figure 11 - Packet Flow Diagram

Part V - DCS Smart Device Application

1. What's a Smart Device?

A smart device, for the purposes of this book, is any cell phone or tablet that utilizes either the iOS 7.0 or later, or Android 4.0.3 or later, operating system, and has WiFi capability. This includes iPhones and Android smartphones, iPads and Android tablets, and the iPod Touch.

The DCS App is available for iOS (Apple) devices from Apple's iTunes Store, and for Android devices from Google Play. A version of the application for any other cell phone, tablet or other device is not currently scheduled for development.

2. The DCS Application - Overview and Capabilities

The remainder of this section discusses MTH's DCS application. The app is available as both a free and paid version, and downloads directly to Android and iOS smart devices. This book discusses the Premium version of the app that operates on iOS devices. Screens on Android devices may be slightly different. This version, unlike the Free and Standard versions, includes all of DCS' features and functions. At present, it has all of the capabilities of the DCS Remote, however, the DCS Application's functions and features are in a different format from those in the DCS Remote.

Versions of the DCS Application

The Standard version of the application can add, delete and operate DCS engines, and it can utilize many DCS functions and all engine soft key features. The Premium version adds control of AIUs for operation of switch tracks and accessories, Routes or Scenes. It also allows use of the Record/Playback function, operation in Super TIU mode, and operation of conventional engines. The Premium version of the DCS App also allows the contents of the DCS App to be backed up to a PC and restored from a PC.

Although the Free and Standard versions of the DCS Application don't have the same functionality and tactile feel of the DCS Remote, they do bring a completely unique and modern approach to controlling a model railroad. They provide inexpensive (free, even!) methods for operating DCS engines for additional layout operators - individuals who may be more attuned to operating modern smart devices than the multi-button DCS Remote. More importantly, the app provides a more intuitive user interface that makes navigating DCS far easier and faster than does the DCS Remote.

The DCS Application requires the following MTH DCS devices in order to operate:

- The latest version of DCS, currently DCS 6.1
- The latest version of the DCS Loader Program, currently DCS Loader Program 5.0
- #50-1003 DCS TIU
- #50-1002 DCS Remote (for functions not present in the application)
- #50-1034 WiFi Interface Unit
- USB cable (for Rev. L TIU), male USB-B (TIU end) to male USB-A (WiFi Interface Unit end); or
- USB to Serial cable (for all other TIUs). If using a USB to Serial cable and the TIU is already connected to a Lionel command base, then a serial "Y" cable (1 male end, 2 female ends) will also be required.

Note that a WIU may be powered from two alternate power sources, as long as the source has an output of 5 volts DC @1000 mA. Those power sources include a computer's USB 2.0 or 3.0 port or an iPhone or iPad charging block. Either option requires a USB cable with a Type B plug on one end and a Type Mini-b (5-pin) plug on the other end.

Downloading the DCS Application

To download the DCS Application, proceed as follows:

- Ensure that the smart device is connected to the Internet.
- On an iOS device, tap on the icon for the App Store.
- On an Android device, tap on the icon for Google Play.
- Search for applications using keywords "MTH DCS WiFi".
- When applications are displayed, select the "Wi-Fi DCS" application.
- Tap the "Get" or "Download" button to download the DCS Application to your smart device.

Upgrading the DCS Application

To upgrade the Free version of the DCS Application to either the Standard or Premium version, proceed as follows:

- Ensure that the smart device is connected to the Internet.
- Tap the DCS Application's icon. This will display the Home Screen.
- Tap the Run My Trains button. This will display the Engine Control Screen. (Note: disregard any error messages that may appear.)
- At the bottom-right corner of the screen, tap the More... button. This will display the More... Screen.
- Tap the Purchase button on the same line as either the Standard or Premium version that you wish to purchase. Follow the displayed instructions to upgrade the Free version of the application to either the Standard or Premium version.

Installing the DCS Application on Multiple Smart Devices

The Basic (free) version of the DCS Application may be installed on more than one smart device, whether the Smart Device is an iOS or Android device, at no charge. Further, once the DCS Application has been upgraded on one device to either the Standard or Premium version, it may then be upgraded on any additional smart device that has had the Basic version of the DCS Application installed, and that is owned by the same purchaser of the original upgrade.

To do so, simply follow the steps above to upgrade the additional devices, being certain that the devices have the same Apple ID for the Apple App Store or Android Account Number (Google E-mail address) for Google Play, as was used to upgrade the first smart device. There will not be any additional charge for subsequent DCS Application upgrades.

The following section discusses how to setup and configure the DCS Wireless Interface Unit (WIU) to allow a DCS layout to be operated using the DCS Application.

Part VI - DCS WiFi Interface Unit

1. WIU Purpose and Function

This section of the book discusses the DCS WiFi Interface Unit (WIU) in terms of what it does, its controls and its installation.

What the WIU Does

The DCS Application communicates with TIUs using WiFi (802.11n) wireless communication. This is exactly the same type of communication as is used by computers communicating over a wireless local area network (LAN).

All smart devices already have WiFi capability. However, the TIU does not. To add this capability to the TIU, it's necessary to connect the TIU's USB port (Rev. L TIU) or serial port (older TIU) to an MTH WiFi Interface Unit. If the layout has multiple TIUs, one WiFi Interface Unit is required for each TIU on the layout to control engines using the DCS Application.

In effect, the communication process between the TIU and the DCS Application is simple and straightforward:

- The DCS Application sends commands wirelessly to the WiFi Interface Unit
- The WiFi Interface Unit forwards commands from the DCS Application to the TIU's serial port
- The TIU passes acknowledgements to the WiFi Interface Unit via the TIU's serial port
- The WiFi Interface Unit forwards acknowledgements wirelessly to the DCS Application.

There are two ways to install and wirelessly connect the DCS Application to the WiFi Interface Unit. The first method, connecting to the WiFi Interface Unit as an access point, is very simple. The second method, connecting to the WiFi Interface Unit via a local area network (LAN), while more involved, has several advantages. Both methods will be discussed below. Note that if any of the following instructions conflict with the manual that accompanies the MTH WiFi Interface Unit, the manual's instructions should be followed instead.

Figure 12 - MTH WiFi Interface Unit (WIU)

2. Setup and Configuration for Using the DCS Application

Connecting to the WiFi Interface Unit in MTH WiFi Network Mode

If you don't already have a local area network (LAN) in place, this is the suggested method to use to wirelessly connect the DCS Application to the WiFi Interface Unit.

This method takes advantage of the mini-WiFi network generated by the WiFi Interface Unit to wirelessly and directly connect the DCS Application on the smart device to the WiFi Interface Unit. You should be aware, however, that although this is very easy to setup, it has two disadvantages.

The smart device is unable to access any other wireless devices, such as the Lionel iCab or LCS applications that allow control of TMCC and Legacy engines, without switching to the mini-networks that are generated by those application's Legacy command base-interfacing hardware. If there are no other WiFi applications present, this is not relevant.

An Internet connection is not possible using this method, precluding use of the DCS Application's ancillary News, Search, and Catalog functions.

To connect the DCS Application to one or more WiFi Interface Units in MTH WiFi Network Mode, proceed as follows for the first WiFi Interface Unit:

- Set the WiFi Interface Unit's MTH/Home selector switch to MTH.
- Connect the WiFi Interface Unit to the TIU by connecting the USB Port on a Rev. L TIU to the USB Port on the WiFi Interface Unit. If the TIU is an older model, use a Serial to USB conversion cable to connect the two devices. In this case, refer to Part XII - DCS Upgrading and Remote Backup/Restore, 4. Required Cables and Connectors earlier in this book for a description of the cable that's required.
- Attach the included antenna, and plug the WiFi Interface Unit's power supply into an AC outlet and the power supply's cable into PWR port on the WiFi Interface Unit. Wait a minute or two for the WiFi Interface Unit's PWR, Wi-Fi and TIU LEDs to light.
- On the smart device, open the device's settings.
- Select the MTH DCS network from the smart device's list of wireless networks.
- Enter the MTH DCS network password: mthdcswifi
- The smart device should indicate that it is connected to the WiFi Interface Unit's mini WiFi network.

To connect additional WiFi Interface Units for use with additional TIUs, follow the instructions below for connecting these additional WIUs in Home Network mode.

Connecting Additional WiFi Interface Units in MTH Network Mode

To connect additional WiFi Interface Units for use with additional TIUs in MTH Network mode, follow the instructions below:

- Set the second WiFi Interface Unit's MTH/Home selector switch to Home.
- Connect the second WiFi Interface Unit to the second TIU by connecting the USB Port on a Rev. L TIU to the USB Port on the WiFi Interface Unit. If the TIU is an older model, use a Serial to USB cable to connect the two devices. In this case, refer to Part XII - DCS Upgrading and Remote Backup/Restore, 4. Required Cables and Connectors later in this book for a description of the exact cable that's required.
- Attach the included antenna, and plug the second WiFi Interface Unit's power supply into an AC outlet and the power supply's cable into PWR port on the WiFi Interface Unit.
- Wait a minute or two for the WiFi Interface Unit's PWR, Wi-Fi and TIU LEDs to light.
- On the first (master) WiFi Interface Unit, press the WPS button. The white WPS LED will begin flashing.

- Immediately press the WPS button on the second WiFi Interface Unit. The WPS button must be pressed within 1 minute. The white WPS LED will begin flashing.
- Wait for the white WPS LED on the second WiFi Interface Unit to come on steadily, and then turn off.
- Select and open WiFi settings on the smart device.
- Choose the MTH WiFi network from the smart device's list of wireless networks.
- The smart device should indicate that it is connected to the MTH WiFi network.

Repeat the above steps for any additional WiFi Interface Units.

By using this method, these additional WiFi Interface Units will connect to the WiFi Interface Unit that was set to MTH mode as if it was a router, thus allowing the DCS Application to connect to the additional WiFi Interface Units though the WiFi Interface Unit that was set up in MTH mode.

Connecting to the WiFi Interface Unit in Home WiFi Network Mode

This method connects one or more WiFi Interface Units to the DCS Application by connecting the smart device to a wireless local area network (LAN). If you already have a local area network in place or are knowledgeable enough to set one up, this is the preferred method to connect the DCS Application to the WiFi Interface Unit. This method has two distinct advantages.

The smart device is able to access other wireless devices, such as the Lionel iCab or LCS applications that allow control of TMCC and Legacy engines, simultaneously without switching wireless networks, assuming that these applications are also connected to the Legacy command base-interfacing hardware via the same local are network as is the DCS Application. If there are no other WiFi applications present, this is not relevant.

An Internet connection is possible using this method, allowing use of the DCS Application's ancillary News, Search and Catalog functions.

Connecting to the WiFi Interface Unit Using a Router With a WPS Button

If your router has a "WPS" button, use this procedure to connect the DCS Application to the WiFi Interface Unit in Home WiFi Network Mode:

- Set the WiFi Interface Unit's MTH/Home selector switch to Home.
- Connect the WiFi Interface Unit to the TIU by connecting the USB Port on a Rev. L TIU to the USB Port on the WiFi Interface Unit. If the TIU is an older model, use a Serial to USB cable to connect the two devices. In this case, refer to Part XII - DCS Upgrading and Remote Backup/Restore, 4. Required Cables and Connectors later in this book for a description of the exact cable that's required.
- Attach the included antenna, and plug the WiFi Interface Unit's power supply into an AC outlet and the power supply's cable into PWR port on the WiFi Interface Unit. Wait a minute or two for the WiFi Interface Unit's PWR, Wi-Fi and TIU LEDs to light.
- On your network router, press the WPS button and then the WPS button on the WiFi Interface Unit.
- Wait for the white WPS LED on the WiFi Interface Unit to come on steadily, and then turn off.
- Select and open WiFi settings on the smart device.
- Choose the desired WiFi local area network from the smart device's list of wireless networks.
- The smart device should indicate that it is connected to the desired WiFi local area network.

By repeating the above procedure, additional WiFi Interface Units that are connected to other TIUs on the layout may also be connected to the home WiFi local area network.

Connecting to the WiFi Interface Unit Using a Router Without a WPS Button

If the router does not have a WPS button, proceed as follows to connect the DCS Application to the WiFi Interface Unit in Home WiFi Network Mode:

- Set the WiFi Interface Unit's MTH/Home selector switch to MTH.
- Attach the included antenna, and plug the WiFi Interface Unit's power supply into an AC outlet and the power supply's cable into PWR port on the WiFi Interface Unit. Wait a minute or two for the WiFi Interface Unit's PWR, Wi-Fi and TIU LEDs to light.
- Using any computer with WiFi capability, navigate to see the available wireless networks and connect to the network named MTH_DCS-XXXX, where XXXX may be any 4 characters. This is the same network name that's printed on the bottom of the WIU.
- When prompted, enter the network password (network key) mthdcswifi in all lower case. The network key is also printed on the bottom of the WIU.
- Open a web browser and enter the following IP address in the url address line at the top of the browser's window: 192.168.143.1 This will open LuCI, the MTH DCS web interface.
- Enter the password mthdcs in all lower case and press the keyboard ENTER or RETURN key. Do not change the username from ROOT.
- Click on the STATION MODE tab at the top of the screen
- Select WIRELESS from the drop-down menu.
- Locate the ESSID field and enter the home network name (SSID) to which the WIU is to be connected. This is the same network to which your smart device is to be connected.
- If your network requires a password, select the network's encryption type from the drop down menu. If the encryption type is not known, select the last choice in the list, mixed mode. If that doesn't work, obtain the encryption type from your router.
- Enter your home network password in the KEY field. Then, click the SAVE AND APPLY button on the lower-right of the screen.
- Remove power from the WIU and close the browser.
- Set the WiFi Interface Unit's "MTH/Home" selector switch to "Home".
- Connect the WiFi Interface Unit to the TIU by connecting the USB Port on a Rev. L TIU to the USB Port on the WiFi Interface Unit. If the TIU is an older model, use a Serial to USB cable to connect the two devices. In this case, refer to Part XII - DCS Upgrading and Remote Backup/Restore, 4. Required Cables and Connectors later in this book for a description of the exact cable that's required.
- Attach the included antenna, and plug the WiFi Interface Unit's power supply into an AC outlet and the power supply's cable into PWR port on the WiFi Interface Unit. Wait a minute or two for the WiFi Interface Unit's PWR, Wi-Fi and TIU LEDs to light.
- The WIU will now automatically connect to your home network each time it is powered up.

Connecting to the WiFi Interface Unit Using Wired Ethernet

To connect with the home network using a wired Ethernet connection:

- Connect the WiFi Interface Unit's LAN port to your network router using a standard Ethernet cable.
- Set the WiFi Interface Unit's MTH/Home selector switch to MTH.
- Connect the WiFi Interface Unit to the TIU by connecting the USB Port on a Rev. L TIU to the USB Port on the WiFi Interface Unit. If the TIU is an older model, use a Serial to USB cable to connect the two devices. In this case, refer to Part XII - DCS Upgrading and Remote Backup/Restore, 4. Required Cables and Connectors earlier in this book for a description of the exact cable that's required.
- Attach the included antenna, and plug the WiFi Interface Unit's power supply into an AC outlet and the power supply's cable into PWR port on the WiFi Interface Unit. Wait a minute or two for the WiFi Interface Unit's PWR, Wi-Fi and TIU LEDs to light.
- Select and open WiFi settings on your smart device.

- Choose the desired WiFi local area network from the smart device's list of wireless networks. If requested, enter the password for the desired WiFi local area network.
- The smart device should indicate that it is connected to the desired WiFi local area network.

If the Smart Device Loses its WiFi Connection to the WiFi Interface Unit

If the smart device is connected to the WIU in MTH mode and the smart device's network connection often spontaneously changes to the home network connection, the DCS Application will report that it cannot find any TIUs. If this happens, use the smart device's WiFi network settings to "forget" the home network. Going forward, the smart device will not to attempt to join the home network unless specifically told to do so.

On an iOS device, this is accomplished by doing the following:

- Turn off the "Ask to Join Networks" option in WiFi settings
- Tap on the home network's entry in the list of available networks and then tap on the "Forget This Network" option.

Android users should do the equivalent of the above on their smart devices.

This should prevent the smart device from spontaneously switching from the WIU's network to the home network.

Resetting the WiFi Interface Unit

If it becomes necessary at any time to reset the WIU to its initial factory settings, such as to de-install and reinstall the WIU to move it to another layout or before giving it to someone else, the process to reset the device is straightforward:

- Power-on the WiFi Interface Unit normally and wait a minute or two for its PWR, Wi-Fi and TIU LEDs to light
- Press the Reset button on the WiFi Interface Unit for a full 10 seconds
- Disconnect the WiFi Interface Unit from the TIU
- Unplug the WiFi Interface Unit's power supply from its AC outlet.

The WiFi Interface Unit has now been reset to the exact condition that it was in when it came from the factory.

Part VII - Engine Operation Using the DCS Application

When the DCS Application is launched for the very first time after having been installed, the Home Screen is displayed briefly and then control automatically transfers to a device selection screen where the operator chooses which WiFi device will be used with the DCS Application, either the WiFi Interface Unit (WIU) or the DCS Explorer. Once a selection is made, control transfers back to the Home Screen. Subsequent launches of the DCS Application will not request that a WiFi device be selected.

The selection of WiFi device may be changed by using the Application Settings Screen. How to access the Application Settings Screen is discussed in Part XI - The DCS Application's More... Screen, 2. DCS Application Settings Screen later in this book.

The Home Screen's only function is to provide access to the DCS Application's main functions. In order to do so, this screen has four buttons. One to access the DCS Applications function screens and three to transfer to a web browser to access one of MTH's websites. These buttons are as follows:

- Run My Trains button - transfers the user to the DCS Application's Engine Control Screen.
- News button - transfers the user to MTH's News web page.
- Search button - transfers you to MTH's Advanced Search web page.
- Catalog function - transfers you to MTH's Catalogs web page.

The News, Search, and Catalog buttons all require Internet access in order to be functional.

Figure 13 - DCS Application Home Screen

1. DCS Application Engine Operation Screens

The DCS Application has three main screens that are used to control and configure DCS engines.

The DCS Application's engine operation screens are:

- Engine Control Screen
- Engine Features Screen
- Engine Settings Screen

DCS Application Engine Control Screen

The DCS Engine Control Screen allows control of the selected DCS engine. From this screen, you can access the engine roster to select a DCS engine and then return to the Engine Control Screen to start it up and operate it.

The table on the next page describes the functions available on the Engine Control Screen.

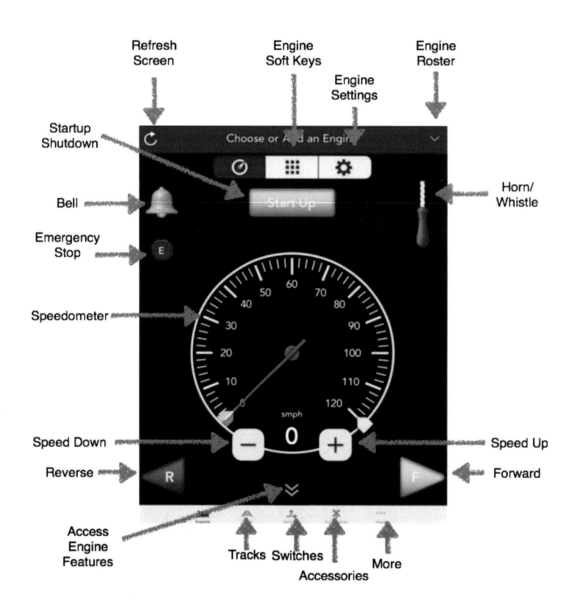

Figure 14 - DCS Application Engine Control Screen

	Engine Control Screen
PURPOSE:	Allows control of DCS engines in command mode.
HOW TO GET IT:	Tap the Run My Trains button on the Home Screen.
INFORMATION DISPLAYED:	Active DCS Engine ID# and Name, and engine controls *Note that some features and controls that are present for DCS engines may be different or altogether absent for TMCC and Legacy engines.*
BUTTONS:	Tap Refresh to refresh the app's contents.
	Tap on the active engine's name to toggle betwen that engine and the previously active engine.
	Tap Engine Soft Keys or swipe left to transfer control to Engine Soft Keys Screen.
	Tap Engine Settings or swipe right to transfer control to the Engine Settings Screen.
	Tap Engine Roster transfers control to the DCS Engine Roster Screen.
	Tap Shutdown/Startup to start up or shut down the active engine.
	Tap Bell to start or stop the engine's bell.
	Slide down on the Horn/Whistle to sound the horn or whistle. If the engine has a Playable Whistle, slide down and up incrementally to "play" the whistle.
	Tap Emergency Stop to shut down power through all TIU channels and reset the power to all TIUs.
	Slide clockwise or tap on the Speedometer to increase the engine's speed. Slide counter-clockwise or tap to reduce the engine's speed.
	Tap the bezel (outer white ring) of the speedometer to gradually accelerate or decelerate the engine to the selected speed. The speedometer needle will follow the actual speed.
	Quickly double-tap the bezel (outer white ring) of the speedometer to quickly accelerate or decelerate the engine to the selected speed. The speedometer needle will follow the actual speed.
	If the DCS engine is traveling in a forward direction, tap the Reverse button to bring the DCS engine to a complete stop and place it in a reverse direction. This will also cause the "R" arrow to turn orange.
	If the DCS engine is traveling in a reverse direction, tap the Forward button to bring the DCS engine to a complete stop and place it in a forward direction. This will also cause the "F" arrow to turn green.
	Tap Tracks to transfer control to the Track Control Screen.
	Tap Switches to transfer control to the Switch Track Control Screen.
	Tap Accessories to transfer control to the Accessories Control Screen.
	Tap More to transfer control to the More... Screen.
	Slide screen up from the bottom to access the Engine Features Screen.

DCS Application Engine Roster Screen

The DCS Engine Roster Screen displays a list of all DCS engines that are on powered tracks and are available for operation. From this screen, you can select a DCS engine to operate and then return to the Engine Control Screen to start it up and operate it.

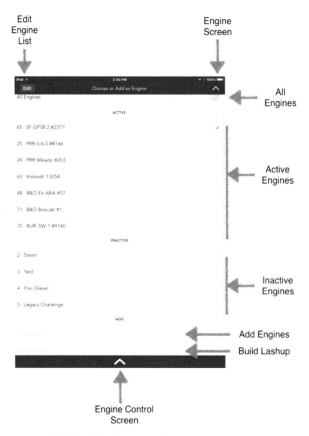

Figure 15 - DCS Application Engine Roster Screen

The following table describes the functions available on the Engine Roster Screen.

Engine Roster Screen	
PURPOSE:	Allows selection of a DCS engine for operation in command mode.
HOW TO GET IT:	Tap the Engine Roster button on any screen where it appears.
INFORMATION DISPLAYED:	Selected DCS Engine ID# and Name, and DCS engine rosters.
BUTTONS:	Tap Edit to move a DCS engine in the Inactive Engine Roster to the Active Engine Roster. (Refer to DCS Application Edit Engine Roster later in this book.)
	Tap a DCS engine in the Active Engine Roster to make that DCS engine active. If all DCS engines aren't visible, scroll down to view the rest of the DCS engines. Tap the Edit button to transfer control to the Edit Engine Screen.
	Tap the All Engines box to select All Engines operation.
	Slide down on the Engine Roster Screen to move all engines on powered tracks to the Active Engine Roster.
	Tap Add Engines to transfer control to the Add Engine Screen to allow a DCS, TMCC or Legacy engine to be added to the Active Engine Roster.
	Tap Build Lashup to transfer control to the Build Lashup Screen.
	Tap Engine Screen (iOS only) or Engine Control Screen to transfer to the Engine Control Screen.

DCS Application Engine Features Screen

The DCS Engine Features Screen allows you to activate any of the active DCS engine's features, and then return to the Engine Control Screen.

The following table describes the functions available for activation on the Engine Features Screen.

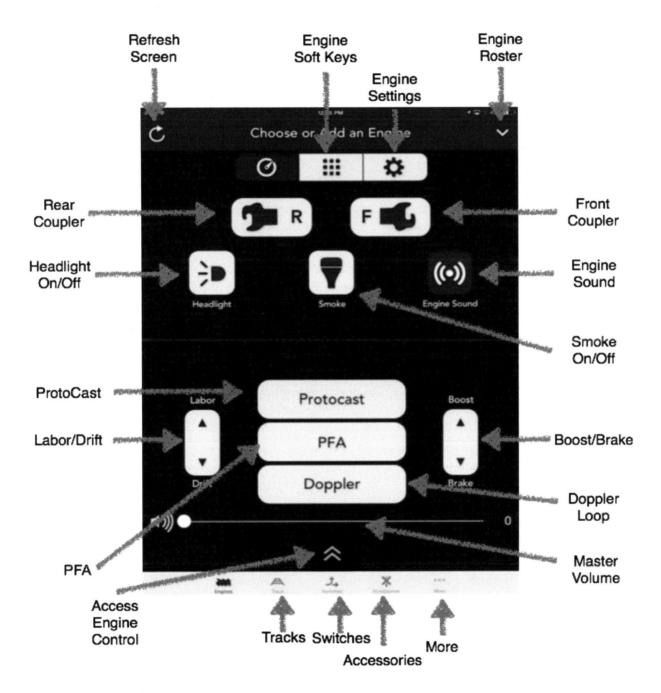

Figure 16 - DCS Application Engine Features Screen

Engine Features Screen	
PURPOSE:	Allows activation of a DCS, TMCC or Legacy engine's features in command mode.
HOW TO GET IT:	Tap the Access Engine Features button on the Engine Control Screen.
INFORMATION DISPLAYED:	Active Engine ID# and Name, and engine features. *Note that some features and controls that are present for DCS engines may be different or altogether absent for TMCC and Legacy engines.*
BUTTON	Tap Refresh Screen to refresh the screen.
	Tap on the active engine's name to toggle between that engine and the previously active engine.
	Tap Engine Soft Keys or swipe left to transfer control to Engine Soft Keys Screen.
	Tap Engine Settings or swipe right to transfer control to the Engine Settings Screen.
	Tap Engine Roster ensure that it's on a powered track and slide to transfer control to the DCS Engine Roster Screen.
	Tap Rear Coupler to operate the rear coupler, if present.
	Tap Front Coupler to operate the front coupler, if present.
	Tap Headlight On/Off to turn the engine's headlight on or off
	Tap Smoke On/Off to turn the engine's smoke on or off, for engine's that have smoke
	Tap Engine Sounds to turn the engine's sounds on or off
	Tap PFA to start playing Passenger Station Sounds or Freight Yard Sounds.
	Tap ProtoCast, Doppler Loop, Labor/Drift, or Boost/Brake to activate that feature.
	Tap Access Engine Control to transfer to the Engine Control Screen.
	Tap Tracks to transfer control to the Track Control Screen.
	Tap Switches to transfer control to the Switch Track Control Screen.
	Tap Accessories to transfer control to the Accessories Control Screen.
	Tap More to transfer control to the More... Screen.
	Slide screen up from the bottom to access the Engine Control Screen.

DCS Application Engine Settings Screen - DCS Engines

The DCS Engine Settings Screen allows you to change any of the settings for an active DCS engine and then return to the Engine Control Screen.

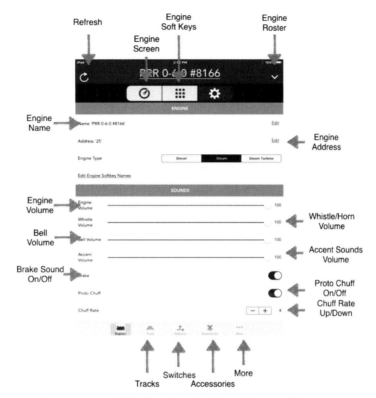

Figure 17a - DCS Engine Settings Screen (1)

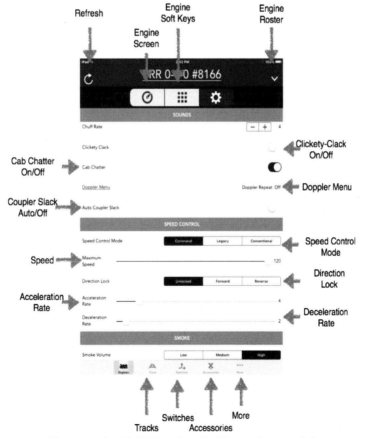

Figure 17b - DCS Engine Settings Screen (2)

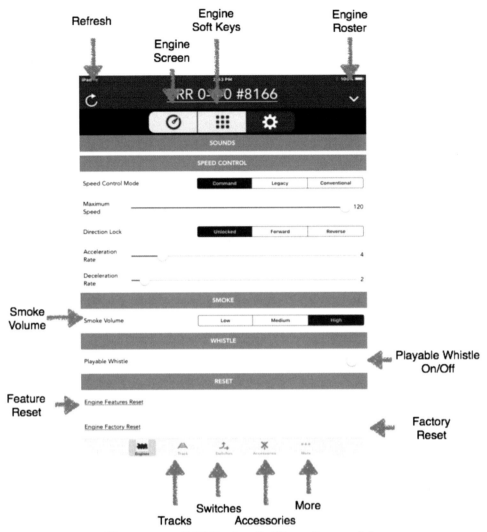

Figure 17c - DCS Engine Settings Screen (3)

The following table describes the functions available to be modified on the Engine Settings Screen for DCS engines.

DCS Engine Settings Screen

PURPOSE:	Allows you to change a DCS engine's settings.
HOW TO GET IT:	Tap Engine Settings on any screen where it appears.
INFORMATION DISPLAYED:	The Active DCS Engine ID# and Name, and engine settings.
BUTTONS:	Tap Refresh to refresh the app.
	Tap Engine Screen or swipe left to transfer control to the Engine Control Screen.
	Tap Engine Soft Keys or swipe right to transfer control to Engine Soft Keys Screen.
	Tap Engine Roster to transfer control to the DCS Engine Roster Screen.
	Tap Engine Name to change the DCS engine's name.
	Tap Engine Address to change the DCS engine's DCS ID#.
	Slide Engine Volume, Whistle/Horn Volume, Bell Volume, or Accent Sounds Volume to adjust that volume up or down.
	Tap Brake Sound On/Off, Proto Chuff On/Off or On/Off to turn that setting on or off.
	Tap Chuff Rate Up/Down to adjust the Chuff Rate.
	Tap Clikity-Clack On/Off, Cab Chatter On/Off or Coupler Slack Auto/Off to adjust that setting accordingly.
	Tap Speed Control Mode according to the type of engine.
	Tap Direction Lock to lock the engine into forward or reverse.
	Use the Acceleration Rate and Deceleration Rate sliders to set the desired rates.
	Tap Smoke Volume to set smoke to Low, Medium or High.
	Tap Tracks to transfer control to the Track Control Screen.
	Tap Switches to transfer control to the Switch Track Control Screen.
	Tap Accessories to transfer control to the Accessories Control Screen.
	Tap Playable Whistle On/Off to set it accordingly.
	Tap More to transfer control to the More... Screen.

DCS Application Engine Settings Screen - TMCC or Legacy Engines

The TMCC/Legacy Engine Settings Screen allows you to change any of the settings for an active TMCC or Legacy engine and then return to the Engine Control Screen.

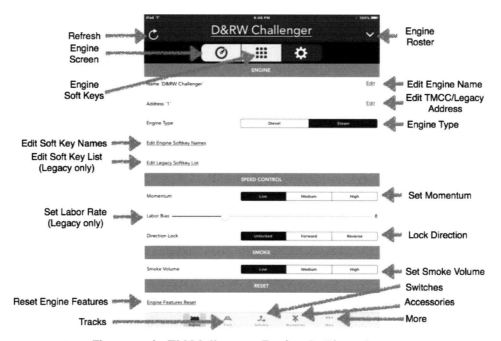

Figure 17d - TMCC/Legacy Engine Settings Screen

The following table describes the settings available to be modified using the Engine Settings Screen.

TMCC/Legacy Engine Settings Screen	
PURPOSE:	Allows you to change a TMCC or Legacy engine's settings.
HOW TO GET IT:	Tap Engine Settings on any screen where it appears.
INFORMATION DISPLAYED:	The Active TMCC or Legacy engine's DCS Engine ID# and Name, and engine settings. Note that TMCC and Legacy engines may display different engine settings.
BUTTONS:	Tap Refresh to refresh the app.
	Tap Engine Screen or swipe left to transfer control to the Engine Control Screen.
	Tap Engine Soft Keys or swipe right to transfer control to Engine Soft Keys Screen.
	Tap Engine Roster to transfer control to the DCS Engine Roster Screen.
	Tap Edit Engine Name to change the TMCC/Legacy engine's name.
	Tap Edit Engine Address to change the TMCC/Legacy engine's ID#.
	Tap Engine Type to set the engine's type accordingly.
	Tap Edit Soft Key Names to modify the names of the engine's soft keys.
	Tap Edit Soft Key List to modify a Legacy (only) engine's soft keys.
	Tap Set Labor Rate to change a Legacy (only) engine's labor rate.
	Tap a Set Momentum button to set the engine's momentum to Low, Medium or High.
	Tap a Lock Direction button to lock the engine into the desired direction.
	Tap a Set Smoke Volume button to set the engine's smoke volume to Low, Medium or High.
	Tap a Speed Control Mode to set the TMCC engine's speed mode. This option is only visible for TMCC engines and will not appear for Legacy engines.
	Tap Tracks to transfer control to the Track Control Screen.
	Tap Switches to transfer control to the Switch Track Control Screen.
	Tap Accessories to transfer control to the Accessories Control Screen.
	Tap More to transfer control to the More... Screen.

Operating the Lionel TMCC Crane Car

The Lionel TMCC crane car is a fun piece of rolling stock to operate and its operation, as a TMCC engine, using the DCS Application is easy to do.

First, set the crane car's Speed Control Mode to Default. Then, control the crane from the Engine Control Screen as follows:

- Use the Speedometer to rotate the crane's cab. Continuously rotating the Speedometer clockwise or counter-clockwise will rotate the cab in the same direction.
- Tap AUX-2 and #1, and use Boost/Brake to move the boom up and down.
- Tap AUX-2 and #2, and use Boost/Brake to move the main hook up and down.
- Tap AUX-2 and #3, and use Boost/Brake to move the small hook up and down.
- Tap AUX-2 and #4 to turn the work lights on and off.
- Tap AUX-2 and #5 to turn the head light on and off.
- Tap AUX-2 and #6 to deploy the outriggers.

DCS Application Engine Soft Keys Screen - DCS Engines

The DCS Engine Soft Keys Screen allows you to adjust any of the soft keys of the active DCS engine and then return to the Engine Control Screen.

The following table describes the settings available to be modified using the DCS Engine Soft Keys Screen.

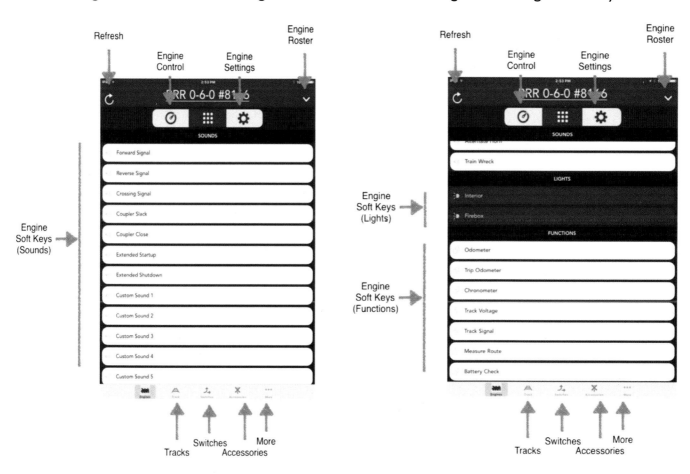

Figure 18a - DCS Engine Soft Keys Screen (1)   Figure 18b - DCS Engine Soft Keys Screen (2)

DCS Engine Soft Keys Screen	
PURPOSE:	Allows adjustment of a DCS engine's soft keys in command mode.
HOW TO GET IT:	Tap Engine Soft Keys button on any screen where it appears.
INFORMATION DISPLAYED:	Active DCS Engine ID# and Name, and engine soft keys
BUTTONS:	Tap Refresh to refresh the app's data.
	Tap Engine Control or swipe right to transfer control to the Engine Control Screen.
	Tap Engine Settings or swipe left to transfer control to the Engine Settings Screen.
	Tap Engine Roster to transfer control to the DCS Engine Roster Screen.
	Tap on an Engine Soft Key button to allow changing that soft key's setting.
	Tap Tracks to transfer control to the Track Control Screen.
	Tap Switches to transfer control to the Switch Track Control Screen.
	Tap Accessories to transfer control to the Accessories Control Screen.
	Tap More to transfer control to the More... Screen.

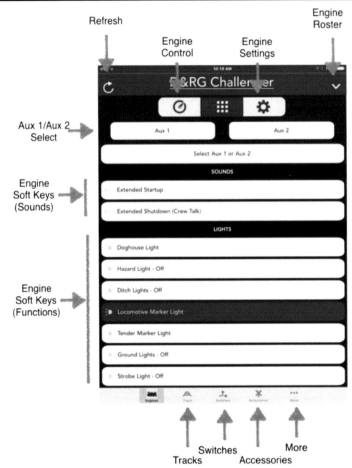

Figure 19 - TMCC/Legacy Engine Soft Keys Screen

DCS Application Engine Soft Keys Screen - TMCC/Legacy Engines

The TMCC/Legacy Engine Soft Keys Screen allows you to adjust any of the soft keys of the active TMCC or Legacy engine and then return to the Engine Control Screen.

The following table describes the settings available to be modified using the TMCC/Legacy Engine Soft Keys Screen.

TMCC/Legacy Engine Soft Keys Screen	
PURPOSE:	Allows adjustment of a TMCC or Legacy engine's soft keys in command mode.
HOW TO GET IT:	Tap Engine Soft Keys button on any screen where it appears.
INFORMATION DISPLAYED:	Active TMCC or Legacy Engine ID# and Name, and engine soft keys.
BUTTONS:	Tap Refresh to refresh the app's data.
	Tap Engine Control or swipe right to transfer control to the Engine Control Screen.
	Tap Engine Settings or swipe left to transfer control to the Engine Settings Screen.
	Tap Engine Roster to transfer control to the DCS Engine Roster Screen.
	Tap Aux 1 or Aux 2 to select the soft keys associated with either Aux 1 or Aux 2.
	Note that the following soft keys, that are not associated with Aux 1 or Aux 2, only appear for Legacy engines and not for TMCC engines.
	Tap on an Engine Soft Key button to allow changing that soft key's setting.
	Tap Tracks to transfer control to the Track Control Screen.
	Tap Switches to transfer control to the Switch Track Control Screen.
	Tap Accessories to transfer control to the Accessories Control Screen.
	Tap More to transfer control to the More... Screen.

DCS Application Add Engine Screens

The DCS Add Engine Screen allows you to add a new DCS, TMCC or Legacy engine to the DCS Application and then return to the Engine Control Screen or Engine Roster Screen. This is accomplished using screens that are different depending upon whether the engine being added is a DCS, or TMCC or Legacy engine.

Regardless of which type of engine is being added, the process begins with the Add Engine Screen.

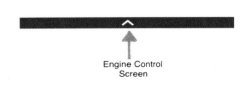

Figure 20 - Add Engine Screen

Add Engine Screen	
PURPOSE:	Allows DCS, TMCC and Legacy engines to be added to the DCS Application.
HOW TO GET IT:	Tap Add Engines button on the Engine Roster Screen.
INFORMATION DISPLAYED:	Type of engine to be added to the DCS Application.
BUTTONS:	Tap Add MTH Engine to see new available MTH engines.
	Tap Add TMCC or Legacy Engine to see new available TMCC and Legacy engines.
	Tap either Engine Control Screen or swipe up on the screen to transfer control to the Engine Control Screen.
	Tap Engine Roster to return to the Engine Roster Screen.

If a DCS engine is to be added, the DCS Application will display the Add MTH Engine Screen so that a new DCS engine may be selected.

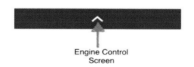

Figure 21a - Add MTH Engine Screen

The following table describes the use of the Add MTH Engine Screen.

Add MTH Engine Screen	
PURPOSE:	Allows DCS engines to be added to the DCS Application.
HOW TO GET IT:	Tap Add MTH Engine button on the Add Engine Screen.
INFORMATION DISPLAYED:	New DCS engines that may be added to the DCS Application.
BUTTONS:	Tap either Engine Control Screen or swipe up on the screen to transfer control to the Engine Control Screen.
	Tap Engine Roster to return to the Engine Roster Screen.
	Tap on a New MTH Engine add it to the DCS Application.
	You will then have the option to then add another engine (if one is available), run the engine just selected, or return to the Engine Roster Screen.

To add a new MTH engine to the DCS Application, proceed as follows:

- Tap the Engines icon at the bottom of any DCS Application Screen where it appears to select the Engine Control Screen.
- Tap the Engine Roster button to display the Engine Roster Screen.
- Tap the Add Engine button to display the Select Engine Type Screen.
- Tap the Add MTH Engine button to search all powered tracks for new MTH engines.
- A list of new MTH engines is displayed.
- Tap on an engine in the list to select it.
- You may then choose to add another engine, run the engine just selected or return to the Engine Roster Screen. If you choose to run the selected engine, the Engine Control Screen will be displayed with the new engine as the active engine.

DCS knows a DCS engine by it's DCS ID# and name. This can cause a problem hen adding a DCS engine that is identical to an engine that's already in the DCS Application's engine list, i.e., the engine has the *exact same engine name* as an engine previously added to the DCS Application.

In order for the second engine to be added successfully, it's necessary to ensure that *before* the second engine is added, that it has a DCS ID# *that is different from the DCS ID# that DCS assigned to the first engine*. If not, the second engine will not be seen as being available to be added to the DCS Application's engine list.

If necessary, change the DCS ID# of the first engine to a one that is different than that of the first engine.

If a TMCC or Legacy engine is to be added, the DCS Application will display all of the layout's available TIUs to which a Lionel command base may be connected. *It's extremely important that the correct TIU is selected!*

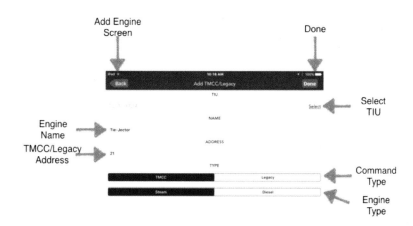

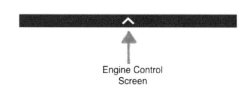

Figure 21b - Add TMCC/Legacy Engine Screen

The following table describes the use of the Add TMCC/Legacy Engine Screen.

Add TMCC/Legacy Engine Screen	
PURPOSE:	Allows TMCC or Legacy engines to be added to the DCS Application.
HOW TO GET IT:	Tap Add TMCC/Legacy Engine button on the Add Engine Screen.
INFORMATION DISPLAYED:	Information that's required to add a TMCC or Legacy engine to the DCS Application.
BUTTONS:	Tap Add Engine Screen to return to the Add Engine Screen.
	Tap Done to complete the add engine TMCC or Legacy engine process.
	Tap Engine Name to name the TMCC or Legacy engine.
	Tap TMCC/Legacy Address to enter the engine's TMCC or Legacy ID#.
	Tap Command Type to identify this engine as a TMCC or Legacy engine.
	Tap Engine Type to identify this engine as a steamer, or diesel or electric.
	Swipe up on the screen to transfer control to the Engine Control Screen.

To add a new TMCC or Legacy engine to the DCS Application, proceed as follows:

- Tap the Engines icon at the bottom of any DCS Application Screen where it appears to select the Engine Control Screen.
- Tap the Engine Roster button to display the Engine Roster Screen.
- Tap the Add Engine button to display the Select Engine Type Screen.
- Tap the Add TMCC/Legacy Engine button to add a new TMCC or Legacy engine.
- Select the TIU to which the Lionel command base is connected. The Add TMCC/Legacy Screen is displayed.
- Tap Engine Name and enter the engine's name using the on-screen keyboard.
- Tap on the engine's command type to select it.
- Tap on the Engine Type to select Steam or Diesel/Electric.
- Tap Done to return to the Engine Roster Screen.

Note that although TMCC and Legacy engines are assigned a DCS ID#, that DCS ID# is only a placeholder and cannot be changed. However, the engine's TMCC/Legacy ID# can be changed on the Engine Settings Screen.

To delete an engine from the engine list on the DCS Application's Engine Roster Screen:

- Tap on the Edit Engine List button at the top left of the screen to enter edit mode.
- Tap on the red dot to the left of the engine's name.
- Tap on the Delete button to the right of the engine's name.
- Tap on the Done button to exit edit mode.

To move an engine from the Inactive Engine List to the Active Engine List:

- Tap on the Edit Engine List button at the top left of the screen to enter edit mode.
- Tap and hold on the active engine's parallel-bars icon, and slide it up into the Active Engine List.
- Tap on the Done button to exit edit mode.

To move an engine from the Active Engine List to the Inactive Engine List:

- Tap on the Edit Engine List button at the top left of the screen to enter edit mode.
- Tap and hold on the active engine's parallel-bars icon, and slide it down into the Inactive Engine List.
- Tap on the Done button to exit edit mode.

DCS Application Edit Engine Roster Screen

The DCS Edit Engine Roster Screen allows deleting an engine from the DCS Application, and moving engines between the Active and Inactive engine lists.

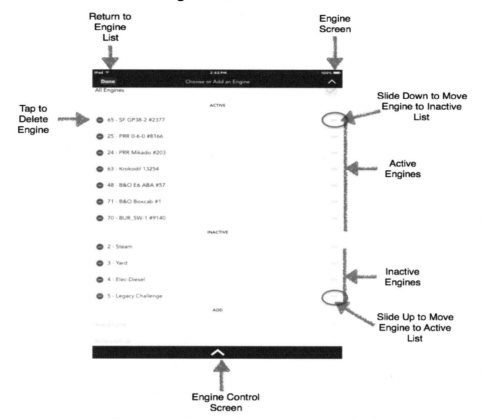

Figure 22a - Edit Engine Roster Screen (iOS)

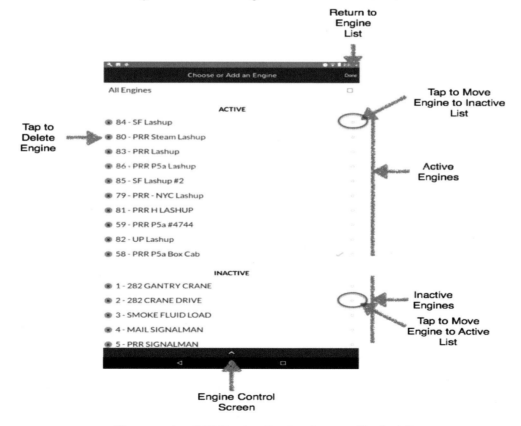

Figure 22b - Edit Engine Roster Screen (Android)

The following table describes the use of the Edit Engine Roster screen.

Edit Engine Roster Screen	
PURPOSE:	Allows DCS, TMCC and Legacy engines, and their lashups, to be moved between the Active Engine List and the Inactive Engine List, or deleted entirely from the DCS Application.
HOW TO GET IT:	Tap Edit button on the Engine Roster Screen.
INFORMATION DISPLAYED:	All engines available in the DCS Application.
BUTTONS:	Tap Engine Control Screen to transfer control to the Engine Control Screen.
	Tap on an engine's red dot to delete that engine from the DCS Application.
	Using the iOS version of the DCS App, slide an engine's parallel-bars icon to move it between the Active and Inactive engine lists.
	Using the Android version of the DCS App, tap on an engine's up arrow or down arrow to move it between the Active and Inactive engine lists.
	In order to move a DCS engine into the Active Engine List, it must be on a powered track.
	In order to move a DCS lashup into the Active Engine List, all of its member engines must be on powered tracks.
	In order to move a TMCC or Legacy engine, or a TMCC or Legacy lashup, into the Active Engine List, the TIU to which the Lionel command base is connected must be in active.
	Tap the Done button to return to the Engine Roster Screen.
	Tap Engine Control Screen to transfer to the Control Screen.
	Tap Engine Screen to transfer to the Engine Control Screen (iOS version only).

How the Active and Inactive Engine Lists Are Maintained

Whenever the DCS Application refreshes the engine roster, it "sorts" all engines and lashups as follows:

- All DCS engines on powered tracks are moved to the Active Engine List.
- All DCS engines on unpowered tracks are moved to the Inactive Engine List.
- All DCS lashups are automatically moved to the Inactive Engine List.
- All TMCC or Legacy engines are automatically moved to the Inactive Engine List.
- All TMCC and Legacy lashups are automatically moved to the Inactive Engine List.

This is exactly the same way that a READ command issued by a DCS Remote works.

It's then necessary to use the Edit Engine Screen to move any of these engines back into the Active Engine List before attempting to operate them.

Further, when a lashup is moved to the Active Engine List, any of its members that were in the Active Engine List are automatically moved to the Inactive Engine List, when the lashup is started up.

Conversely, when an engine that's a member of a lashup is moved to the Active Engine List, any lashups of which it's a member that were in the Active Engine List, are automatically moved to the Inactive Engine List when the member engine is started up.

2. Controlling Command Control Engines Using the DCS Application

To begin using the DCS Application to control command control engines, launch the application and then, when the Home Screen appears, tap the Run My Trains button. This causes the Engine Control Screen to be displayed. Wait about 2 minutes for the WIUs to come online, and for each WIU to connect to its TIU. Then, tap the Refresh button (curved arrow) at the top-left of the screen.

If the engine displayed as the active engine is not the DCS, TMCC or Legacy engine that is desired to be started up and operated, tap the Engine Roster button to transfer to the Engine Roster Screen.

On the Engine Roster Screen, select from the list of available engines the one to be operated. If all of the DCS, TMCC and Legacy engines aren't visible, scroll down the screen to view the rest of the engines.

Ensure that the desired engine is on a powered track. If the engine is in the Inactive Engine List, tap the Edit button and, if using an iOS device, use the slider icon to move it into the Active Engine List and make it active. If using an Android device, tap the up arrow to move it into the Active Engine List and make it active. Then, tap the Done button.

Tap the engine in the Active Engine List to select it and the Engine Control Screen will appear. The selected engine's name will be displayed.

On the Engine Control Screen, tap on the Startup/Shutdown button to start up the active engine.

Once the engine is started up, it can be operated using the buttons on the Engine Control Screen. Swiping clockwise on the Speedometer, or tapping on the Speed Up button, will increase speed and swiping counter-clockwise, or tapping on the Speed Down button, will reduce speed. Tapping the Reverse button while the engine is moving forward will stop and reverse the engine. Tapping the Forward button while the engine is moving in reverse will stop the engine and place it in a forward orientation. The Bell, Horn/Whistle, and Emergency Stop buttons behave the same way as do their equivalent buttons on the DCS Remote.

Engine features may be accessed by tapping the Access Engine Features button to bring up the Engine Features Screen. Tap the desired feature on the Engine Features Screen to activate that feature, or use the Master Volume slider to adjust the overall engine sounds volume. Tapping the Access Engine Control button returns to the Engine Control Screen. Engine soft keys may be accessed in a similar fashion by tapping on the Engine Soft Keys button to access the Engine Soft Keys Screen.

Settings may be changed by tapping the Engine Settings button, modifying settings on the Engine Settings Screen, and then tapping the Engine Control Screen button to return to the Engine Control Screen.

3. Where Information is Stored

DCS stores information in three places: the DCS Application, the TIU, and DCS Engines. The following discussion indicates where different information is stored.

DCS Application

DCS Application contents on different smart devices need not all be the same, and DCS Application on different smart devices are not aware of each other's contents. The following information is stored in the DCS Application:

- DCS engine names
- TIU Associations With DCS Engines
- TMCC and Legacy engine names
- Accessories

- Switch tracks
- Scenes
- Routes
- TIU Tracks
- Custom soft key lists and DCS engine maximum speed values.

When a DCS Application's content is reset, all of the information stored in the DCS Application is deleted. Each of the items stored in the DCS Application is discussed below.

DCS Engine Names

Engine names are listed by DCS ID#. When a DCS engine is added to a DCS Application, the DCS Application will place the engine into its engine list with a DCS ID# that is the same as what is in the engine, if it is available. If the engine's DCS engine ID# is already in use in the DCS Application, the first (lowest) available DCS engine ID# will be selected.

TMCC engines and Legacy engines must have their actual commands system ID# entered at the time that the engine is added to the DCS Application. These engines will also be assigned a "dummy" DCS ID# that is the lowest unused DCS ID# that is available in the DCS Application.

Regardless, the engine will be assigned its new engine ID# and will respond to commands using that ID#, however, the new engine ID# will not become permanent in a DCS engine's on-board memory until track power is removed from the engine. When track power is removed from the engine, the engine uses its on-board battery (PS2 engines) or super capacitor (PS3 engines)to write its new engine ID# into its memory. If a PS2 engine's battery is too low to write back a newly-assigned new DCS ID#, the DCS Application will not be able to access the engine the next time you attempt to Start Up the engine after power is restored.

If a DCS engine is added to DCS Applications on multiple smart devices, it will not necessarily be assigned the same DCS ID# in all copies of the DCS Application, but rather, a DCS engine will have the DCS ID# assigned to it by the last DCS Application to which it was added. This is the DCS ID# by which the engine must be addressed. Any DCS Application that has the engine with an ID# different from the one in the engine's memory will be unable to command the engine and will get errors when it attempts to do so. Therefore, it is always advisable to keep all DCS Applications on all smart devices in sync by ensuring that DCS engines have the same DCS ID# in all DCS Applications.

If engines are to be added to DCS Applications on multiple smart devices, it's important that they always have the same engine ID# in each DCS Application. When adding an engine, first add it to a DCS Application on one smart device and then repeatedly add the engine to each additional DCS Application. If you follow this process starting with the first engine you add to DCS and continue it with all subsequent engines, your DCS Applications will always be in sync with regard to engine ID#s.

When changing an engine ID# of an engine already in one or more DCS Applications, ensure that the engine ID# to which you desire to change the engine is available in all DCS Applications where the engine resides. To keep DCS engines in sync when changing their DCS ID#s in multiple DCS Applications, first change the engine ID# in the first DCS Application. Once the engine ID# has been changed in the first DCS Application, delete the engine from the second DCS Application and re-add it to the second DCS Application. Repeat these steps for each additional DCS Application in which the engine's DCS ID# is to be changed.

TIU Associations With DCS Engines

Each DCS engine is associated with one and only one TIU. An association occurs when a DCS engine is added to a DCS Application. The TIU that is controlling the track where the DCS engine is added is automatically associated with that DCS engine.

Engine associations are temporary and can be moved from TIU to TIU, and the association will change whenever the engine is re-added to the same DCS Application or added to a different DCS Application. Further, the association will also change to whichever TIU is controlling the powered track upon which the DCS engine resides when a DCS Application refreshes its engine list. Only the last TIU association for a DCS engine is stored in the DCS Application.

TMCC and Legacy Engine Names

TMCC and Legacy engine names are listed by DCS engine ID#, however, the DCS ID# for TMCC and Legacy engines is not critical. The critical factor for TMCC and Legacy engines is the engine's actual TMCC/Legacy ID#. When a TMCC or Legacy engine is added to a DCS Application, the DCS Application will place the engine into its engine list using the lowest DCS ID# that is available.

If a TMCC or Legacy engine is added to more than one DCS Application, it will not necessarily be assigned the same DCS ID# in all DCS Applications. Again, this is not a problem for TMCC or Legacy engines.

Accessories

Although accessory names are listed by DCS ID#, they are assigned to AIU ACC ports. Unlike DCS engines, accessories need not have the same DCS ID#s when entered into multiple DCS Applications.

What identifies an accessory is the TIU, AIU and ACC port to which the accessory is connected. These assignments must be the same for any accessory that is listed in more than one DCS Application.

Switch Tracks

Although switch track names are listed by DCS ID#, they are assigned to AIU SW ports. Unlike DCS engines, switch tracks need not have the same DCS ID#s when entered into multiple DCS Applications.

What identifies a switch track is the TIU, AIU and SW port to which the switch track is connected. These assignments must be the same for any switch track that is listed in more than one DCS Application.

Scenes

Scenes are collections of accessories that may be turned on or off as a group and are displayed at the end of the same list as accessories, by DCS ID#. Scenes in one DCS Application can be numbered the same as, or different from, Scenes in another DCS Application.

Routes

Routes are collections of switch tracks that may be activated as a group and are displayed at the end of the same list as switch tracks, by DCS ID#. Routes in one DCS Application can be numbered the same as, or different from, Routes in another DCS Application.

TIU Tracks

TIU Tracks must be assigned before the remote can control a Variable TIU Channel. Each TIU Track is assigned to one TIU Variable Channel.

Custom DCS Engine Soft Key Lists

Custom DCS engine soft key lists are stored along with DCS engine information. This includes the maximum speed at which a DCS engine may be operated when using this DCS Application, as well as any changes made to the order of the DCS engine soft key list in this DCS Application.

TIU

Each TIU used with a layout must have a unique TIU ID# of 1 through 5. Numbering TIUs is required by DCS. Numbering of TIUs is accomplished through the DCS Application's System Settings, TIU Settings Screen.

TIU contents need not all be the same and TIUs are not aware of each other's contents. The following information is stored in the TIU:

- Associations With DCS Engines
- Custom Sounds
- Record/Playback Sessions.

When a TIU is Feature Reset, all of the information stored in the TIU is deleted, however, the TIU retains its DCS ID#. When a TIU is Factory Reset, all of the information stored in the TIU is deleted and the DCS ID# is restored to 1. Each of the items stored in the TIU is discussed below.

Associations With DCS Engines

Although DCS engine information is not saved in the TIU, each DCS engine is associated with one and only one TIU. An association occurs when a DCS engine is added to a DCS Application. The TIU that is controlling the track where the DCS engine is added is automatically associated with that DCS engine.

Engine associations are temporary and can be moved from TIU to TIU, and the association will change whenever the engine is re-added to the same DCS Application or added to a different DCS Application. Further, the association will also change to whichever TIU is controlling the powered track upon which the DCS engine resides whenever the DCS Application's Engine Roster is refreshed. Only the last TIU association for a DCS engine is stored in the TIU.

Custom Sounds

Up to three Custom Sounds may be stored in each TIU on the layout for a maximum total of 15 Custom Sounds.

While being recorded, a Custom Sound may play for only 11 seconds and then stop playing the sound out of the engine. This is because the processor in the TIU runs out of buffer space that it needs to save the audio that's being recorded. The Custom Sound is still being recorded in the TIU, however, it just isn't being played out of the engine.

The 11 second initial playback while recording is to confirm that the Custom Sound is acceptable and should be recorded. After 11 seconds the TIU discontinues playing the Custom Sound so that it can preserve buffer space in memory to record the audio. Regardless, the TIU records up to a maximum of 174 seconds of the Custom Sound.

Record/Playback Sessions

Up to three Record/Playback sessions may be stored in each TIU on the layout for a maximum total of 15 Record/Playback sessions. The total of all three Record/Playback sessions cannot exceed 90 minutes or 500 button presses, or a combination of the two.

DCS Engines

DCS engines store the engine's feature settings and other information in the memory of the DCS engine's PS2 or PS3 board. These include:

- DCS engine ID#
- Lighting, including headlight, marker lights, interior lights, number board lights, ditch lights, and beacon
- Sounds appropriate to the engine, such as idle sounds, cab chatter, horn, whistle, bell, passenger station sounds, freight yard sounds, transit station announcements, and others
- Sound levels, including engine sounds, horn/whistle, bell, and accent sounds
- Chuff rate and Proto Chuff setting
- Smoke level
- Acceleration and deceleration rates
- Original soft key settings
- Custom Name, if assigned
- Engine statistics, including Chronometer, Odometer, Measured Route, and battery condition

Performing a Feature Reset of a DCS engine will restore all settings, except for Custom Name, Chronometer, Odometer, and DCS engine ID#, to their original, factory settings. Performing a Factory Reset will additionally delete the engine's Custom Name, reset the engine's DCS ID# to 1 and delete the engine from the DCS Application.

Part VIII - Accessory and Switch Track Control

1. How the AIU Works

The AIU is the DCS component that is used to control switch tracks and accessories from the DCS Application. The AIU is, quite simply, a box that contains relays to control switch tracks and accessories. These relays operate just like toggle switches and push buttons, except that they are controlled from the DCS Application.

Switch tracks are connected to AIU SW ports and accessories are connected to AIU ACC ports. Each SW or ACC port has 3 terminals, labeled 1, 2 and IN.

Switch tracks or accessories are programmed into each DCS Application by entering the switch track or accessory path from the TIU to the AIU to the SW or ACC port. When the switch track or accessory name is selected in the DCS Application and its button is tapped, the switch track or accessory is activated.

Switch tracks are activated briefly to throw the switch and then cease activation, while accessories may be activated continuously until stopped or momentarily only as long as a button is pressed.

AIUs are connected to TIUs in a chain-like manner, using cables supplied with each AIU, i.e., TIU to AIU #1 to AIU #2 to AIU #3 to AIU #4 to AIU #5. Up to 5 AIUs may be connected to a single TIU. Since up to 5 TIUs may be connected to a layout, a layout may have up to 25 AIUs. Since each AIU can handle 10 switch tracks plus 10 accessories, the total number allowable for a layout would be 250 switch tracks and 250 accessories.

If it's necessary to replace an AIU cable, they are standard RJ12, 6 Conductor Cross Wired Modular Telephone Cables.

2. Adding and Controlling Switch Tracks

The Premium version of the DCS Application allows for complete control of switch tracks, including operating, adding, deleting, and changing of switch track information. This is accomplished by using the Switch Tracks Control Screen.

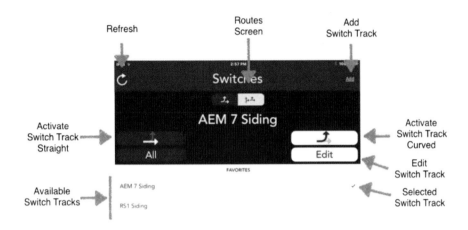

Figure 23 - Switch Tracks Control Screen

How to access the Switch Tracks Control Screen, as well as a description of its functions, is described in the following table.

Switch Tracks Control Screen	
PURPOSE:	Allows Control of Switch Tracks.
HOW TO GET IT:	Tap Switches Soft Keys button on any screen where it appears.
INFORMATION DISPLAYED:	A list of switch tracks that are programmed into all of the layout's TIUs.
BUTTONS:	Tap Refresh Screen to refresh the screen.
	Tap Routes Screen, or swipe left or right to transfer control to the Routes Screen.
	Tap Add Switch Track or Route to add a new switch track or Route.
	Tap a switch track in the Available Switch Track list to select it.
	Tap Activate Switch Track Straight to set the selected switch track to its straight orientation.
	Tap Activate Switch Track Curved to set the selected switch track to its curved orientation.
	Tap All to set all of the switch tracks in the SWITCHES list to their default orientation.
	Tap Edit Switch Track to edit the selected switch track's name, or the TIU/AIU/SW port of the selected switch track.
	Tap Engines to transfer control to the Engine Control Screen.
	Tap Track to transfer control to the Track Control Screen.
	Tap Accessories to transfer control to the Accessory Control Screen.
	Tap More... to transfer control to the More... Screen.

3. Operating Switch Tracks Using the DCS Application

It's strongly recommended that a separate transformer be used for powering switch tracks. This ensures that the DCS signal never has to travel through the windings of a switch motor or a circuit board. If the DCS signal travels through switch motor windings or circuit boards, serious degradation of the signal may occur.

In order to program a switch track into the DCS Application, the Add Switch or Route Screen is used.

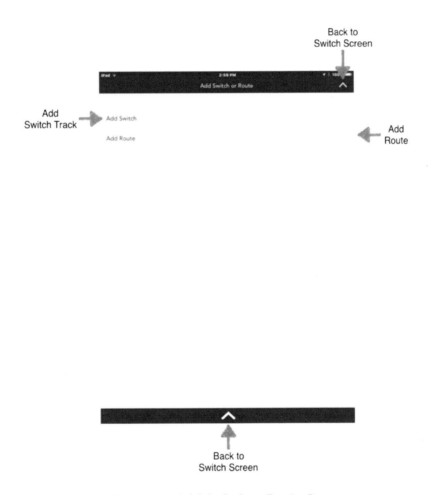

Figure 24 - Add Switch or Route Screen

How to access the Add Switch or Route Screen, as well as a description of its functions, is described in the following table.

Add Switch or Route Screen	
PURPOSE:	Add Switch Tracks and Routes.
HOW TO GET IT:	Tap Add on Switches Screen.
INFORMATION DISPLAYED:	Buttons to add a switch track or a Route.
BUTTONS:	Tap Add Switch Track to add a switch track.
	Tap Add Route to add a Route.
	Tap Back to Switch Screen to return to the Switches Control Screen.

Programming Switch Tracks Into the DCS Application

To add a switch track to the DCS Application, proceed as follows:

- Tap the Switches icon at the bottom of any DCS Application screen where it appears to select the Switch Tracks Control Screen.
- Tap the Add icon at the top right of the Switch Tracks Control Screen. The Add Switch or Route Screen is displayed.
- Tap Add Switch.
- A list of available TIUs is displayed. Tap the TIU that's connected to the AIU where the switch track is connected.
- A list of available AIUs connected to the TIU is displayed. Tap on the AIU to which the switch track is connected.
- A list of the TIU's SW ports is displayed. Tap on the SW port that's connected to the switch track.
- Use the on-screen keyboard to enter the name of the switch track. Tap on DONE to save the switch track's name, and to be returned to the Switch Tracks Control Screen.

Testing Switch Track Operation

To test the accessory or accessory functions, proceed as follows:

- Tap the Switches icon at the bottom of any DCS Application screen to select the Switch Tracks Control Screen.
- Tap the switch track in the SWITCHES list to select it.
- Tap the Straight button to throw the switch track to its straight orientation.
- Tap the Curved button to throw the switch track to curved orientation.
- If the switch track switches to the wrong orientation, swap the wires connected to terminals 1 and 2 of the SW port and test again.
- If the switch track fails to operate, first ensure that it is wired as described above. Next, delete the switch track from the DCS Application by tapping the Edit button and then deleting the switch track. Then, re-enter it. If problems persist, refer to Switch Track Control Problems in the Troubleshooting Problems section of this book.

If it's necessary to change the programmed assignment of a switch track to a different TIU, AIU or SW port on the same AIU, tap the Edit button to proceed.

4. Adding and Controlling Accessories

The Premium version of the DCS Application allows for complete control of accessories, including operating, adding, deleting, and changing of accessory information. This is accomplished by using the Accessories Control Screen.

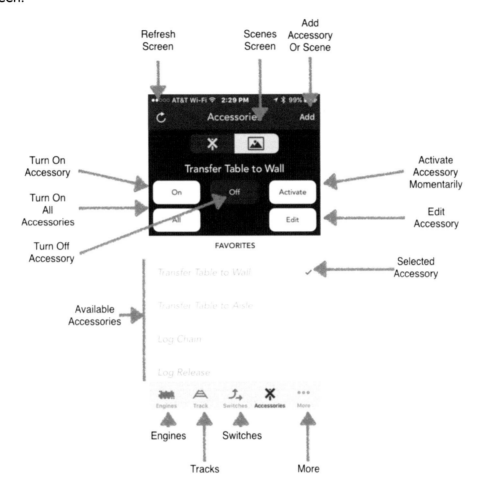

Figure 25 - Accessories Screen

How to access the Accessories Control Screen, as well as a description of its functions, is described in the following table.

Accessories Screen	
PURPOSE:	Allows Control of Accessories
HOW TO GET IT:	Tap Accessories Soft Keys button on any screen where it appears.
INFORMATION DISPLAYED:	A list of accessories and Scenes that are programmed into all of the layout's TIUs.
BUTTONS:	Tap Refresh Screen to refresh the screen.
	Tap Scenes Screen, or swipe right or left to transfer control to the Scenes Screen.
	Tap Add to add a new accessory or Scene.
	Tap an accessory or Scene in the Available Accessories list to select it.
	Tap On to turn on the selected accessory.
	Tap Off to turn off the selected accessory.
	Tap Activate to turn on the selected accessory momentarily as long as the button is pressed.
	Tap Edit Accessory or Scene to edit the name of a selected accessory or Scene, or the TIU/AIU/ACC port path of the selected accessory.
	Tap Engines to transfer control to the Engine Control Screen.
	Tap Track to transfer control to the Track Control Screen.
	Tap Switches to transfer control to the Switch Track Control Screen.
	Tap More... to transfer control to the More... Screen.

5. Operating Accessories Using the DCS Application

DCS can, through the AIU, control just about any accessory. In general, each accessory uses one AIU ACC port. However, some accessories that have multiple functions that happen independently of each other require that each operation be treated as a separate accessory. An example of this would be the MTH Operating Track section, where one function activates the uncoupling magnet and another activates the control rails, independently of each other. These types of accessories require the use of multiple AIU ACC ports, one port for each independent function.

Accessories that do several things at the same time, however, can generally be wired using the same AIU port. An example of this would be the MTH Operating Car Wash or Operating Firehouse, where a car or fire truck moves while lights turn on.

It's strongly recommended that a separate transformer be used to power accessories. This ensures that the DCS signal never has to travel through the windings of a motor or circuit board. If the DCS signal travels through motor windings or circuit boards, serious degradation of the signal may occur.

In order to program a switch track into the DCS Application, the Add Switch or Route Screen is used.

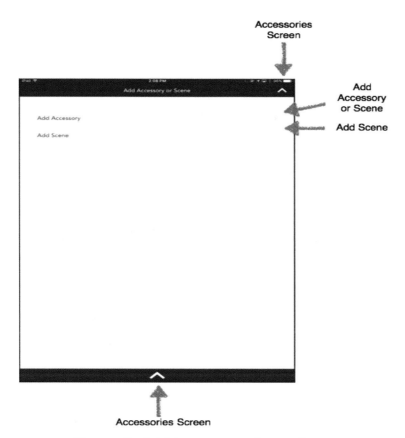

Figure 26 - Add Accessory or Scene Screen

How to access the Add Accessory or Route Screen, as well as a description of its functions, is described in the following table.

Add Accessory or Route Screen	
PURPOSE:	Add Accessories and Scenes.
HOW TO GET IT:	Tap Add on Accessories Control Screen.
INFORMATION DISPLAYED:	Buttons to add an accessory or a Scene.
BUTTONS:	Tap Add Accessory to add an accessory.
	Tap Add Scene to add a Scene.
	Tap the up arrow at the top-right to return to the Accessories Control Screen.
	Tap the up arrow at the bottom-middle to return to the Accessories Control Screen.

Programming Accessories Into the DCS Application

To add a connected accessory or accessory function to the DCS Application, proceed as follows:

- Tap the Accessories icon at the bottom of any DCS Application screen where it appears to select the Accessories Control Screen.
- Tap the Add icon at the top right of the Accessories Control Screen. Then, tap Add Accessory on the next screen.
- A list of available TIUs is displayed. Tap the TIU that's connected to the AIU where the accessory is connected.
- A list of available AIUs connected to the TIU is displayed. Tap on the AIU to which the accessory is connected.
- A list of the TIU's ACC ports is displayed. Tap on the ACC port to which the accessory is connected.
- Use the on-screen keyboard to enter the name of the accessory. Tap on DONE to save the accessory's name, and to be returned to the Accessories Control Screen.

Testing Accessory Operation

To test the accessory or accessory functions, proceed as follows:

- Tap the Accessories icon at the bottom of any DCS Application screen where it appears to select the Accessories Control Screen.
- Tap the On button to turn on the selected accessory or function.
- Tap the Off button to turn off the selected accessory or function.
- Tap the Activate button to turn on the selected accessory or function momentarily, until the Activate button is released.
- If the accessory or accessory function fails to operate, first ensure that it is wired as described above. Next, delete the accessory function from the DCS Application by tapping the Edit button and then tapping Delete accessory. Then, re-enter it. If problems persist, refer to Accessory Control Problems in the Troubleshooting Problems section of this book.
- Repeat the above for each additional accessory or accessory function that was connected to the AIU.

If it's necessary to change the programmed assignment of an accessory or accessory function to a different TIU, AIU or SW port on the same AIU, tap the Edit button and then Edit accessory path to proceed.

6. Parallel Control of Switch Tracks and Accessories

Depending upon the size and configuration of the O gauge layout, it may be advantageous to operate switch tracks or accessories from either the DCS Application or the control panel, depending upon the situation. This is achieved by wiring the AIU and control panel in parallel.

Parallel Operation of Switch Tracks

There are times when it is advantageous to be able to throw switch tracks very quickly. This can often prevent an impending problem, such as a pair of trains on a collision course or a train that's been turned around a reversing loop and is heading towards its own siding via an incorrectly oriented switch track.

On the other hand, in order for switch tracks to be included in Routes or Record/Playback sessions, (Routes and Record/Playback are discussed in detail later in this book in Part IX - Advanced Features and Functions), they must first be connected to an AIU's SW port and programmed into the DCS Application.

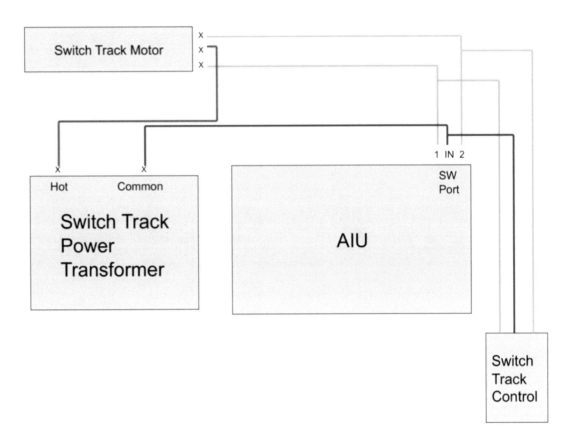

Figure 27 - Parallel Connection of Switch Tracks

Parallel Operation of Accessories

There are times when it's good to be able to operate accessories manually, such as when young children are visiting the layout. Very little fingers may sometimes have trouble manipulating the DCS Application, however, it's generally much easier for small children to push a button or throw a switch to make something on the layout happen. Some adults who are not comfortable using a DCS Application would also benefit.

However, in order for accessories to be included in Scenes or in Record/Playback sessions (Scenes and Record/Playback are discussed in detail later in this book in Part IX - Advanced Features and Functions), they must first be connected to the AIU's ACC port and programmed into the DCS Application. This may be accomplished for the great majority of accessories, however, there are some situations where this is not possible.

In some cases, connecting an accessory to both an AIU ACC port and also the accessory's controller may cause a conflict that can only be resolved by either disconnecting the accessory from the AIU or from its controller. This occurs when the controller uses a latching type relay or other device that continues to apply power to the accessory even after the manual control is released.

Two examples of this are MTH's Operating Passenger Station and Operating Freight Station.

In order to wire accessories in parallel, proceed as follows:

- First, connect the accessory to the AIU as described earlier in the section Operating Accessories Using DCS and ensure that it's operating properly from the DCS Application.
- Next, mount the accessory's manual controller in the desired location on the control panel.
- Following the instructions in the accessory's instruction manual, connect the necessary wires between the accessory's wires or terminals and the accessory's manual controller.

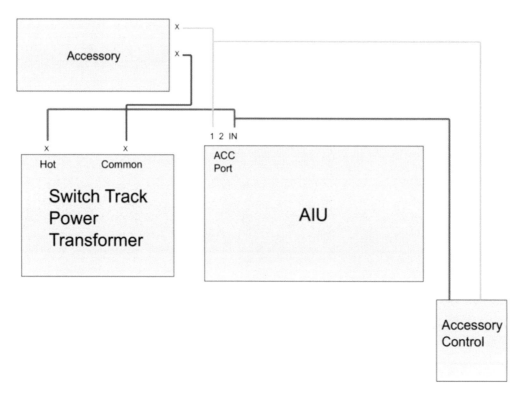

Figure 28 - Parallel Connection of Accessories

7. Special AIU Applications

Atlas Turntable

Dave Hikel, of Hikel O Gauge Layouts and Trains (www.hikelogauge.com), developed a method for operating the Atlas #6910 turntable from the DCS Application using two AIU ACC ports. The turntable determines in which direction to rotate based upon the nature of the DC voltage with which it's supplied. If it "sees" a positive (+) voltage it will rotate in one direction. If it "sees" a negative (-) voltage it will rotate in the opposite direction.

A diode is a small semiconductor device, available at Radio Shack and other electronic parts suppliers, that converts AC voltage to DC voltage. Depending upon which end of the diode the AC voltage enters, either DC + or DC - voltage comes out of the other end. Dave Hikel's method works as follows:

- Connect a transformer's AC Hot terminal (10-18 volts) to the IN terminal of an AIU ACC port.
- The output of this AIU ACC port is filtered by placing a pair of diodes at its 1 and 2 terminals. The preferred diode is IN4001 or equivalent (Radio Shack part #276-1653). The diodes should be connected so that their orientation is reversed end-for-end with respect to each other.
- Since the AIU ACC port will output through the 1 terminal when the port is turned on from the DCS Application (by tapping the "On button on the Accessory Control Screen) and will output through the 2 terminal when the port is turned off from the DCS Application (by tapping the Off button on the Accessory Control Screen), only a positive or negative DC voltage can be output by the port at any time.
- Since only one or the other of ports 1 and 2 will have an output DC voltage at any time, depending upon which soft key is pressed, the other ends of the two diodes can be safely connected to each other without the fear of creating a short circuit. The connected pair of diodes is now connected to the IN terminal of a second AIU ACC port.
- Connect the output of the second AIU's ACC port IN terminal to one terminal of the Atlas turntable.
- Connect the transformer's AC Common terminal to the other terminal of the Atlas turntable.

The DCS WIFI Companion

- Program the DCS Application for the two AIU ACC ports in the usual manner as described in Part VIII - Accessory and Switch Track Control, 5. Operating Accessories Using the DCS Application, Programming Accessories Into the DCS Application earlier in this book.

To operate the Atlas turntable, use the first AIU port to select the direction of rotation by tapping either its On or Off button. Then start and stop the rotation with the second ACC port by using its On or Off button.

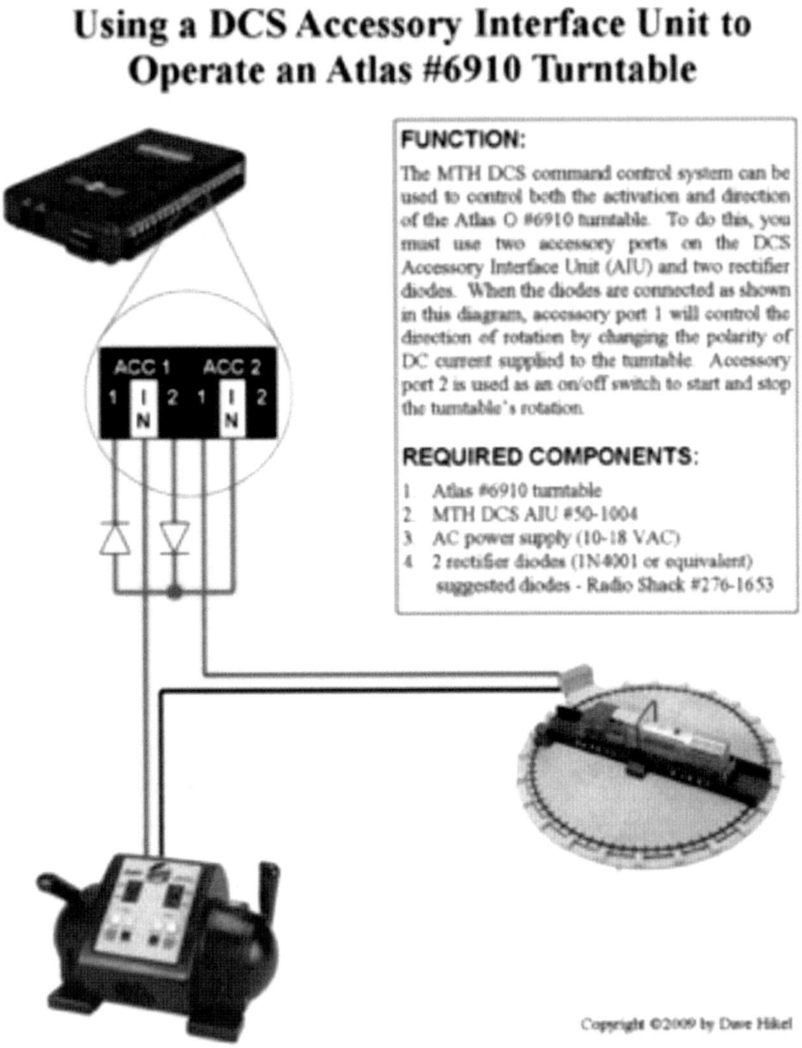

Figure 29 - Atlas Turntable

Tortoise Switch Machines

Previously, a method was discussed for using Tortoise switch machines with latching relay-type devices between the switch machine and the AIU's SW port. The purpose of such a device was to allow a longer activation period to throw a switch using the Tortoise switch machine. A less expensive way to activate switches using Tortoise switch machines through the AIU is to use the AIU's ACC ports rather than its SW ports.

The Tortoise motor determines in which direction to throw the switch based upon the nature of the DC voltage with which it's supplied. If it "sees" a positive (+) voltage it will throw the switch in one direction. If it "sees" a negative (-) voltage it will throw the switch in the other direction.

A diode is a small semiconductor device, available at Radio Shack and other electronic parts suppliers, that converts AC voltage to DC voltage. Depending upon which end of the diode the AC voltage enters, either DC + or DC - voltage comes out of the other end.

Using a pair of diodes, wire the Tortoise motor to an AIU ACC port as follows:

- Connect a transformer's AC Hot terminal (10-20 volts) to the IN terminal of an AIU ACC port.
- The output of this AIU ACC port is filtered by placing a pair of diodes at its 1 and 2 terminals. The preferred diode is IN4001 or equivalent (Radio Shack part #276-1653). The diodes should be connected so that their orientation is reversed end-for-end with respect to each other.
- Since the AIU ACC port will output through the 1 terminal when the port is turned on from the DCS Application by tapping the On button on the Accessory Control Screen) and will output through the 2 terminal when the port is turned off from the DCS Application (by tapping the Off button on the Accessory Control Screen), only a positive or negative DC voltage can be output by the port at any time.
- Since only one or the other of ports 1 and 2 will have an output DC voltage at any time, depending upon which soft key is pressed, the other ends of the two diodes can be safely connected to each other without the fear of creating a short circuit. The connected pair of diodes is now connected to one terminal of the Tortoise switch motor.
- Connect the transformer's AC Common terminal to the other terminal of the Tortoise switch motor.
- Program the DCS Application for the AIU ACC port in the usual manner as described in Part VIII - Accessory and Switch Track Control, 5. Operating Accessories Using the DCS Application, Programming Accessories Into the DCS Application earlier in this book.

To operate the switch track, throw the switch one way by pressing soft key ON and the other way by pressing soft key OFF.

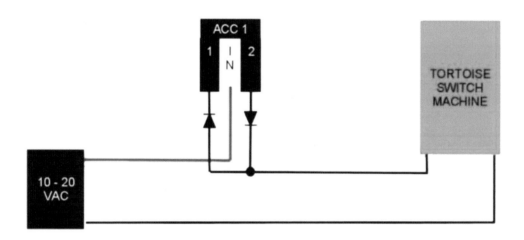

Figure 30 - Alternate Method for Wiring a Tortoise Switch Machine

Controlling Track Power Using the AIU

The AIU can be used to control track power safely using two different methods. The first method is for the AIU to switch the power to the track directly, using its own ACC port relays to carry power. In this case, the following rules apply:

- The AIU's relays are rated for no more than 4 amps. If more than 4 amps are passed through an AIU's relay the relay can be damaged. Therefore, the expected amp draw for any tracks controlled by an AIU relay must be less than 4 amps.
- There is no internal protection for the AIU's relays. Therefore, a 4 amp, fast blow fuse must be inserted in the Hot wire between the output of the AIU and the track.

Using the method of having the AIU switch power to the track directly, wire as follows:

- Connect the Hot wire from either a TIU output channel or a terminal block connected to a TIU output channel, to either terminal of a 4 amp fuse.

- Connect the other terminal of the 4 amp fuse to the AIU's ACC port's IN terminal.
- Connect the same ACC port's I terminal to the center rail of the track that will have its power controlled by the AIU.
- Connect the Common wire from the same TIU output channel or terminal block connected to a TIU output channel, to one of the outside rails of the track that will have its power controlled by the AIU.
- Program the DCS Application for the AIU ACC port in the usual manner as described in Part VIII - Accessory and Switch Track Control, 5. Operating Accessories Using the DCS Application, Programming Accessories Into the DCS Application earlier in this book.

To control power to the track, first select the associated accessory entry on the DCS Application's Accessory Control Screen. Then, turn the track's power on and off by tapping the On and Off buttons, respectively. The buttons will activate and deactivate the AIU's internal relay, and turn power to the track on and off, as desired.

The second method of controlling a track's power using the AIU's ACC port requires that the AIU control a relay, external to the AIU, that will do the actual switching of track power. In this case, the following rules apply:

- The external relay must be able to handle a minimum of 10 amps continuous load and be of the non-latching type.
- A power supply for the relay itself must be available on the layout. Therefore, it's wise to choose a relay that is powered by AC rather than DC at a voltage that is close to the voltage available from one of the layout's accessory transformers.
- As for all track power, ensure that the power to the track to be controlled by the AIU is protected by either a fast-acting fuse of no more than 10 amps or a circuit breaker that has similar characteristics to such a fuse.

Using the method of having the AIU switch power to the track using an external relay, wire as follows:

- Connect one of the wires from the relay's power supply directly to one of the terminals that supply power for the relay itself (not for the tracks).
- Connect the second of the wires from the relay's power supply to the AIU's ACC port's "IN" terminal.
- Connect the same ACC port's "I" terminal to the other one of the terminals that supply power for the relay itself (not for the tracks).
- Connect the Hot wire from either a TIU output channel or a terminal block connected to a TIU output channel, to one of the relay's input switching terminals.
- Connect the corresponding one of the relay's output terminals to the center rail of the track that will have its power controlled by the AIU.
- Connect the Common wire from the same TIU output channel or terminal block connected to a TIU output channel, to the other of the relay's input switching terminals.
- Connect the corresponding one of the relay's output terminals to an outside rail of the track that will have its power controlled by the AIU.
- Program the DCS Application for the AIU ACC port in the usual manner as described in Part VIII - Accessory and Switch Track Control, 5. Operating Accessories Using the DCS Application, Programming Accessories Into the DCS Application earlier in this book.

To control power to the track, first select the associated accessory entry on the DCS Application's Accessory Control Screen. Then, turn the track's power on and off by tapping the "On" and "Off" buttons, respectively. The buttons will activate and deactivate the AIU's internal relay, and turn power to the track on and off, as desired.

Lionel #350 Transfer Table

(This information appeared in an article in O Gauge Railroading magazine, Run 236 June/July 2009 entitled Creative Extensions for Lionel's No. 350 Transfer Table)

The Lionel #350 Transfer Table may be operated from the DCS Application using two AIU ACC ports. There are two caveats if the transfer table is to be wired to use the AIU:

- It will be necessary for the operator to line up the transfer table at its sidings by eye rather than using the light on top of the table.
- The control box that accompanies the transfer table may not be used if the table is wired to operate using the AIU. To control power to the track, first select the associated accessory entry on the DCS Application's Accessory Control Screen. Then, turn the track's power on and off by tapping the On and Off buttons, respectively. The buttons will activate and deactivate the AIU's internal relay, and turn power to the track on and off, as desired.

Wire the Transfer Table as follows:

- Connect transformer Hot from the output of the TIU channel that will control the transfer table yard to the middle of the 5 rails upon which the table rides. This will power the center rail on the table. Placing a toggle switch in this line allows power to the table's center rail to be turned off if necessary, however, this is optional.
- Connect transformer Common from the same TIU channel to the two outermost of the 5 rails. This will provide Common for all table functions, including the outside rails on the table itself.
- Connect a 14 volt AC accessory transformer Hot to the inputs of two AIU ACC ports on terminal In of each. This will provide power for the motors that move the table.
- Connect terminal 1 of one of the two AIU ACC ports to rail #2 of the 5 rails. Connect the other AIU ACC port terminal 1 to rail #4. It doesn't matter which side you count rails from, as you'll see below.
- Program the AIU so that the first of the two AIU ports is designated as Table Forward operation and the other for Table Reverse. Program the DCS Application for the AIU ACC port as described in Part VIII - Accessory and Switch Track Control, 5. Operating Accessories Using the DCS Application, Programming Accessories Into the DCS Application earlier in this book.
- Wire each siding's center rail to one point on a rotary switch or to a separate toggle switch for each siding. Rotary switches are preferred if panel space is at a premium, however, toggle switches will allow many of the engines to be powered up at the same time.
- Wire the rotary switch input tab to the TIU channel output Hot that was previously connected to the middle of the 5 rails upon which the table rides. If using more than one rotary, or multiple toggles, wire the inputs of all the switches back to that same TIU channel Hot.
- Wire one outside rail of each siding back to the TIU channel output Common that was connected to the two outermost of the 5 rails upon which the table rides.

Transfer Table Wiring Diagram

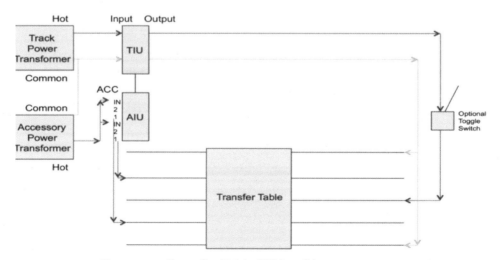

Figure 31 - Transfer Table Wiring Diagram

Sidings Wiring Diagram

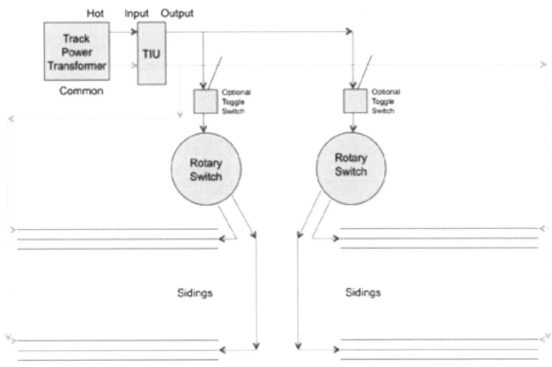

Figure 32 - Transfer Table Sidings Wiring Diagram

To operate the transfer table, do the following:

- Turn on power to the table and also to the siding upon which the engine you want to operate resides. Note that when the table's center rail has power, the red light on top of the table will be on.
- Using the DCS Application's Accessory Control Screen, select the forward or reverse table entry. Use the On, Off and Activate buttons to line up the table with a siding. Using the Activate button will allow a nudge-like function for precise lineup. You'll find that the table rolls at a very slow speed so precise line up is easy.
- In the Engine Roster Screen, select the desired engine, go to the Engine Control Screen, start it up, and run it onto the table.
- Go back to the Accessory Control Screen and select the forward or reverse table entry. Use the On, Off and Activate buttons to line up the table with the lead-in track.
- Go to the Engine Control Screen and drive the engine off the table.

Controlling Switch Tracks Using AIU ACC Ports

An AIU's SW ports are normally reserved for operating switch tracks and its ACC ports are normally reserved for operating accessories. However, many layouts have more switch tracks than accessories and often a DCS operator will be forced into purchasing additional AIUs just to add additional switch tracks, while the existing AIUs have ACC ports that are not being used.

When this occurs, it is possible, depending upon the nature of the switch track's motor, to use ACC ports to operate switch tracks. In order to do this, the switch track motor must be of the kind that, once the switch has been thrown, the motor turns off. An example of this type of motor would be the DZ1000 or DZ2500 switch motors, manufactured by Z-Stuff and most often used with Ross and Gargraves, and sometimes as replacement motors for Atlas, switch tracks. However, even with these motors, the automatic non-derailing feature must not be implemented. The reason why the automatic non-derailing mechanism must not be implemented is due to the difference in the action of the relays within the AIU itself.

When an AIU SW port is activated, the relay is closed for only a second or two, long enough to cause the motor of most switch tracks (Tortoise motors being the exception) to throw the switch.

However, when an AIU ACC port is activated, it may be activated in one of two ways:

- If activated using the ON soft key, the relay will be activated and stay closed. If the motor does not turn off after throwing the switch, it will eventually burn out.
- If activated using the ACT soft key, the relay will activate only momentarily, however, it will then revert to its pre-activation state, throwing the switch back to its previous orientation.
- If automatic non-derailing is implemented for a switch track wired to an AIU's ACC port, when the automatic non-derailing mechanism is activated by a passing train, the motor will attempt to throw the switch in both directions at the same time, since the AIU's relay will have been locked into a position to throw the switch in the opposite direction.

For similar reasons, if a switch track is wired for operation using an AIU ACC port, it may not also be wired for operation using a manual controller.

The subject of using AIU ACC ports to control switch tracks may be summarized as follows

- Only switch track motors, such as Z-Stuff's DZ1000 or DZ2500, that shut themselves off after throwing the switch, may be used.
- The switch track must not be wired for automatic non-derailing operation.
- The switch track must not be operated using the ACT soft key, rather, it must be operated using the ON soft key.
- The switch track may not also be wired for operation using a manual controller.

To wire the switch track to an AIU's ACC port, proceed as follows:

- Identify the wire or terminal on the switch track motor that should be connected to transformer Hot and connect it to a Hot terminal of the switch track power transformer.
- Identify the one of the two remaining operational wires or terminals that is used to throw the switch track to the straight orientation and connect it to an AIU ACC port using the terminal labeled "1." If you're unsure as regards which terminal is the correct one, simply choose one or the other.
- Identify the other of the two remaining operational wires or terminals that is used to throw the switch track to the curved orientation and connect it to the same AIU ACC port using the terminal labeled "2".
- Connect the AIU ACC port terminal labeled "IN" to a Common terminal of the switch track power transformer.

Program the switch track into the DCS Application and test it as if it was an accessory, as described in Part VIII – Accessory and Switch Track Control, 4. Adding and Controlling Accessories, Programming Accessories Into the DCS Application and Testing Accessory Operation earlier in this book.

Part IX - Advanced Features and Functions

In earlier sections of this book we've discussed DCS in enough detail that an O gauge operator should be able to get DCS running on a layout with complete control over DCS engines, switch tracks and operating accessories. In this section we'll explore some of the more advanced features and functions of DCS, including the following:

- External TIU Power
- ALL engines operation
- Lashups
- Subways and trolleys
- Routes
- Scenes
- Record/Playback
- Import/Export of DCS Application Contents
- DCS Engine Recovery
- DCS System Settings
- Super TIU Mode
- Passive TIU Mode
- Using Passenger Station and Freight Yard Announcements (PFA).

1. External TIU Power

Providing Power to the TIU

Like any other electronic component, the TIU requires a power source. MTH designed the TIU so that it can be powered in two different ways.

One way is to use the track power that is present at the inputs to TIU Fixed Channel #1. This power source is available whenever the O gauge operator is running trains on tracks connected to Fixed Channel #1.

Another way to power the TIU is to use a separate power supply that is plugged into the TIU's Aux. Power port. In this case, the TIU would have power all the time. Any power supply that provides between 12 and 22 volts AC or DC at 1.5 amps or greater, equipped with a compatible barrel plug, may be used.

If the TIU is a Rev. L (or later) that has a USB port, the TIU may alternately be powered via the USB port. However, this should only be done when using the TIU solely to update TIU or DCS Remote software. In order to perform DCS engine sound file transfers, DCS Remote backup or recovery, DCS engine operation, or activation of switch tracks or accessories connected to a TIU's AIUs, power must come from either the Aux. Power port or Fixed Channel #1 Input.

When the TIU is powered through Fixed Channel #1 Input, every time the power to the tracks controlled by Fixed Channel #1 is interrupted for any reason, the TIU turns itself off. However, when the TIU is powered through the Aux. Power port, the TIU remains turned on regardless of the state of power applied to the tracks controlled by Fixed Channel #1.

Advantages to Powering the TIU Through the Aux. Power Port

Essentially, the TIU is a computer. This means that each time its power is interrupted, it must reboot when power is restored. This reboot process takes a small amount of time, during which commands sent by the DCS Application cannot be received by the TIU. If the TIU is powered by power present on Fixed Channel #1, turning off this power, even momentarily, will cause the TIU channels to behave in different ways. Although commands from the DCS Application sent on any channel cannot be received while the TIU is turned off, the various TIU channels will react as follows:

- Trains connected to Fixed Channel #1 will simply stop running.
- Variable channels will shut down and not pass power to the tracks. Trains running on tracks controlled by these channels will also simply stop running.
- Power will continue to pass through Fixed Channel #2. Trains running on tracks connected to this channel will continue to operate. DCS (or TMCC) engines will continue doing whatever they were last doing when power to the TIU was turned off. However, the operator will have no control of these trains from the DCS Application.

If the TIU is powered through Fixed Channel #1 rather than the Aux. Power port and there's a derailment on the tracks connected to Fixed Channel #1, the following will occur:

- The TIU will immediately stop receiving commands from the DCS Application.
- All trains running on tracks connected to Fixed Channel #1 or to a Variable Channel will come to a halt when the TIU's internal fuse or an external fuse for Fixed Channel #1 blows, or the transformer or other external circuit breaker trips.
- All trains running on tracks connected to Fixed Channel #2 will continue to operate, however, they will not respond to commands from the DCS Application.

The above scenario will continue with some trains stopped and others unable to be controlled until the power to the TIU is restored or all track power is shut down. Further, the E-Stop button on the DCS Application will not be useable. Not a good situation!

TIU Aux. Power Sources

There are several sources of power that may be used to power the TIU through the Aux. Power port. In general, any AC or DC power supply that provides 1.5 amp of power at a voltage between 12 and 22 volts and has a suitable connector that fits the Aux. Power port will work.

One source of power for the TIU's Aux. Power port is any one of the smaller MTH transformers, such as the Z500, Z750 or Z1000, or the MTH #50-240 Z-DC24 power supply. Their barrel plugs exactly fit the TIU's Aux. Power port. If using one of these power supplies, it is important not to use the Z-Controller that may be included with them.

Another source of power for the TIU's Aux. Power port is the Radio Shack #273-331 Enercell™ Switchable 18/24 VAC 1 AMP Power Adapter with #273-344 Enercell™ Adaptaplug™ M. It should be used on the 18 volt setting. However, since this power supply is rated for only 1.0 amp, it should be used only to power a TIU to which AIUs are not connected.

A third source of power for the TIU's Aux. Power port is the 14 volt output of an MTH Z4000 transformer using an appropriate barrel connector. It should be noted that if the Z4000's 14 volt output is used, it should be used solely for this purpose and not used to power any other device.

Although the polarity of the power source for the Aux. Power port is typically not a concern, there are two caveats in that regard that are noteworthy:

- If the Z4000's 14 volt output is used to power the TIU via the TIU's Aux. Power port, polarity is important and must be correctly observed. If polarity is reversed, and one or both of the Z4000's handles are used to power the TIU's channels, a short circuit through the Z4000 can result.
- If a brick-type transformer is used to power the TIU via the TIU's Aux. Power port and the non-accessory output of the brick is being used for other purposes, including powering a TIU channel or powering switch tracks that use non-derailing mechanisms, polarity is important and must be correctly observed. Otherwise, a short circuit through the brick-type transformer can result.

2. ALL Engines Operation

What is ALL Engines Operation?

DCS allows control of several DCS engines and/or DCS lashups operating at the same time. The ALL Engines feature of DCS allows all active DCS engines and lashups to be controlled from the same Engine Control Screen at the same time. This is called ALL engines operation. During an ALL engines operating session, DCS engine commands issued by the DCS Application are executed by all of the DCS engines and DCS lashups that are participating in the ALL engines operation.

Advantages and Limitations of ALL Engines Operation

When running an ALL engines operating session, the DCS operator can have any number of DCS engines and lashups operating at the same time, and can control their speed, direction, bell, whistle or horn, or other operation, as if they were one engine. They will all move in the same direction and at the same speed. There are several advantages to operating using the ALL engines function of DCS.

When all DCS engines are operating the same way and responding to the same DCS commands, the stress of managing several engines at once is greatly reduced and there's more time to interact with visitors as you show off your layout. If desired, ALL engines operation can be interrupted so that an individual DCS, TMCC or conventional engine can be operated separately while the other DCS engines continue running as a group.

There are, however, a few limitations when operating an ALL Engines session. The ALL engines function attempts to operate all of the engines in the Active Engine List simultaneously. If any engine in the Active Engine List is not powered up when a command is issued to ALL Engines, the DCS Application may report error messages. TMCC and Legacy engines, and conventional engines cannot be included in an ALL engines operating session, although they can be operated separately while DCS engines are engaged in ALL engines operations.

ALL Engines operation may be used either with Normal TIU mode or Super TIU mode. Although ALL Engines operation may require that a TIU be selected, if that TIU is in Super TIU mode then all TIUs that are in Super TIU mode are included. If it is not in Super TIU mode then only those engines associated with the selected TIU are included in the ALL Engines operating session.

Starting an All Engines Session

When starting an ALL engines session, it is important to first ensure that all of the engines that are to participate in the ALL engines session are on tracks that are receiving power and are in DCS mode. Next, tap the Refresh button on the Engine Roster Screen. This will ensure that only those engines that are drawing power will participate in the ALL engines operation by moving those engines that are drawing power to the Active Engine List and those that are not to the Inactive Engine List. Look at the Active Engine List on the Engine Roster Screen. If DCS lashups are to be included in the operating session, move them from the Inactive Engine List to the Active Engine List. This will cause their member engines to move to the Inactive Engine List.

If any engines are in the Active Engine List that are not to be included in the ALL engines operations, they should be moved to the Inactive Engine List. Then tap the ALL Engines box at the top of the Engine Roster Screen to initiate the ALL engines session. If there is more than one TIU on the layout a list of TIUs may be displayed. If operating in Normal TIU mode, select the TIU whose engines will participate in the session. If operating in Super TIU mode, select any TIU. Regardless, the Engine Control Screen will be displayed showing an engine name of ALL.

Operating an ALL Engines Session

The ALL engines session is operated in the same manner as operating an individual DCS engine. The only difference is that when a command is issued from the DCS Application that is running the session, all of the DCS engines that are participating in the session will respond. Tapping any key on the DCS Application that pertains to DCS engine operation will simultaneously send that command to all of the DCS engines that are participating in the ALL engines operating session.

While running an ALL engines session, you can single out one or more DCS or TMCC engines for individual operation while ALL Engine operation continues, whether or not the engine is participating in the session. This is accomplished as follows for each engine that is to be individually operated during the ALL engines session:

- Tap the Engine Roster button on the Engine Control Screen to view the engine roster, consisting of the Active Engine List and the Inactive Engine List.
- Select any DCS engine or lashup that is operated individually during the ALL engines operating session. Ensure that the engine or lashup is on a powered track that's connected to one of the TIUs being used in the ALL Engines session.
- If the engine is in the Inactive Engine List, tap the Edit button and then slide the engine's parallel-bars icon to move it to the Active Engine List. Tap the Done button.
- Return to the Engine Control Screen.
- The selected engine will appear in the DCS Application's Engine Control Screen and may be operated separately, even if it is a member of the ALL operation.

By following the above procedure it's possible to use the Engine Roster button to view the Active Engine List and choose between operating ALL Engines, or an individual engine or lashup.

3. Lashups

What's a Lashup?

Real railroads combine multiple engines that are run as a single engine when the makeup of the consist itself (number of cars, weight, etc.) or the route (grades or other factors) demand more pulling power than can be provided by a single engine alone. DCS provides the ability to simulate real-world engine combinations by allowing you to combine multiple DCS engines into lashups that are controlled as a single engine.

Up to 10 DCS engines can be members of a lashup. Regardless of how many DCS engines are included in the lashup, one engine will always be the head engine, another will be the tail engine and up to 8 additional engines, as many as track power can support, may be designated as middle engines. A DCS engine may be the member of more than one lashup, however, only one of the lashups of which it is a member may be operated at the same time. Each lashup will have a unique DCS engine ID#.

Creating a Lashup

Before creating a lashup, it's a good idea to ensure that all of the DCS engines that are to be members of a particular lashup operate at close to the same speed. As discussed in Part XIII - Troubleshooting Problems, 5. Engine Control Problems, Speed Control Problems, sometimes a DCS engine may run too slow or too fast. Fortunately, there's a simple test to ensure that all of the members of a DCS lashup can operate well together:

- Place the engines about 2 feet apart on a loop of track.
- Power up the track, select the first member engine for operation on the Engine Control Screen and tap the Start Up button.
- Select the second member engine and tap the Start Up button.
- Start the first engine moving at about 20 SMPH.

- Immediately start the second engine moving at 20 SMPH.
- Observe the engines and see if one engine catches up or falls behind, and how quickly it does.
- If the engines only lose or gain 2-3 inches every 10 feet or more, they're within about 2% of each other at 20 SMPH and shouldn't fight each other in a lashup. If there are any other engines to be members of this lashup, repeat the procedure using the new engine and one of the previous engines.

To create a lashup, it is necessary to first ensure that all of the engines that are to be members of the lashup are on powered tracks. Then, ensure that they are all in the Active Engine List. This is accomplished as follows:

- If the DCS Application is not already displaying the Engine Control Screen, navigate to it.
- Tap the Engine Roster button to display the Active Engine List and the Inactive Engine List.
- If there are any engines in the Inactive Engine List that are to be members of the lashup, ensure that they are all on powered tracks of the same TIU and pull down on the Engine Roster Screen to refresh it to move these DCS engines to the Active Engine List.
- Press the Engine Control Screen button on the Engine Roster List Screen to return to the Engine Control Screen.

To begin building a lashup, navigate first to the Engine Control Screen and then to the Engine Roster Screen. These screens are described earlier in this book in Part VII - Engine Operation Using the DCS Application. On the Engine Roster Screen, tapping Build Lash Up accesses the Select Lashup Type Screen, the build Lashup Screen and the Select Lashup Member Screen. Each of these screens, including a description of their functions, are shown below.

How to access the Build Lashup Screen, as well as a description of its functions, is described in the tables that follow the screens.

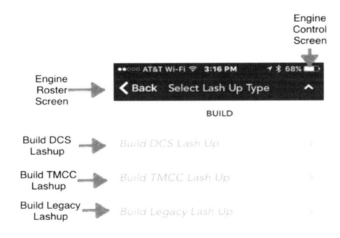

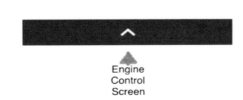

Figure 33 - Select Lashup Type Screen

Select Lashup Type Screen	
PURPOSE:	Build a Lashup.
HOT TO GET IT:	Tap Build Lashup on the Engine Roster Screen.
INFORMATION DISPLAYED:	Choice of lashup type, DCS or TMCC or Legacy.
BUTTONS:	Tap Engine Roster Screen to return to the Engine Roster Screen.
	Tap Build DCS Lash Up to build a lashup using DCS engines.
	Tap Build TMCC Lashup to build a lashup using TMCC engines.
	Tap Build Legacy Lashup to build a lashup using Legacy engines.
	Tap Engine Control Screen to return to the Engine Control Screen.

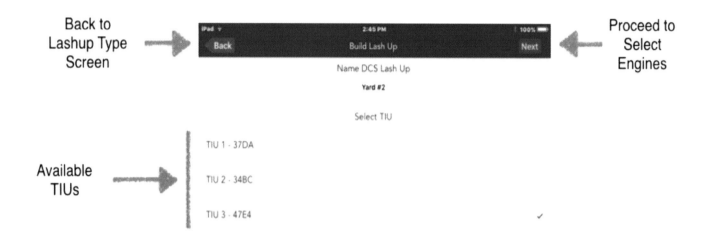

Back to Lashup Type Screen

Proceed to Select Engines

Available TIUs

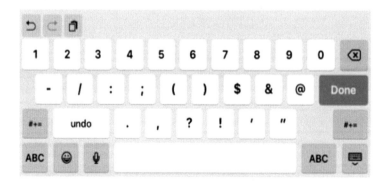

Figure 34 - Build DCS Lashup Screen

Build Lashup Screen	
PURPOSE:	Name Lashup and select member engine's TIU.
HOW TO GET IT:	By tapping Build DCS Lashup on the Build Lashup Screen.
INFORMATION DISPLAYED:	Available layout TIUs.
BUTTONS:	Select the TIU to which the member engines are currently associated.
	Enter the lashup's name.
	Tap Proceed to Select Engines when ready to do so.
	Tap the box to the right of an engine to add that engine to the lashup.
	Tap Back to Lashup Type Screen to return to the Lashup Type Screen.

Back to
Lashup Type
Screen

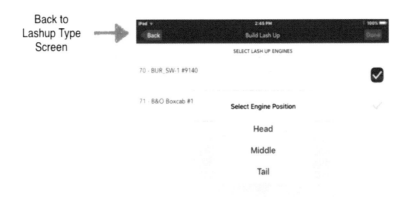

Figure 35 Select Lashup Member Screen

Select Lashup Member Screen	
PURPOSE:	Add Lashup Member Engines.
HOW TO GET IT:	By tapping Build DCS Lashup, or Build TMCC Lashup or Build Legacy Lashup on the Build Lashup Screen.
INFORMATION DISPLAYED:	Active Engine List of engines available to be included in a lashup on the selected TIU.
BUTTONS:	When requested, tap on the engine's position in the lashup, Head, Middle or Tail.
	When requested tap on the engine's facing direction in the lashup, Forward or Backward.
	Tap the box to the right of an engine to add that engine to the lashup.
	Tap Engine Control Screen to return to the Engine Control Screen.

Once all DCS engines that are to be members of the lashup are on powered tracks and are in the Active Engine List, proceed as follows to create the lashup:

- Tap the Build Lash Up button on the Engine Roster Screen to bring up the Select Lashup Type Screen.
- On the Select Lashup Type Screen, tap Build DCS Lashup to bring up the Build DCS Lashup Screen.
- On the Build DCS Lashup Screen, select the TIU to which the lashup's member engines are currently associated.
- Enter the lashup's name using the on-screen keyboard.
- Tap on Proceed to Select Engines. The Select Lashup Member Screen will be displayed.
- Tap on the box belonging to an engine in the Active Engine List to select it as a lashup member.
- Determine whether this engine will be a Head, Middle or Tail engine by tapping on its desired position.
- Determine if this member engine will be facing Forward or Reverse by tapping on its desired orientation.
- Repeat the above steps for all other member engines of the lashup. If you make a mistake adding a member engine, uncheck the member engine's box to remove it from the lashup.
- Tap on Done to create the lashup.

The lashup will now appear as the active engine on the Engine Control Screen. After the lashup is created, member engines may not be added or deleted, although the lashup itself may be deleted, or its name or address edited, as with any other DCS engine. It may be selected and operated as if it were an ordinary DCS engine.

Effect on Member Engines

Initial settings for lashup member engines are always the same for all lashups. These include turning off all interior, marker and number board lights, and all accent sounds, for all lashup members other than the head engine. Only the front-facing headlight on the head engine and the rear-facing headlight on the tail engine will illuminate to indicate which direction the lashup is moving or about to move. This is done to simulate the way real lashups operate. Additionally, only the front-facing Protocoupler on the head engine and the rear-facing Protocoupler on the tail engine will respond to commands from the DCS Application.

However, individual member engine settings may be changed after the lashup has been created and started up. This may be accomplished as follows:

- After the lashup is started up, press the Engine Roster button on the Engine Control Screen to view the Active Engine List and the Inactive Engine List.
- If the member engine whose settings are to be changed is in the Inactive Engine List, tap the Edit button and then slide the engine's parallel-bars icon to move it to the Active Engine List. Tap the Done button.
- Tap on the member engine whose lashup settings are to be changed to return to the Engine Control Screen with this engine as the Active Engine.
- DO NOT START UP THE ENGINE!
- Use Engine Soft Keys and/or Engine Settings Screens to make whatever changes are desired to the lashup settings for the selected DCS member engine. These settings will become active as you select them.
- Return to the Engine Control Screen and tap the Engine Roster button to display the Active Engine List. If the lashup is in the Inactive Engine List, tap the Edit button and then slide the lashup's parallel-bars icon to move it to the Active Engine List. Tap the Done button.
- Tap on the lashup to return to the Engine Control Screen with the lashup as the Active Engine.

Note that the sound level settings of any lashup member engine that was modified will be retained for that member engine every time it is operated, either when it is part of the lashup or started up individually. This will persist until these sound level settings are again changed.

The changed settings will be in effect every time you start up the lashup until the lashup is broken down into member engines. This occurs whenever one of the member engines is selected in the Engine Control Screen and the Start Up key is pressed. At this time, each member engine has its feature settings reset to factory defaults, except for the engine's DCS ID# and Custom Name, if one was assigned. This is necessary since there is room in the DCS engine's onboard memory to store only one set of engine settings at a time, the lashup settings or the DCS engine's settings.

When the lashup settings are placed in the DCS board's memory, they overlay any previously changed settings for the member engines. When the lashup is broken down, the engine's default factory settings overwrite the lashup settings. When selecting the individual member engines of a DCS lashup, any settings that are changed in the member engine will stay with the engine when the lashup is subsequently started up.

A lashup may not be operated at the same time that any of its member engines are being operated individually, since this would necessitate starting up the member engine and breaking down the lashup. If a member engine of a lashup is deleted from a DCS Application or is Factory Reset, all lashups of which it was a member are also deleted. Like individual DCS engines, a lashup may be created in more than one DCS Application, however, unlike DCS engines it need not have the same DCS ID# in all DCS Applications in which it is entered.

Missing the Watchdog Signal

If individual DCS engines miss seeing the watchdog signal, they can be either brought directly into DCS active mode by tapping the Start Up button or put into DCS stealth mode by tapping the Shut Down button. However, this is not the same for lashups.

If a lashup is powered on after the watchdog signal has come and gone, perhaps if its siding was toggled on after voltage appeared at the TIU channel outputs connected to its siding, there are two ways to put the lashup into DCS mode. One way to put the lashup into DCS mode is to turn off power to the inputs for the TIU channel that is connected to the track upon which the lashup resides, toggle on the siding and then re-apply power. The other way is to first select the lashup in the DCS Application's Active or Inactive Engine list. Then, flip the toggle switch and immediately tap the lashup to select it. It will come up in DCS stealth mode, dark and silent. This also works with individual DCS engines.

TMCC and Legacy Lashups

The DCS Application allows the creation of lashups between two or more TMCC or Legacy engines. The process of creating a TMCC or Legacy Lashup is similar to that of creating a lashup of DCS engines, with the exception that the Build TMCC Lashup or Build Legacy Lashup button is tapped. When the lashup is created, it will be assigned the first available DCS ID# in the range 91 through 99. This will equate to a TMCC Train number of 1 through 9. TMCC lashups are subject to the following rules:

- If there is not an available DCS ID# 91 through 99, the lashup creation will fail.
- If the same lashup is created in more than one DCS Application, the lashup's DCS ID#, and therefore its TMCC Train number, must be the same in all DCS Applications in which the lashup appears. If not, only the last occurrence of the lashup that was created will operate from the DCS Application in which it was created.
- A TMCC or Legacy engine may not be a member of more than one lashup. If it is, only the last lashup in which the engine was included will be able to be operated.

4. Subways and Trolleys

Station Stop Technology for Transit Station Announcements

Generally, all DCS engines have either Passenger Station Sounds or Freight Yard Sounds. These are predetermined sound sequences that a DCS engine will cycle through when the PFA button on the DCS Application is tapped. DCS subways and trolleys, however, have much more extensive sound sequences that are triggered differently than using the PFA key. Further, they are programmed sequences that allow determination of exactly which stations are included on a subway or trolley route. These Transit Station Announcements are very different from Passenger Station Sounds or Freight Yard Sounds.

How it Works

Transit Station Announcements are actually more similar to the Record/Playback function except that only a single DCS subway or trolley is involved. This DCS function allows you to set up automatic operation using a series of pre-programmed subway or trolley routes.

Every DCS subway or trolley engine has in its DCS board memory a series of 9 or more station stops that are based on the route of the prototype subway or trolley. The DCS operator can choose any or all of these stops to create a custom route where the subway or trolley actually stops at stations on the layout. The route can consist of 2 or more stops. The subway or trolley memorizes a route on the layout by counting motor revolutions using the timing stripes on the motor's flywheel as the engine proceeds along its route. Each time the engine is stopped a station name is selected and remembered in the engine's DCS board memory. When the route is completed the entire sequence of motor revolutions and station stops is saved as either an out-and-back or looped route.

Only one route may be saved in a DCS subway or trolley. Once you begin to create a new route, the previous route no longer exists. DCS subways and trolleys come from the factory with a looped or out-and-back route pre-programmed. Once you program a route, this factory-provided route is lost and may only be restored by performing a Factory Reset of the DCS subway or trolley. It's generally a good idea to see how a route performs by running the factory-provided route before programming a route of your own. This is accomplished by following the instructions below in Operating Subway and Trolley Routes.

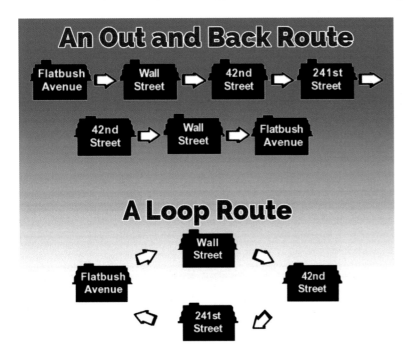

Programming Station Stops

There are two kinds of station stop routes that can be programmed, either out-and-back or looped routes. Out-and-back routes cause the subway or trolley to proceed in one direction making stops. After the last stop, the subway or trolley reverses direction and proceeds back along the route making stops at the same stations, ending at the original, first stop. Looped routes cause the subway or trolley to proceed in one direction making stops until it arrives back at the original, first stop. Upon completing either the out-and-back or looped route, the subway or trolley repeats the route until you stop it. Out-and-back and looped routes are programmed in a similar fashion. All that's different is the way the route is saved.

Figure 36 - Subway and Trolley Routes

Subways and Trolleys Learn Mode

DCS engines that have Transit Station Announcements can be programmed by using a set of special soft keys that are accessed via the Trolley/Subway Control soft key that is present only for DCS subways, trolleys and certain other DCS engines.

Figure 37 - Subway and Trolley Soft Keys Screen

When the Trolley/Subway Control soft key is tapped, the Trolley/Subway Control menu is displayed, as shown below.

Figure 38 - Subway and Trolley Menu

How to access the Subway and Trolley Menu, as well as a description of its functions, is described in the following table.

Subway and Trolley Menu	
PURPOSE:	Program and Operate routes Using Transit Station Announcements.
HOW TO GET IT:	By tapping the Trolley/Subway Control button in the Functions area of the active subway's or trolley's Soft Keys Screen.
INFORMATION DISPLAYED:	Transit Station Announcements control functions.
BUTTONS:	Tap Auto Mode to operate the subway or trolley in Auto mode, making pre-programmed station stops and announcements. The Engine Control Screen is displayed.
	Tap Learn Mode to program station stops and announcements for the subway or trolley. The Learn Mode Menu is displayed.
	Tap Manual Mode to return the subway or trolley to manual control. The Engine Control Screen is displayed.
	Tap Exit Trolley Sequence to return to the Soft Keys Screen.
	Tap Cancel to cancel the current command sequence.

Before programming a subway or trolley route, it is necessary to first ensure that the DCS subway or trolley to be programmed is on a powered track. Then, ensure that it's in the Active Engine List.

This is accomplished as follows:

- If the DCS Application is not already displaying the Engine Control Screen, navigate to that screen.
- Tap the downward arrow to navigate to the Engine Roster Screen to display the Engine List.
- If the DCS subway or trolley is in the Inactive Engine List, ensure that it's on a powered track and pull down on the Engine Roster Screen to refresh it and to add the engine to the Active Engine List.
- Select the DCS subway or trolley in the Engine List and tap on it to return to the Engine Control Screen.

Programming the transit station route is accomplished by using the Learn Mode Menu.

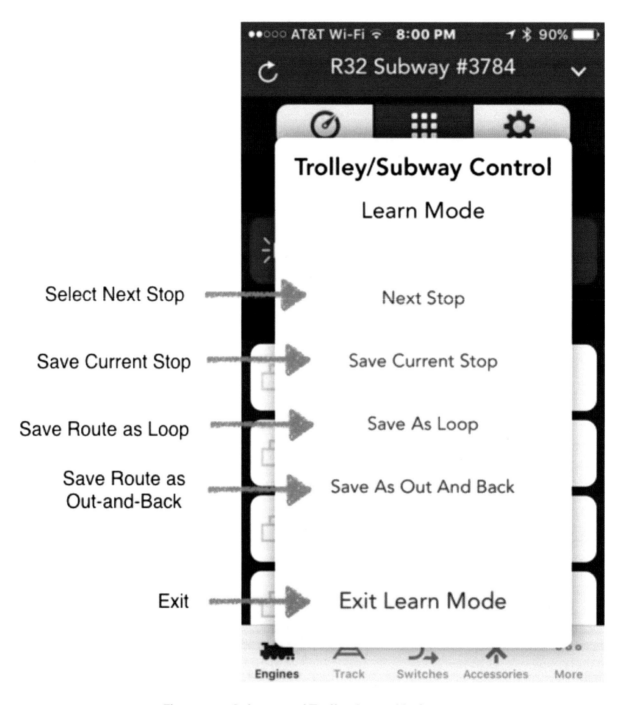

Select Next Stop → Next Stop

Save Current Stop → Save Current Stop

Save Route as Loop → Save As Loop

Save Route as Out-and-Back → Save As Out And Back

Exit → Exit Learn Mode

Figure 39 - Subway and Trolley Learn Mode

How to access the Learn Mode Menu, as well as a description of its functions, is described in the following table.

Learn Mode Menu	
PURPOSE:	Program transit station stops and announcements.
HOW TO GET IT:	By tapping the Learn Mode button in the Subway and Trolley Menu.
INFORMATION DISPLAYED:	Program buttons for building a subway or trolley route.
BUTTONS:	Tap Select Next Stop to hear announcements for upcoming stations on the route.
	Tap Save Current Stop to add the current station to the subway or trolley route.
	Tap Save Route as Loop to save the completed route as a looped route. The Engine Control Screen is displayed.
	Tap Save Route as Out-and-Back to save the completed route as a out-and-back route. The Engine Control Screen is displayed.
	Tap Exit to exit learn mode and cancel the current command sequence.

Next, proceed as follows to select the DCS subway or trolley and program the route:

- Press Start Up on the DCS Application to place the DCS subway or trolley into DCS command mode. Ensure that it is facing forward and ready to proceed forward. If it is a subway, ensure that all the subway cars that will normally be attached to the subway are attached.
- Note as closely as possible exactly where the front of the engine is located in the station.
- Then, drive it to the first station at the beginning of the route.
- Navigate to the engine's Soft Keys Screen and scroll down to the Trolley/Subway Control button. Tap on the button to display the Subway and Trolley Menu.
- Tap the Learn Mode button. The engine will announce, "Learn Mode", and the Learn Mode Menu will be displayed.
- Tap Select Next Stop repeatedly to announce the names of the stations that may be programmed on the route, in the order in which they appear. Note that as many station names as there are stops on the route must be assigned and that they must be assigned in the order in which they are announced. When the desired name for the first station is announced, tap Save Current Stop to assign it. The engine will announce, "Saved", and the Engine Control Screen will be displayed.
- Drive the subway or trolley to the next stop of the route.
- Navigate to the engine's Soft Keys Screen and scroll down to the Trolley/Subway Control button. Tap on the button to display the Learn Mode Menu Screen
- Repeat step 6-8 above for each of the other stops on the route slowly enough that it can be stopped at a precise location.
- When the engine arrives at the last stop on the route, name that station as in step 6 above.
- Depending on whether the route is a loop or an out-and-back route, do one of the following:
1. If the route is an out-and-back route, complete programming the route by tapping the Save as Out-and-Back. The engine will announce, "Saved". Then, tap the button again. The engine will announce, "Saved complete". Tap the Exit Learn Mode button to return to the Engine Control Screen.
2. If the route is a Looped route, tap Save Current Stop and then continue to drive the DCS subway or trolley forward until it returns to the original, starting station. Stop the engine as close as possible to the place where it was when you began programming the route.
- Navigate to the engine's Soft Keys Screen and scroll down to the Trolley/Subway Control button. Tap on the button to display the Learn Mode Menu.
- Complete programming the route by pressing the Save as Loop button. The engine will announce, "Saved Complete". Tap the Exit Learn Mode button to return to the Engine Control Screen.

Operating Subway and Trolley Routes

Now that the route has been programmed into the DCS subway or trolley, the subway or trolley can automatically traverse the route once or as many times as desired. The process of running the programmed route is as follows:

- Power up the track where the DCS subway or trolley resides to 18 volts.
- Navigate to the Engine Control Screen and tap the downward arrow to navigate to the Engine Roster Screen and to display the Engine List.
- Tap on the DCS subway or trolley in the engine list. If it was in the Inactive Engine List, tap it again. The Engine Control Screen will be displayed.
- Press Start Up to place the DCS subway or trolley into DCS command mode and drive it to the first station at the beginning of the route. Ensure that it is facing forward and ready to proceed forward. If it is a subway, ensure that all the subway cars that will normally be attached to the subway are attached.
- Position the engine as closely as possible to exactly where the front of the engine was located in the station when the route was programmed.
- Navigate to the engine's Soft Keys Screen and scroll down to the Trolley/Subway Control button. Tap on the button to display the Subway and Trolley Menu.
- Tap the Auto Mode button. The engine will announce, "Auto Mode", and the Auto Mode Menu will be displayed.
- Tap the button for the appropriate Route type, Loop or Out And Back.
- Tap the All Stops button to make all stops on the route or tap the Random Stops button to stop at only a random number of stops on the route.
- Tap the Start Auto Mode button to start auto mode and return to the Engine Control Screen.
- Start the DCS subway or trolley moving at a speed close to the speed at which the route was programmed. The engine will now repeat the route as it was programmed, stopping at each programmed station.

As the engine approaches each programmed station, it will announce the station name and then stop at the station. When the subway or trolley stops, it will make sounds, including doors opening and station activity, followed by the doors closing. The subway or trolley will then proceed to the next stop. This will be repeated for all stations programmed in the route.

When the last station stop of an out-and-back route is completed, the engine will reverse direction and travel back along the route to the first station, stopping at each station in turn, until it stops in the original, first station. The route will then repeat.

When the last station stop of a looped route is completed, the engine will travel forward to the first station, stopping at its original starting point. The route will then repeat.

This activity will continue until the route program is ended by navigating to the engine's Soft Keys Screen, scrolling down to and tapping on the Trolley/Subway Control button to display the Auto Mode Menu. Tap the Stop Auto Mode button to end auto mode and then tap the Close button to return to the Engine Control Screen.

Caveats and Additional Subway and Trolley Features

Custom Names

Subways and trolleys may not have Custom Names. This is because the DCS board memory where a Custom Name would reside is used instead for subway and trolley Transit Station Announcements.

Accuracy

In general, the auto mode feature that allows subways to run pre-programmed out-and-back or looped routes is very accurate, however, it is not 100% perfect. Small variations can occur for several reasons:

- Minute variability in the DCS subway or trolley gears.
- Slippage of wheels on rails over the course of a route.
- Changes in voltage or areas of poor traction due to track work problems.

Larger variations can occur for other reasons, such as including grades on the route.

If the DCS subway or trolley tends to end the route a little bit ahead or behind its original starting point, run the route for several iterations and observe if the variation is a one-time occurrence (only off a bit once but there's no accumulative effect) or occurs every time the loop is run (the difference from the starting point increases with each loop iteration). Each of these problems generally has a different remedy.

If the difference is a one-time occurrence, adjust the starting point of the route by the difference between where the engine should have stopped and where it actually stopped and run the route again, noting if the accuracy improves.

When a DCS subway or trolley tends to overshoot an out-and-back route each time the route is run, attempt to re-program the route so that any pushing against a bumper on the return is minimized. When a DCS subway or trolley tends to end a looped route a little bit ahead or behind its original starting point and the difference from the starting point increases with each loop iteration, attempt to reprogram and start the DCS subway or trolley a little bit farther back.

There are a few additional things that can be done to improve accuracy, although it's unlikely that any route will run perfectly for an infinite number of loops. Accuracy can be improved by doing the following:

- Take great care to end the loop exactly where it started.
- Go slow and brake gradually when entering each station.
- Ensure that all traction tires are in place and not overly slick or worn.
- Check the tracks carefully for any power or conductivity issue that can cause the subway or trolley to pause or stutter during its playback in Auto mode.
- Stop the DCS subway or trolley and note as closely as possible exactly where the beginning of the engine is located in the station.
- Keep the tracks clean.
- When playing back the route, keep the speed to 20 or 25 SMPH.

Selecting All Stops vs. Random Stops

While operating a DCS subway or trolley over a programmed route, the operator can choose between having the engine stop at all of the programmed stations or only at some of them, where the stations are chosen on a random basis. In other words, the entire route will be run, however, only some, but not all stops will be made.

Manual Station Stops

In manual mode, the operator can initiate a station stop sequence while the DCS subway or trolley is under operator control rather than in auto mode. This is accomplished as follows:

- With the subway or trolley as the active engine on the Engine Control Screen, press Start Up to place the DCS subway or trolley into DCS command mode and start it moving in either forward or reverse.
- Navigate to the engine's Soft Keys Screen and scroll down to and tap on the Trolley/Subway Control button to display the Subway and Trolley Menu.
- Tap the Manual Mode button to display the Manual Mode Menu.

- Tap the Next Stop button repeatedly to hear all of the station stops that are available on the route until the desired station is announced.
- Tap the Arm button to return to the Engine Control Screen.
- Stop the engine at the desired station to hear the sound sequence for that station. Sounds will start when the engine comes to a stop and will continue until the engine leaves the station.
- When the engine leaves that station, it will automatically play the announcement for the next station.
- If it is desired that the engine stop at that station, repeat the steps above.
- If it is not desired to stop at that station, do nothing.

5. Routes

The Routes feature allows the DCS operator to set up frequently used switch track routes on a layout. Each Route is a script that when run, instructs TIUs to throw switch tracks connected to AIUs according to pre-programmed instructions. Routes allow the operator to program multiple switch tracks to throw sequentially with a single command. Each Route can contain up to 250 switch tracks and each DCS Application can contain up to 15 Routes.

Each switch track in a Route must first be connected to an AIU. Switch tracks that are part of a Route can still be operated individually from the DCS Application.

Routes are created starting with the Switch Track Control Screen and the Add Switch Track or Route Screen. Both of these screens are described in Part VIII - Accessory and Switch Track Control, 5. Operating Switch Tracks Using the DCS Application earlier in this book. Actual building of the Route is accomplished using the Add Route Screen.

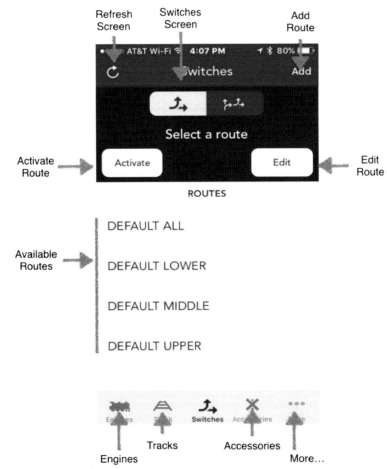

Figure 40 - Routes Screen

Save Route

Cancel Route

Name Route

Mark as favorite?   Favorite

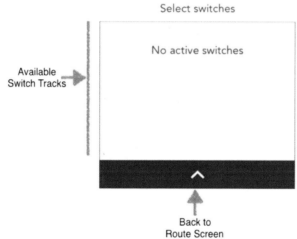

Select switches

Available Switch Tracks

No active switches

Back to Route Screen

Figure 41 - Add Route Screen

How to access the Add Route Screen, as well as a description of its functions, is described in the following table.

Add Route Screen	
PURPOSE:	Create Routes of Switch Tracks.
HOW TO GET IT:	By tapping the Add Route button in the Add Switch or Route Screen.
INFORMATION DISPLAYED:	All of the layout's switch tracks that are programmed into the DCS Application.
BUTTONS:	Tap Cancel Route to exit back to Switches Screen without creating a new Route.
	Tap Save to save the new Route and return to the to Switches Screen.
	Tap Name Route to enter a name for the new Route.
	Tap the Favorite box to mark this Route as a Favorite.
	Tap on a switch track in the Available Switch Track List to add it to the Route.
	Tap Back to Route Screen to exit back to Switches Screen without creating a new Route.

Creating a Route

Before creating a Route, ensure that each of the switch tracks that will compose the Route is already wired to the AIU and is programmed into the DCS Application. It's a good idea to test that each switch is wired and programmed correctly before actually creating the Route.

Once all the switch tracks in the Route have been proven to work properly from the DCS Application, take note of what will be each switch track's orientation in the Route, curved or straight.

Routes are created starting with the Switch Tracks Control Screen and the Add Switch or Route Screen. Both of these screens are described in Part VIII - Accessory and Switch Track Control, 2. Adding and Controlling Switch Tracks earlier in this book. Actual building of the Route is accomplished using the Add Route Screen.

Programming a Route

To program a Route, proceed as follows:

- Navigate the DCS Application to the Switch Track Control Screen.
- Tap the Add Switch or Route button. The Add Switch or Route Screen is displayed.
- Tap the Add Route button. The Add Route Screen is displayed.
- Enter the Route's name using the on-screen keyboard. A Route's name may be up to 16 characters long. Tap Done. You may also check the box indicating that this Route is to be listed as a Favorite.
- A list of all the switch tracks that are connected to all AIUs and programmed into the DCS Application is displayed in order of each switch track's number and name.
- Scroll through the list to the first switch in the list that is to be included in the Route and tap the button, Straight or Curved, corresponding to the orientation of the switch when it's used by the Route.
- Repeat this for all of the other switch tracks in the Route. If you mistakenly add a switch track to the Route, scroll back to it and tap its Remove button to remove the switch from the Route.
- When all the switch tracks have been added to the Route, tap the Save button to complete building the Route.

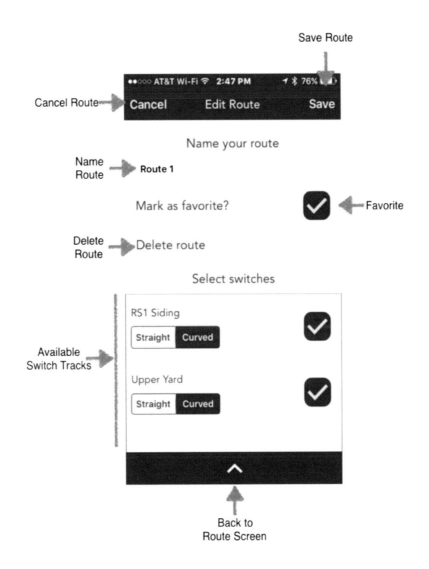

Figure 42 - Edit Route Screen

How to access the Edit Route Screen, as well as a description of its functions, is described in the following table.

Edit Route Screen	
PURPOSE:	Edit Routes of Switch Tracks.
HOW TO GET IT:	By tapping the Routes Screen button followed by the Edit button in the Switches Screen.
INFORMATION DISPLAYED:	All of the information about a Route, including all of the layout's switch tracks that are programmed into the DCS Application.
BUTTONS:	Tap Cancel Route to exit back to Switches Screen.
	Tap Save to save changes to the Route and return to the to Switches Screen.
	Tap Name Route to enter a new name for the Route.
	Tap the Favorite box to mark or unmark this Route as a Favorite.
	Tap on a switch track in the Available Switch Track List to add, change or delete it in the Route.
	Tap on Delete Route to delete the entire Route.
	Tap Back to Route Screen to exit back to Switches Screen without creating a new Route.

Testing a Route

To test a Route, first navigate to the DCS Application's Switch Track Control Screen. Tap on the Routes Screen button. Tap on the Route's name and then tap on the Activate button. Each switch track in the Route should activate and switch to the orientation dictated by its setting in the Route.

Changing the Switch Tracks in a Route

If it's determined that a switch track was omitted from a Route, or the wrong switch track was added to a Route or was oriented incorrectly, the Route may be edited to correct any such errors. Proceed as follows to edit the switch tracks in a Route:

- Navigate the DCS Application to the Switch Track Control Screen and tap on the Routes Screen button.
- Locate and tap on the Route's name to select it.
- Tap the Edit button to edit that Route. All of the Route's information and a list containing all of the switch tracks in all AIUs is displayed.
- Scroll to a switch track that needs to be added, deleted, or whose orientation in the Route is to be changed. Switch tracks that are currently in the Route have a check mark in the Select Box to the right of the switch track.
- To change the orientation of a switch that's already in the Route, tap the button for the correct orientation, Straight or Curved.
- To add another switch to the Route, scroll to that switch and tap its select box to add a check mark. Then tap its desired orientation button, Straight or Curved.
- To remove a switch from the Route, scroll to that switch and tap its select box to remove the check mark.
- Repeat the above to add or delete a switch from the Route, or to change the orientation of any other switch tracks in the Route.
- Tap the Save Route button to save the changes.

Renaming a Route

If an error was made when naming a Route, the Route's name may be changed. Proceed as follows to rename a Route:

- Navigate the DCS Application to the Switch Track Control Screen and tap the Routes Screen button.
- Locate and tap on the Route's name to select it.
- Tap the Edit button to edit that Route. All of the Route's information and a list containing all of the switch tracks in all AIUs is displayed.
- Tap on the Route's name to change it.
- Enter the Route's new name using the on-screen keyboard. A Route's name may be up to 16 characters long.
- Tap the Save Route button to save the name change.

Deleting an Entire Route

If it's necessary to delete an entire Route, proceed as follows:

- Navigate the DCS Application to the Switch Track Control Screen and tap on the Routes Screen button.
- Locate and tap on the Route's name to select it.
- Tap the Edit button to edit that Route. All of the Route's information and a list containing all of the switch tracks in all AIUs is displayed.
- Tap the Delete button to delete the Route.
- Confirm by tapping Continue. The entire Route will be deleted.

6. Scenes

The Scenes feature groups several accessories that can be activated together, rather than having to select them individually from the Accessory list. Each Scene is a script that, when run, instructs TIUs to turn on accessories connected to AIUs according to pre-programmed instructions. Scenes allow the operator to turn on accessories as groups with a single command. Each Scene can contain up to 250 accessories, and each DCS handheld can store up to 15 Scenes. Accessories, remote control tracks, or lights must first be connected to an AIU. Note that accessories that are part of a Scene can still be operated individually from the DCS Application.

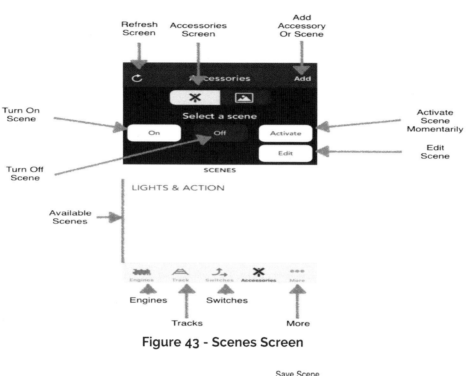

Figure 43 - Scenes Screen

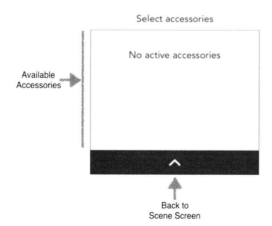

Figure 44 - Add Scene Screen

Scenes are created starting with the Accessories Control Screen and the Add Accessory or Scene Screen. Both of these screens are described in Part VIII - Accessory and Switch Track Control, 5. Operating Accessories Using the DCS Application earlier in this book. Actual building of the Scene is accomplished using the Add Scene Screen.

Add Scene Screen	
PURPOSE:	Create Scenes of Accessories.
HOW TO GET IT:	By tapping the Add Scene button in the Add Accessory or Scene Screen.
INFORMATION DISPLAYED:	All of the layout's accessories that are programmed into the DCS Application.
BUTTONS:	Tap Cancel Scene to exit back to Accessories Screen without creating a new Scene.
	Tap Save to save the new Scene and return to the to Accessories Screen.
	Tap Name Scene to enter a name for the new Scene.
	Tap the Favorite box to mark this Scene as a Favorite.
	Tap on an accessory in the Available Accessory List to add it to the Scene.
	Tap Back to Scene Screen to exit back to Accessories Screen.

Creating a Scene

Before creating a Scene, ensure that each of the accessories to be included in the Scene is already wired to the AIU and is programmed into the DCS Application. It's a good idea to test that each accessory is wired and programmed correctly before actually creating the Scene.

Once all the accessories in the Scene have been proven to work properly the Scene can be created.

Programming a Scene

To program a Scene, proceed as follows:

- Navigate the DCS Application to the Accessories Control Screen.
- Tap the Add Accessory or Scene button. The Add Accessory or Scene Screen is displayed.
- Tap Add Scene. The Add Scene Screen is displayed.
- Enter the Scene's name using the on-screen keyboard. A Scene's name may be up to 16 characters long. Tap Done. You may also check the box indicating that this Route is to be listed as a Favorite.
- A list of all the accessories that are connected to all AIUs programmed into the DCS Application is displayed in order of each accessory's number and name.

Scroll through the list to the first accessory that is to be included in the Scene and tap its select box to add a check mark.

- Repeat this for all of the other accessories in the Scene.
- If you mistakenly add an accessory to the Scene, scroll to that accessory and tap its select box to remove the check mark.
- When all the accessories have been added to the Scene, tap the Save button to complete building the Scene.

Testing a Scene

To test a Scene, first navigate to the DCS Application's Accessories Control Screen and tap the Scenes Screen button. Locate the Scene's name in the list of Scenes. Tap on the Scene's name and then tap on the On button. Each accessory in the Scene should activate.

Tap the Off button to turn off the Scene. Tap and hold the Activate button to momentarily activate the Scene as long as the button is depressed.

Changing the Accessories in a Scene

If it's determined that an accessory was omitted from a Scene, or the wrong accessory was added to a Scene, the Scene may be edited to correct any such errors. Proceed as follows to edit the accessories in a Scene:

- Navigate the DCS Application to the Accessories Control Screen. Tap on the Scenes Screen button.
- Scroll to the Scene and tap the Edit button to edit that Scene. A list containing all of the information regarding the Scene, as well as all accessories in all AIUs is displayed.
- Scroll to an accessory that needs to be added or deleted from the Scene.
- To add another accessory to the Scene, tap its select box to add a check mark.
- To remove an accessory from the Scene, tap its select box to remove its check mark.
- Repeat the above to add or delete any other accessories from the Scene, and then tap the Save button.

Renaming a Scene

If an error was made when naming a Scene, you can change the Scene's name. Proceed as follows to rename a Scene:

- Navigate the DCS Application to the Accessories Control Screen. Tap on the Scenes Screen button.
- Scroll to the Scene and tap the Edit button to edit that Scene. A list containing all of the information regarding the Scene, as well as all accessories in all AIUs is displayed.
- Tap on the Scene's name to change it.
- Enter the Scene's new name using the on-screen keyboard. A Scene's name may be up to 16 characters long. Tap the Save button to save the new name.

Deleting an Entire Scene

If it's necessary to delete an entire Scene, proceed as follows:

- Navigate the DCS Application to the Accessories Control Screen. Tap on the Scenes Screen button.
- Scroll to the Scene and tap the Edit button to edit that Scene. A list containing all of the information regarding the Scene, as well as all accessories in all AIUs is displayed.
- Tap the Delete button to delete the Scene. Tap Delete to confirm and delete the Scene.

7. Record/Playback

DCS has a terrific feature that allows trains to run automatically while going through pre-scripted operations. Passenger trains can pull into stations, make announcements and pull out again. Freight trains can stop in the yard and go through maintenance routines before moving back out onto the mainline. A train might stop at a cross track so that another train can pull through, sound a whistle or horn at a railroad crossing, or ring the bell to alert rail fans to get out of the way.

Engines can follow complicated routes, execute sound effects such as coupler slack and other sounds, and couple and uncouple their consists, all simply by pressing a few keys on the DCS Application. This feature is called Record/Playback and all that's required to run trains this way is a DCS Application and TIU. Add an AIU to include switch tracks and accessories, as well.

Using Record/Playback is a great way to entertain visitors to the layout without having to continuously operate trains to show off the layout. Instead, the operator can start a session and carry on a discussion about layout features and operation while the layout shows itself off. The DCS Application allows the operator to include ALL engines operation in Record/Playback sessions.

The Record/Playback feature is initially accessed via the DCS Application's More.. Screen followed by the Advanced Features Screen. Since the More...Screen has many other functions that are unrelated to actual DCS operation and merely acts as a pass-through to get to the Record/Playback Screen, a full discussion of the More... Screen is deferred until later in this book.

How to access the Advanced Features Screen, as well as a description of its functions, is described in the following table.

Figure 45 - Advanced Features Screen

Advanced Features Screen	
PURPOSE:	Access DCS Advanced features.
HOW TO GET IT:	Tap Advanced Features on the More... Screen.
INFORMATION DISPLAYED:	A list of advanced DCS features.
BUTTONS:	Tap Record/Playback to access the Record/Playback Screen.
	Tap Import/Export to transfer the contents of the DCS Application to or from a personal computer.
	Tap Recover Engines to recover a DCS engine whose DCS ID# has fallen outside of the normal DCS ID# range of 1-99.
	Tap System Settings to view or edit the DCS Application's settings.

Record the Session

Use DCS to position engines for the start of the recording session, ensure that transformer power is on for all tracks on which trains will be run, and set switch tracks included in the session to their starting orientation. Recording a session is accomplished via the DCS Application's Record/Playback Screen.

How to access the Record/Playback Screen, as well as a description of its functions, is described in the following table.

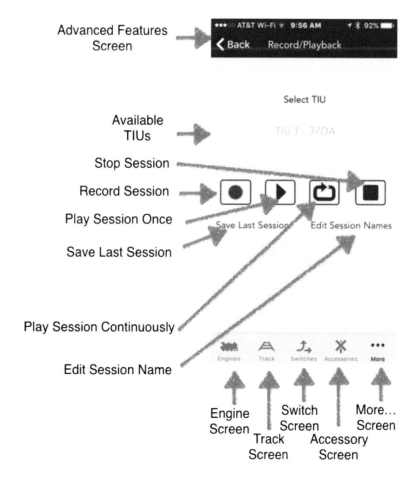

Figure 46 - Record/Playback Screen

Record/Playback Screen	
PURPOSE:	Record and playback DCS operating sessions.
HOW TO GET IT:	Tap Record/Playback on the Advanced Features Screen.
INFORMATION DISPLAYED:	Buttons to record and playback DCS operating sessions.
BUTTONS:	Tap Advanced Features Screen to return to the Advanced Features Screen.
	Tap Record Session to start or stop recording a session just recorded, or to stop a session that's being played back.
	Tap Stop Session to stop recording a session.
	Tap Play Session Once to play back a recorded session one time.
	Tap Play Session Continuously to play back a recorded session indefinitely.
	Tap Save Last Session to save the session just recorded.
	Tap Edit Session Name to edit a session's name.
	Tap Engine Screen to transfer control to the Engine Control Screen.
	Tap Track Screen to transfer control to the Track Control Screen.
	Tap Switch Screen to transfer control to the Switch Control Screen.
	Tap Accessory Screen to transfer control to the Accessory Control Screen.
	Tap More... Screen to transfer control to the More... Screen.

Use the DCS Application to start recording a session as follows:

- Navigate the DCS Application to the More... Screen. This screen can be accessed by tapping the More... button at the bottom of any screen where it appears. The More... button can be found at the bottom of the Engine Control Screen, Track Control Screen, Switch Control Screen, and Accessory Control Screen.
- Tap Advanced Features at the top of the More... Screen to display the Advanced Features Screen.
- Tap Record/Playback to display the Record/Playback Screen.
- Tap on the TIU where the Record/Playback session will be later saved. If operating in Super TIU mode, regardless of the TIU selected, the recorded session will be saved in all the TIUs on the layout.
- Begin the recording session by tapping on the Record Session button. A message will indicate that the recording has been started and that the application will go to the Engine Control Screen.

Using only DCS engines and lashups that are on tracks connected to the TIU selected above, or all TIUs if operating in Super TIU mode, begin to operate your trains as you normally would in exactly the way that you want them to operate when the session is played back.

Operate as many DCS engines as you desire. You can start up a passenger train, get it rolling forward and, as it approaches a station, tap the PFA button to begin the Passenger Station Sounds sequence. Tap the Forward button to have the train glide into the station and then tap Forward again every 30 seconds to go through the sequence, and have the train start up and leave the station. You can do the same thing with a freight train as it approaches the yard, and you can switch back and forth between two or more engines so that they are executing their PFA sounds simultaneously.

Sound the bell, whistle, or horn on any DCS engines wherever they are at any time, play the forward or reverse signals at will, and put the engines through their paces for up to 90 minutes or 500 button presses, or a combination of the two. Uncouple a train from an engine, stop the engine, back it up, re-couple the train, and pull out again. Put the trains through as complicated an operating session as you like.

If there are switch tracks and accessories connected to AIUs and programmed into the DCS Application they can also participate in the session. Simply operate them through the DCS Application, switching tracks to put trains through complicated maneuvers and turning accessories on and off as desired. If there are Routes or Scenes programmed into the DCS Application they also can be part of the operating session by activating Routes consisting of multiple switch tracks to be thrown as a group and Scenes with multiple accessories to be turned on or off together.

It's important to understand that when a Record/Playback session includes a Scene or a Route, the Scene or Route is included as a series of independent accessory or switch track activations for those items that are in the Scene or Route. If the Scene or Route is changed after making a Record/Playback session, the session will not reflect the changes that were made. Further, if the Scene or Route is deleted after recording a session, the session will still include and activate the accessories that were originally in the Scene and the switch tracks that were originally in the Route.

You can even include conventional trains operated via the Track Control Screen in the Record/Playback session, as long as care is taken to ensure that track voltage is always sufficient to effectively operate the DCS engines.

When the session is completed, use the DCS Application to stop the trains. If engines are stopped as close as possible to where they started, it will allow the option to run the session continuously when it's played back. If the session will not be run continuously on playback, it's a good idea to use the Shut Down button for each engine after it's been stopped. Reset any switch tracks to their starting orientation and turn off any accessories or Scenes.

Stop and Save the Session

Navigate to the Record/Playback Screen and the tap the Stop Session button to stop the Record/Playback session. To save the session for future playback, tap the Save Last Session button and select one of the 3 session names listed to save this session with that name. If operating in Super TIU mode, the session will be saved in all TIUs on the layout.

If there was a previously saved session under the selected session name, the new session will replace the saved session. If it's necessary to change a recorded session's name, tap the Edit Session Name button.

When a session is saved in the DCS App, it is available to all DCS Apps used with the layout as the same numbered session in the TIU where it was saved, or in all layout TIUs that are in Super TIU mode. However, the actual name of the session is only saved in the DCS App where the session was saved or the session name was changed. While the session is available to all copies of the DCS App used with the layout, it may have a different name when accessed by different DCS Apps operating on different smart devices.

Play Back the Session

Start by using DCS to position engines where they're supposed to be at the start of the session and ensure that transformer power is on for all the tracks on which trains will be run. Set any switch tracks to their desired starting orientation. Next, use the DCS Application to start playing back the session:

- Navigate the DCS Application to the More... Screen. This screen can be accessed by tapping the More... button at the bottom of any screen where it appears. The More... button can be found at the bottom of the Engine Control Screen, Track Control Screen, Switch Control Screen, and Accessory Control Screen.
- Tap Advanced Features at the top of the More... Screen. The Advanced Features Screen will be displayed.
- Tap Record/Playback to display the Record/Playback Screen.
- Playback the recorded session once by tapping the Play Session Once button.
- To play back a session continuously, instead of tapping the Play Session Once button, tap the Play Session Continuously button. This will cause the session to play back repeatedly, over and over again. Either way, the trains, switch tracks and accessories will perform just the way they did when the session was recorded.

To stop playback at any time, navigate to the Record/Payback Screen and stop the recorded session by tapping the Stop Session button.

8. Import and Export of DCS Application Contents

The Import/Export feature is initially accessed via the DCS Application's More... Screen followed by the Advanced Features Screen. Since the More... Screen has many other functions that are unrelated to actual DCS operation and merely acts as a pass-through to get to the Import/Export Screen, a full discussion of the More... Screen is deferred until later in this book.

Use the DCS Application to import or export content from another copy of the DCS Application operating on a different smart device, or from a DCS Remote, as follows:

- Navigate the DCS Application to the More... Screen. This screen can be accessed by tapping the More... button at the bottom of any screen where it appears. The More... button can be found at the bottom of the Engine Control Screen, Track Control Screen, Switch Control Screen, and Accessory Control Screen.
- Tap Advanced Features at the top of the More... Screen. The Advanced Features Screen will be displayed.
- Tap Import/Export to display the Import/Export Screen.

The Import/Export Screen allows the DCS Application's contents, including engines, switch tracks, accessories, Routes, and Scenes, to be backed up to a personal computer or directly transferred to another iOS or Android device. A backup file may later be restored to the same DCS Application or a different DCS Application on a different smart device, effectively making a clone of the first DCS Application on the second smart device.

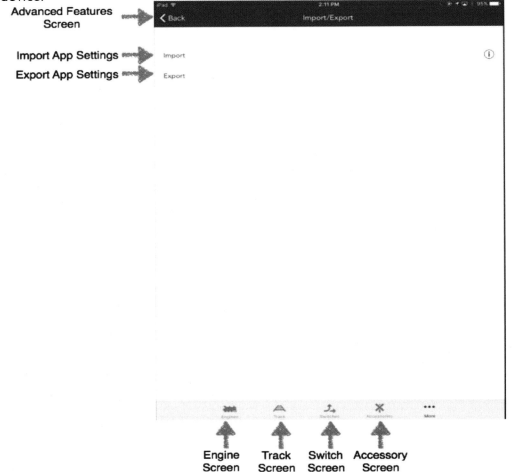

Figure 47 - Import/Export Screen

Exporting the DCS Application's Contents

If you intend to send the exported file to a DCS Application as an E-mail attachment, ensure that Internet access is available and that the recipient's E-mail address is available to the E-mail program on the smart device that receives the file. It may be necessary to temporarily disconnect the smart device from a WIU configured in MTH mode and connect to a home or cellular network. Do not change the WIU from its MTH or Home setting.

After the export process has been completed, if the smart device's network connection was switched away from the WIU, switch it back to the WIU.

To export a DCS Applications contents, proceed as follows:

- Tap the Export button.
- The iOS version of the DCS Application will display a message "Export Complete" along with a Share button. Tap on the Share button.
- The sharing options for the iOS or Android device will be displayed. These will often be different for iOS and Android, and may also differ depending upon the version of the device's operating system.
- Choose an appropriate transfer method. Then follow the device's instructions to transfer the file.

Importing the DCS Application's Contents

To import a previously saved DCS Application's contents, the DCS Application's Import button is not used. If the Import button is tapped, the DCS Application will only display a message explaining how the import function is actually accomplished.

In order to Import a file to replace the contents of the DCS Application via an E-mail attachment:

- Ensure that Internet access is available. It may be necessary to temporarily disconnect the smart device from a WIU configured in MTH mode and connect to a home or cellular network. **Do not change the WIU from its MTH or Home setting.**
- Receive the E-mail using the smart device's E-mail program.
- Tap on the attached export file.
- Select the DCS Application as the receiver of the file.
- A dialog box will appear asking to import the exported file.
- Tap the Import button in the dialog box to import the contents of the exported file. This will completely replace the existing contents of the DCS Application on this smart device. If this was done in error, tap the Close button.
- When the file has been imported, an "Import Successful" message will appear. Click the Close button to complete the process.
- After the import process has been completed, if the smart device's network connection was switched away from the WIU, switch it back to the WIU.
- Refresh the contents of the DCS Application.

Importing a DCS Remote's Contents

To import a DCS Remote backup file, the file must first be made ready for use by the DCS Application. To do so, change the DCS Remote's backup file from having a .txt extension on the end of its name to having a ".mth" extender instead. Next, E-mail the file as an attachment to an E-mail address that is available to the E-mail program on the PC or smart device intended to receive the file.

Then, proceed as described above to receive the file on the smart device.

After a DCS Remote backup file is imported, there may be some DCS engine entries that have an entry with a blank or erroneous engine name. If this happens, the solution is to delete the engine from the DCS Application and then re-add it.

To prevent the problem from reoccurring if the DCS Remote backup file is imported again into the same, or a different, DCS Application, do the following:

- Using the DCS Remote from which the backup file was made, delete and re-add the engine that had the missing or erroneous name.
- Use the DCS Loader Program to recreate and replace the original corrupted backup file.
- Follow the steps above to make the new DCS Remote backup file available to the DCS Application.

When a DCS Remote's backup file is imported into the DCS Application, any Legacy engines that were present in the backup file are added to the Inactive Engine List, as are TMCC engines. However, since the DCS Remote is not capable of recognizing Legacy engines as being any different from TMCC engines, the Legacy engines are added to the DCS Application's Inactive Engine List as TMCC engines.

If these Legacy engines are to be operated as TMCC engines, nothing further is required. However, if the DCS operator desires to use the DCS Application to operate the Legacy engines in full Legacy mode. they must be deleted from the DCS Application and re-added as Legacy engines.

Refer to Part VII - Engine Operation Using the DCS Application, 1. DCS Application Engine Operation Screens, DCS Application Edit Engine Roster Screen and DCS Application Add Engine Screen, respectively, earlier in this book to delete and add the engines.

When a TMCC engine is imported from a DCS Remote, it's speed mode is set to the default, which is Cab-1 mode. If this is not the most desirable choice, the engine's speed mode may be changed by using the Engine Settings Screen.

Importing and Exporting a DCS Application's Contents Using AirDrop

One option when exporting the contents of a DCS Application from an iOS device is to use AirDrop. However, AirDrop is not an option for the DCS Application running on iOS devices using iOS 11.x or later. Fortunately, there's an alternative method to export the file directly to iCloud using an iOS 11.x device:

- After clicking on Share, in the bottom part of the box, select "Save to Files" from the list.
- On the next screen, scroll to and tap on "TextEdit" to highlight it.
- Tap "Add" at the top right of the screen to save the file.

To import the file on an iOS device that uses iOS 11.x:

- From the Home screen, tap on the "Files" icon.
- From the "iCloud Drive" screen, tap on the "TextEdit" icon.
- Look for the icon for the saved export file. There will be two files with the same date and time. The one to use is the one with the MTH icon. The other file may be deleted. The MTH export file may also be renamed.
- Tap on the MTH export file.
- On the next screen, tap on the Share icon in the top right corner.
- Scroll through the list of apps and tap the DCS Application's icon.
- Import the file.

9. DCS Engine Recovery

Occasionally, a DCS engine will have its DCS ID# move to a number outside of the normal DCS engine ID# range of 1-99. When this happens, the DCS Application can no longer access the engine. In order to once again recover the engine by resetting its DCS ID# to a value inside the range of 1-99, it's necessary to use the DCS Application's Recover Engine Screen.

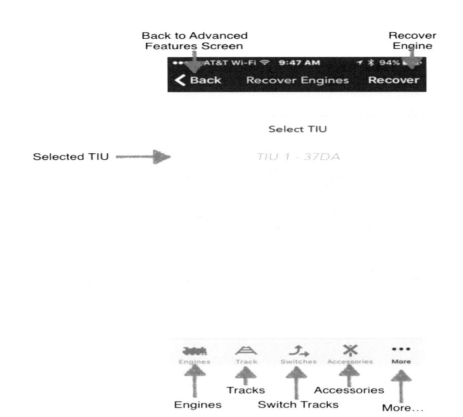

Figure 48 - Recover Engines Screen

How to access the Recover Engines Screen, as well as a description of its functions, is described in the following table.

Recover Engines Screen	
PURPOSE:	Recover a DCS engine whose DCS ID# is outside of the normal range.
HOW TO GET IT:	Tap Recover Engines on the Advanced Features Screen.
INFORMATION DISPLAYED:	The TIU on the layout upon whose tracks the DCS engine to have its DCS ID# recovered is residing.
BUTTONS:	Tap Back to Advanced Features Screen to return to the Advanced Features Screen.
	Tap Recover Engine to attempt to recover a DCS engine.
	Tap Engines to transfer control to the Engine Control Screen.
	Tap Tracks to transfer control to the Track Control Screen.
	Tap Switch Tracks to transfer control to the Switch Control Screen.
	Tap Accessories to transfer control to the Accessory Control Screen.
	Tap More... to transfer control to the More... Screen.

To recover an engine whose DCS ID# has moved out of the normal range of DCS ID#s, 1-99, first ensure that the engine is on a powered track. It does not have to be started up. Then, proceed as follows:

- Tap the icon for the More... Screen at the bottom of any screen on which it appears.
- Tap on the More... Screen's Advanced Features button.
- Tap on the Recover Engines button on the Advanced Features Screen.
- Tap on the TIU upon whose tracks the DCS engine to have its DCS ID# recovered is residing.

- Tap on the Recover Engine button to attempt to recover the engine.
- A dialog box appears stating that the engine was, or was not, recovered.

f the engine is recovered, it will be Factory Reset and must be re-added to the DCS Application in order to be used. Before adding it, ensure to first delete it if it's in the DCS Application's Active List or Inactive Engine List.

10. System Settings

The DCS Application allows the DCS operator to review and adjust a variety of DCS settings. This is accomplished troughthe use of the System Settings Screen.

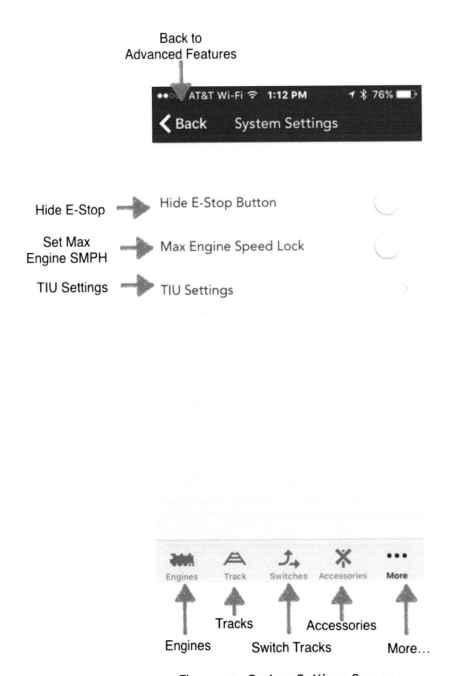

Figure 49 - System Settings Screen

The DCS WIFI Companion

How to access the System Settings Screen, as well as a description of its functions, is described in the following table.

System Settings Screen	
PURPOSE:	Access DCS system settings.
HOW TO GET IT:	Tap System Settings on the Advanced Features Screen.
INFORMATION DISPLAYED:	DCS system settings.
BUTTONS:	Tap Hide E-Stop to hide or show the E-Stop button on the Engine Control Screen and the Track Control Screen.
	Tap Set Max Engine SMPH to set a maximum speed for all DCS engines controlled by the DCS Application.
	Tap TIU Settings to transfer control to the TIU Settings Screen.
	Tap Tracks to transfer control to the Track Control Screen.
	Tap Engines to transfer control to the Engine Control Screen.
	Tap Switch Tracks to transfer control to the Switch Control Screen.
	Tap Accessories to transfer control to the Accessory Control Screen.
	Tap More... to transfer control to the More... Screen.

Hide E-Stop Button

Although many DCS operators consider the E-Stop button to be a very useful feature, others find that it can be annoying if it is tapped accidentally. Therefore, the DCS Application allows the operator to choose whether or not to have the E-Stop button be available.

To change the visibility of the E-Stop button, tap on the selector to the right of Hide E-Stop Button to toggle its visibility on or off. This feature requires the use of a password, as described below.

Set Max Engine SMPH

At times, it can be useful to limit the speed at which a DCS engine may be operated, particularly when a small child or other inexperienced visitor to the layout is operating trains using the DCS Application.

To set a maximum speed for DCS engine operation from the DCS Application, tap on the selector to the right of Set Max Engine Speed Lock to toggle it on or off. Once the setting is on, it is not possible to change the maximum speed of any DCS engine. Note that when the maximum engine speed is set, it is set for this DCS Application only. Other DCS Applications, operating on other smart devices, are not affected. This feature requires the use of a password, as described below.

DCS Application Password

The first time that either of the two selectors above are tapped, the operator is required to establish a password for the DCS Application. Any subsequent modification of either setting will necessitate entering the password. If the operator forgets the password, in order to change either setting it becomes necessary to reset the DCS Application, clearing all of its contents. Resetting the DCS Application is described later in this book in Part XI - The DCS Application's More... Screen, 2. DCS Application Settings Screen.

TIU Settings Screen

The TIU Settings Screen displays information regarding, and allows modification of all of the settings associated with each of the layout's TIUs.

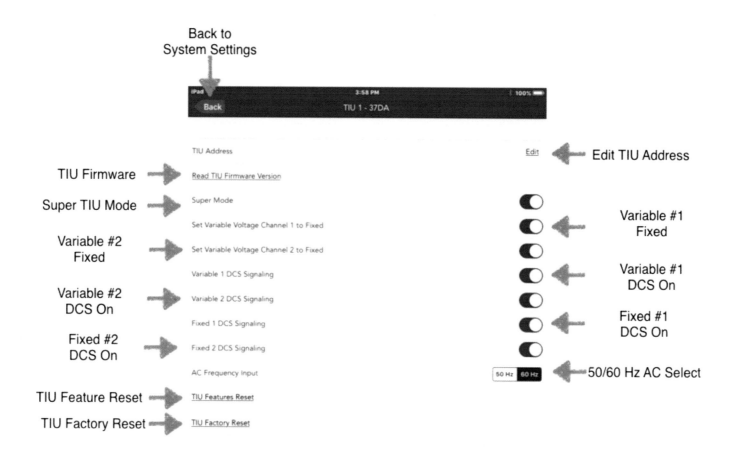

Back to
System Settings

TIU Firmware → Read TIU Firmware Version

Super TIU Mode → Super Mode

Variable #2
Fixed → Set Variable Voltage Channel 2 to Fixed

Variable #2
DCS On → Variable 2 DCS Signaling

Fixed #2
DCS On → Fixed 2 DCS Signaling

TIU Feature Reset → TIU Features Reset

TIU Factory Reset → TIU Factory Reset

TIU Address — Edit ← Edit TIU Address

Set Variable Voltage Channel 1 to Fixed ← Variable #1 Fixed

Variable 1 DCS Signaling ← Variable #1 DCS On

Fixed 1 DCS Signaling ← Fixed #1 DCS On

AC Frequency Input — 50 Hz 60 Hz ← 50/60 Hz AC Select

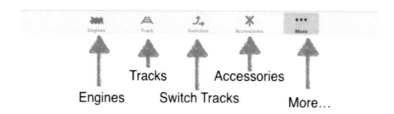

Engines   Tracks   Switch Tracks   Accessories   More…

Figure 50 - TIU Settings Screen

How to access the TIU Settings Screen, as well as a description of its functions, is described in the following table.

TIU Settings Screen	
PURPOSE:	View and modify TIU settings.
HOW TO GET IT:	Tap TIU Settings on the System Settings Screen.
INFORMATION DISPLAYED:	TIU settings for the selected TIU.
BUTTONS:	Tap Back to Advanced Features Screen to return to the Advanced Features Screen.
	Tap Edit TIU Address to change the selected TIU's DCS ID#.
	Tap TIU Firmware to learn the version of the TIU's DCS software.
	Tap the Super TIU Mode selector to toggle Super TIU Mode on or off.
	Tap Variable #1 Fixed selector to toggle Variable #1 fixed or variable.
	Tap Variable #2 Fixed selector to toggle Variable #2 fixed or variable.
	Tap Variable #1 DCS On selector to toggle DCS on or off for Variable #1.
	Tap Variable #2 DCS On selector to toggle DCS on or off for Variable #2.
	Tap Fixed #1 DCS On selector to toggle DCS on or off for Fixed #1.
	Tap Fixed #2 DCS On selector to toggle DCS on or off for Fixed #2.
	Tap 50/60 Hz AC Select to select 50Hz or 60Hz power for the TIU.
	Tap TIU Feature Reset to affect a Feature Reset for the selected TIU.
	Tap TIU Factory Reset to affect a Factory Reset for the selected TIU.
	Tap Engines to transfer control to the Engine Control Screen.
	Tap Tracks to transfer control to the Track Control Screen.
	Tap Switch Tracks to transfer control to the Switch Control Screen.
	Tap Accessories to transfer control to the Accessory Control Screen.
	Tap More... to transfer control to the More... Screen.

Using the TIU Settings Screen, the DCS operator can learn the version of the DCS software running in each layout TIU and modify each TIU's settings. When the TIU Settings button on the System Settings Screen is tapped, a list of all of the layout's TIUs is displayed. When one of the TIUs is tapped, the settings for that TIU are displayed.

The following may be accomplished from the TIU Settings Screen:

- Tap Edit TIU Address to modify the TIU's DCS ID#.
- Tap TIU Firmware to learn the TIU's software version.
- Tap the Super TIU Mode selector to toggle the TIU between Normal TIU mode and Super TIU mode. This must be done using each smartphone or tablet that will be used with this TIU.
- Tap the Variable #1 Fixed selector to toggle Variable Channel #1 between Fixed and Variable mode of operation.
- Tap the Variable #2 Fixed selector to toggle Variable Channel #2 between Fixed and Variable mode of operation.
- Even though the first DCS App to change the Variable channel's setting changes it in the TIU itself, this should be done using each smartphone or tablet that will be used with this TIU in order to avoid any operator confusion as regards what is the status of the variable channel. If it's desired to set a channel to Fixed or Variable operation, it should be done on all devices that will access that TIU's Variable channel
- Tap the Variable #1 DCS On selector to turn on or off the DCS signal on Variable Channel #1.
- Tap the Variable #2 DCS On selector to turn on or off the DCS signal on Variable Channel #2.
- Tap the Fixed #1 DCS On selector to turn on or off the DCS signal on Fixed Channel #1.
- Tap the Fixed #2 DCS On selector to turn on or off the DCS signal on Fixed Channel #2.
- Tap the 50/60 Hz AC selector to set the AC power input for the TIU to 50Hz or 60Hz.
- Tap TIU Feature Reset to perform a Feature Reset of the selected TIU. All Record/Playback sessions and Custom Sounds in the TIU will be deleted.
- Tap TIU Factory Reset to perform a Factory Reset of the selected TIU. All Record/Playback sessions and Custom Sounds in the TIU will be deleted. In addition, the TIU will be returned to factory settings and its DCS ID# will be set to 1.

TIU Replacement Procedure

If it becomes necessary to replace a TIU on a layout, the procedure to do so using a DCS Application is considerably more straightforward than when using a DCS Remote. However, since all Record/Playback sessions and Custom Sounds are saved in the TIUs, rather than in the DCS Application itself, any such Record/Playback sessions and Custom Sounds that were in the TIU being replaced will be lost. However, if done properly, replacing a TIU should not result in the loss of any engine, switch track, accessory, or TIU Track information.

For purposes of the following discussion, the TIU being replaced is referred to as the OLD TIU and the replacement TIU is referred to as the NEW TIU.

First, power on the NEW TIU and count how many times its red LED blinks before it comes on steady. This is the DCS ID# of the NEW TIU. Next, do the same for the OLD TIU to learn its DCS ID#. If the OLD TIU and the NEW TIU have the same DCS ID#, simply replace the OLD TIU with the new TIU.

However, if the OLD TIU and the NEW TIU have different DCS ID#s, proceed as follows:

1. Note for **all** of the layout's TIUs whether each TIU is in Normal or Super TIU mode and whether each TIU channel is set to variable voltage or fixed voltage. (Refer to Part IX - Advanced Features and Functions, 10. System Settings, TIU Settings Screen earlier in this book.)

2. Export the contents of the DCS Application. The method chosen for accomplishing the export is unimportant, as long as the operator is fully conversant with the associated method by which the contents of the DCS Application may be later re-imported..

3. Reset the DCS Application. The entire contents of this DCS Application will be deleted.

4. Ensure that all TIUs and their associated WIUs are powered off.

5. Disconnect the OLD TIU from its WIU and set it aside.

6. Connect the NEW TIU to the OLD TIU's WIU and power-on only the NEW TIU and its WIU

7. Launch the DCS Application, tap Run My Trains and wait for the WIU to stabilize before tapping the Refresh button on the Engine Control Screen.

8. Navigate to the More... Screen, Advanced Features Screen, and then the TIU Settings Screen.

9. Select the NEW TIU from the list of available TIUs. It should be the only TIU in the list. The TIU Settings Screen is displayed. Tap Edit TIU Address and enter the OLD TIU's address to change the NEW TIU's address to the OLD TIU's address.

10. Power on the layout, including the NEW TIU.

11. Import the contents of the DCS Application that was previously saved back into the DCS Application.

12. Wait for the WIUs to stabilize and then refresh the DCS Application.

13. Ensure that **each** of the layout's TIUs has the same settings that they had before the export as regards Normal or Super TIU mode, and whether each TIU channel is set correctly to variable voltage or fixed voltage. Make any changes as appropriate.

14. Repeat the last 4 steps

11. Super TIU Mode

As discussed earlier in this book, DCS engines can usually only be controlled by the DCS Application when they are on tracks that are connected to the TIU with which they were associated the last time the engine was added to that DCS Application. When operating large layouts that utilize more than one TIU, this limitation can result in serious restrictions on where DCS engines can be operated on the layout.

In order to remove these restrictions DCS includes a feature called Super TIU mode that ignores the entire DCS engine/TIU association issue, allowing DCS engines to operate anywhere on the layout. The layout looks to DCS as if there is a single TIU controlling DCS over the entire layout, rather than multiple individual TIUs.

Why Use Super TIU Mode?

Large layouts often require more than one TIU for effective operation of DCS. These large layouts often have a track plan that allows DCS engines to move from tracks connected to their associated TIU to tracks connected to a different TIU, and may also have multiple DCS Applications being used on multiple smart devices simultaneously. On these layouts, the operator would normally lose the ability to control a DCS engine when it crosses from the tracks controlled by one TIU to the tracks controlled by another TIU. Also, DCS Applications that added DCS engines on tracks of different TIUs may be unable to control these engines. Super TIU mode allows all DCS engines on the layout to be controlled from all DCS Applications, regardless of where the engines are on the layout or to which TIU they were last associated.

How Does Super TIU Mode Work?

As previously discussed, DCS engine commands issued by a DCS Application are received by all TIUs on the layout. However, when TIUs are set to normal TIU mode only the TIU with which the DCS engine was last associated actually forwards the command to the engine. If the engine isn't on a powered track connected to its associated TIU, the command cannot be received and the DCS engine does not respond, the DCS Application times out and an error message is displayed on the Engine Control Screen.

When TIUs are in Super TIU mode, all TIUs forward any DCS engine command received from any DCS Application to the DCS engine, regardless of whether or not the DCS engine is associated with the TIU. This ensures that any DCS engine that is powered up and on tracks connected to any TIU on the layout will receive the command.

Turning on Super TIU Mode

In order to operate properly, Super TIU mode must be turned on for each TIU on the layout, from each DCS Application used with the layout. This is accomplished as follows for each of the layout's DCS Applications:

- Navigate to the More… Screen, tap Advanced Features, tap System Settings, tap TIU Settings, and select a TIU from the list of all of the TIUs in the DCS Application by tapping it.
- Tap the Super TIU Mode selector to toggle Super TIU Mode on.
- Repeat the above process for each TIU listed.
- Repeat the above process for all other DCS Applications running on all other smart devices that are used with the layout.

To change back to normal TIU mode of operation, repeat the above process for all TIUs and DCS Applications, tapping the Super TIU Mode selector again to toggle Super TIU Mode off, placing each TIU and DCS Application back into normal TIU mode.

Considerations When Using Super TIU Mode

Generally, there are no real disadvantages to using Super TIU mode. However, there are a few things worth noting:

- When operating in Super TIU mode, all TIUs and all DCS Applications must be in Super TIU mode in order to achieve seamless layout operation.
- When operating in normal TIU mode, all TIUs and all DCS Applications must be in normal TIU mode.
- DCS Applications and TIUs communicate with each other through the use of wireless data packets. When the layout is operating in Super TIU mode, the number of data packets increases significantly. This may cause a very small lag time between a command being issued to a DCS engine and the engine responding. This lag time is on the order of a fraction of a second and is usually not noticeable.
- When passenger trains travel from tracks controlled by one TIU to tracks controlled by another TIU, the passenger car pickup rollers generally bridge the gap between the two TIUs. If a DCS Application issues a command to a DCS engine that is on tracks controlled by either TIU while the gap between the two TIU's is being bridged, it's possible that the DCS engine may not respond to the command.

12. Passive TIU Mode

In a typical DCS layout, TIUs are connected to the layout between the transformers that provide track power and the tracks themselves. Power flows from the transformers to the tracks through the TIUs. However, some operators have determined that it is not entirely necessary to have track power flow through the TIU. Using this connection method, track power transformers and TIUs are connected to the tracks independently of each other and transformer track power does not pass through the TIU. This connection method is called Passive TIU mode.

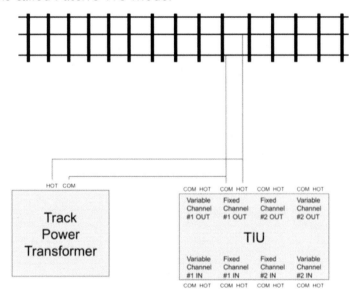

Figure 51 - Passive TIU Mode

Why Use Passive TIU Mode?

In the great majority of cases, the typical DCS operator will never have a real need to use Passive TIU mode of operation. The primary reason for an operator to utilize Passive TIU mode would be to allow more power (amperage not voltage) to be provided to the tracks than can safely be passed through a TIU channel. TIU channels are each rated for a maximum of 10 amps continuous draw and most operators would rarely, if ever, have a need to exceed 10 amps per TIU channel.

If it is expected that 10 amps or higher continuous power is required for any portion of the layout, those TIU channels that are connected to that portion of the layout may be wired for Passive TIU mode of operation.

A secondary reason why TIU channels may be wired for Passive TIU mode of operation would be if a great concern exists that the TIU could be damaged due to short circuits caused by derailments or for other reasons. Generally, these types of concerns are easily resolved through the use of modern transformers with built-in short circuit protection for track power and the disadvantages of utilizing Passive TIU mode of operation are usually greater than the advantages.

Advantages and Disadvantages of Using Passive TIU Mode

The only real advantage gained by wiring for Passive TIU mode of operation is that track power may exceed 10 amps per channel without any concern of damage to the TIU. This allows use of higher capacity toy train transformers or devices that can combine the output of two or more transformers into a single power feed.

There are, however, disadvantages to using Passive TIU mode of operation:

- The E-Stop key on the DCS Application, which is used to shut down the layout in an emergency, works by shutting down TIU channels to turn off power to the tracks. The E-Stop function will not operate when wired for Passive TIU mode of operation since power to the tracks does not pass through the TIU. Instead, only the DCS signal will be turned off. This has the potential to make things worse, since DCS engines would continue doing whatever they were last instructed to do and the operator will lose all control over them.
- Since TIU Variable Channels operate by regulating voltage from transformers to the tracks, it is not possible to use Variable Channels when wired for Passive TIU mode of operation. Again, this is because track power does not pass through the TIU under Passive TIU mode of operation.
- Passive TIU Mode may adversely affect DCS signal strength. Some operators have reported a DCS signal strength decrease of 1-2 points.

The only real difference between wiring TIU channels normally and wiring them for Passive TIU mode of operation is that, instead of transformer power for the tracks being connected to the input terminals of the TIU, transformer power is connected to the output TIU channel terminals or directly to the tracks. All other wiring from TIU output terminals to terminal blocks and to tracks remains the same, and the wiring guidelines presented in the DCS Implementation section should still be followed.

13. Using Passenger Station and Freight Yard Announcements

Every DCS engine that is not a subway or trolley (those engines have Transit Station Announcements as discussed earlier in this book) is equipped with either Freight Yard or Passenger Station Announcements. Each series of announcements consists of 5 linked sound sequences that starts when the PFA button on the DCS Application's Engine Features Screen is tapped. To play the engine's passenger or freight yard announcements, proceed as follows:

- Tap the PFA button to open the Passenger/Freight Announcements window.
- Tap Activate to begin to play the announcement sequences. Activate will change to Arrival.
- Tap the Arrival button to stop the engine and play the first sound sequence. Arrival will change to Segment 1. The engine's reverse unit is temporarily disabled so that the train will not move until the full PFA sequence is completed or cancelled. Also disabled is the use of the Bell and Horn/Whistle buttons.
- After waiting about 30 seconds for the sequence to finish, tap the Segment 1 button to play the next sound sequence. Repeat this for the remaining sound sequences. At the conclusion of the Departure sound sequence, the DCS engine's bell will begin to sound and the engine will resume movement in the same direction that it was going when PFA was initiated.
- Once the bell turns off, the operator regains control of the engine.

Although most of the times that PFA is activated the engine is moving forwards, PFA can also be activated while the DCS engine is either moving backwards or is stationary. If PFA is activated while the engine is stationary, the engine will remain stationary during and after the PFA activation. If it's activated while the engine is moving backwards, at the conclusion of the PFA sound sequences, the engine will move backwards at the same speed at which it was moving when the PFA sound sequences began.

PFA may be terminated at any time by pressing the PFA button on the on the DCS Application's Engine Features Screen.

Part X - Operating Conventional Engines

1. Conventional Engines Defined

A conventional engine is most often thought of as a Lionel postwar engine. In actuality, there are several different kinds of conventional engines. They include:

- Prewar engines from Lionel, Marx and others.
- Postwar engines from Lionel, Marx and others.
- MTH PS1 engines.
- MTH Locosound engines.
- Other engines that lack command control capability, such as current offerings from Lionel, Weaver, Atlas O, 3rd Rail, and others.
- Engines capable of command control using DCS, Legacy or TMCC with command control turned off.

A DCS engine may be operated under conventional control by doing one of three things:

- The DCS engine may be powered on after the DCS signal has been turned off for the TIU channel(s) connected to the tracks upon which it will be operated.
- The DCS engine may be powered up with DCS active, after which the operator can tap the soft key for Legacy Mode to place the engine into conventional mode, with speed control turned off, until the engine's power is turned off and then back on again.
- The DCS engine may be powered up with DCS active, after which the operator can tap the soft key for Conventional Mode to place the engine into conventional mode, with speed control turned on, until the engine's power is turned off and then back on again.

As discussed earlier, command control engines are controlled by keeping power on the tracks at all times and sending digital signals with commands to operate the engine's functions. On the other hand, conventional engines are controlled through changes in track voltage.

The higher the voltage in the tracks, the faster conventional engines will go and the lower the track voltage, the slower they will go. Generally, these engines also contain a mechanical or electronic E-Unit that senses brief voltage interruptions and changes the engine's direction. Conventional engines will go through a cycle of neutral to forward, forward to neutral, neutral to reverse, and reverse back to neutral each time power is interrupted. Many conventional engines will start up in neutral while some will start up in forward. Conventional engines respond to DC pulses in the AC power to ring their bell, or sound their horn or whistle.

2. Controlling Conventional Engines Using the DCS Application

DCS Engines are controlled in conventional mode using the DCS Application through the use of TIU Tracks on TIU Variable Channels by varying voltage to control the tracks. The voltage is varied within the TIU. Further, TIU Variable Channels may not be used with DC voltage and are therefore unsuitable for use with MTH PS3 HO engines that require DC voltage only, or any other conventional engines that operate solely on DC voltage.

Creating TIU Tracks on Variable Channels

TIU Tracks are created to allow the DCS operator to vary the voltage to the tracks through the TIU's Variable Channels. TIU Tracks are created and operated by the DCS Application though the Track Control Screen.

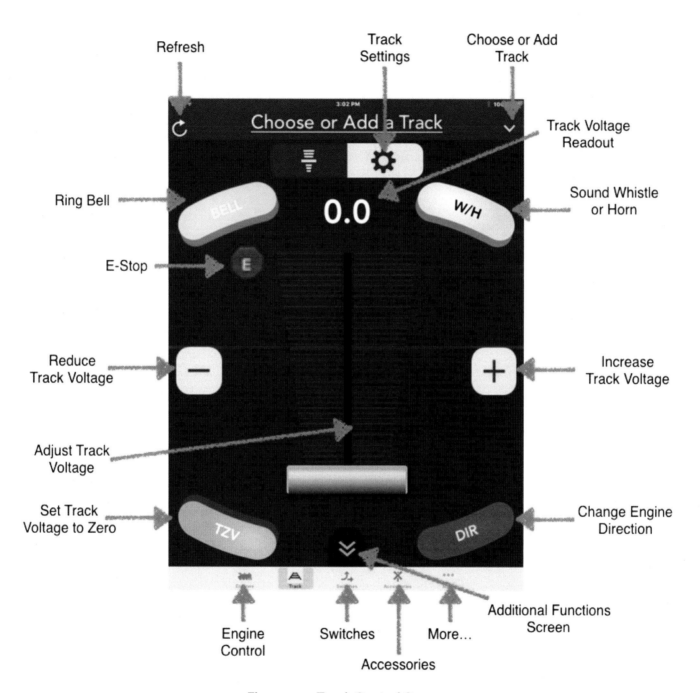

Figure 52 - Track Control Screen

How to access the Track Control Screen, as well as a description of its functions, is described in the following table.

Track Control Screen	
PURPOSE:	Allows Control of Conventional Engines.
HOW TO GET IT:	Tap Track Screen button on any screen where it appears.
INFORMATION DISPLAYED:	Track voltage for the selected TIU Track.
BUTTONS:	Tap Refresh to refresh the screen.
	Tap Track Settings, or swipe left or right to transfer control to the Track Settings Screen.
	Tap Choose or Add Track to see all TIU Tracks or add new TIU Tracks.
	Tap Ring Bell to ring the bell of all conventional engines on this TIU Track.
	Tap Sound Whistle or Horn to blow the horn or blast the whistle of all conventional engines on this TIU Track.
	Tap E- Stop to shut down power through all TIU channels and reset the power to all TIUs.
	Tap Reduce Track Voltage to incrementally lower the voltage to this TIU Track.
	Tap Increase Track Voltage to incrementally raise the voltage to this TIU Track.
	Slide Adjust Track Voltage up or down to continuously increase or decrease track voltage on this TIU Track.
	Tap Set Track Voltage to Zero to lower the track voltage to zero on this TIU Track.
	Tap Change Engine Direction to change direction of all conventional engines on the TIU Track by cycling their E-units.
	Tap Additional Functions Screen to transfer to the Additional Track Functions Screen.
	Tap Engine Control to transfer control to the Engine Control Screen.
	Tap Switches to transfer control to the Switch Control Screen.
	Tap Accessories to transfer control to the Accessory Control Screen.
	Tap More... to transfer control to the More... Screen.
	Slide the screen up to go to the Additional Track Functions Screen.

TIU Tracks may be created for TIU Variable Channels using the Choose or Add a Track Screen, shown below.

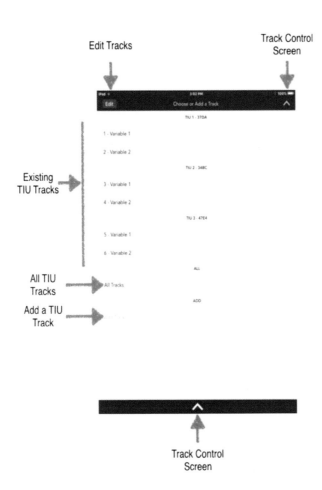

Figure 53 - Choose or Add Track Screen

How to access the Choose or Add Track Screen, as well as a description of its functions, is described in the following table.

Choose or Add Track Screen	
PURPOSE:	Choose an Existing TIU Track or create a new one.
HOW TO GET IT:	Tap Choose or Add Track on the Track Control Screen.
INFORMATION DISPLAYED:	List of existing TIU Tracks.
BUTTONS:	Tap on All TIU Tracks to operate all of the layout's TIU Tracks from a single throttle and return to the Track Control Screen.
	Tap on an existing TIU Track to select it and return to the Track Control Screen.
	Tap Add a TIU Track to create a new TIU Track.
	Tap Track Control Screen to return to the Track Control Screen.

To create a new TIU Track, proceed, as follows:

- Navigate the DCS Application to the Track Control Screen.
- Tap on Choose or Add Track to display the Choose or Add a Track Screen.

- Tap on Add a TIU Track.
- A list of available TIUs is displayed. Tap on the TIU for which a TIU Track is to be created.
- Tap on the Variable Channel for which the TIU Track is to be created, either Variable 1 or Variable 2.
- Use the on-screen keyboard to enter the name of the TIU Track for that Variable Channel. Tap Done to save the new track's name and return to the Choose or Add Track Screen.

Additional conventional operation functions are located on the Additional Track Functions Screen, shown below.

Operating Conventional Engines on TIU Tracks

After one or more TIU Tracks have been created, conventional engines may be operated on those TIU Tracks using the DCS Application's Track Control Screen, as follows:

- Navigate the DCS Application to the Track Control Screen.
- Tap on Choose or Add Track. A list of all TIU Tracks that have been added to the DCS Application will appear, listed by the track names they were assigned.
- Tap on a TIU Track where the conventional engines are located.
- The Track Control Screen is displayed. Use the buttons on the Track Control Screen as if they

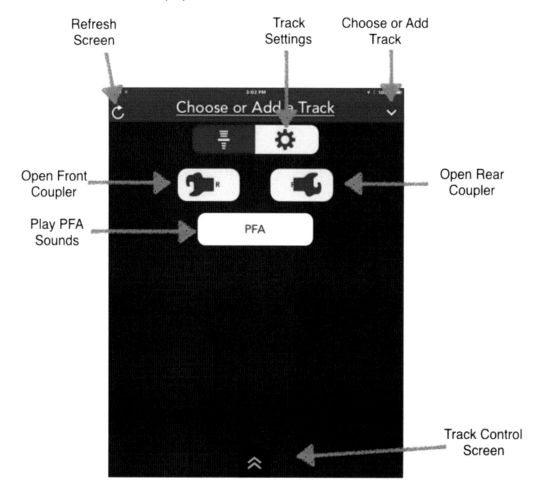

Figure 54 - Additional Track Functions Screen

were buttons on the control panel of a transformer to operate the conventional engines. Tap + to increase voltage to the tracks. The first tap of the button will display .5 Volts and each additional tap will increase voltage by 1/2 volt. Tapping - decreases voltage to the tracks in 1/2 volt increments, until 5 Volts is displayed. The next tap will display 0 volts and power to the tracks will be turned off. Alternately, use the Adjust Track Voltage slider to adjust track voltage.

- The DIR button will cycle conventional engines that have E-Units through their forward-neutral-reverse cycle. The BELL button will ring the bell for engines that have one and the W/H button will sound the whistle or horn for engine's that have one.

- Note that all engines on the same TIU Track will respond to button taps on the Track Control Screen, the same way that they all would respond to button presses on a transformer's control panel. This is the nature of conventional engines. Unlike command control engines, they are not individually controlled.

- When the operating session with conventional engines is completed, tap repeatedly on the - button until the voltage displayed is zero and power to the tracks has been turned off. Alternately, tapping the TZV button or moving the Adjust Track Voltage slider to its lowest position will set track power to 0 volts.

- In the event of a derailment, it's recommend to tap and hold E-Stop until track power through all TIU channels has been turned off. Note that if E-Stop is used, it's necessary to cycle power to the layout in order to resume operations though any TIU channel.

How to access the Additional Track Functions Screen, as well as a description of its functions, is described in the following table.

Additional Track Functions Screen	
PURPOSE:	Allows Control of Conventional Engines.
HOW TO GET IT:	Tap Additional Functions Screen button on the Track Control Screen.
INFORMATION DISPLAYED:	Additional conventional control features and functions.
BUTTONS:	Tap Refresh Screen to refresh the screen.
	Tap Track Settings, or swipe left or right to transfer control to the Track Settings Screen.
	Tap Choose or Add a Track to transfer to the Choose or Add a Track Screen to select an existing track or to create a new track.
	Tap Open Front Coupler to open the front coupler on DCS engines operating in conventional mode.
	Tap Open Rear Coupler to open the rear coupler on DCS engines operating in conventional mode.
	Tap Play PFA Sounds to play Passenger Station Sounds or Freight Yard Sounds on DCS engines operating in conventional mode.
	Tap Engines to transfer control to the Engine Control Screen.
	Tap Switches to transfer control to the Switch Track Control Screen.
	Tap Accessories to transfer control to the Accessory Control Screen.
	Tap More... to transfer control to the More... Screen.
	Slide the screen down to go to the Track Control Screen.

3. How Variable Tracks Manage Voltage

There is a common misconception regarding the method by which Variable Tracks manage voltage. Based on the actual voltage being input to a Variable Channel, the Track Control Screen may display the voltage of TIU Tracks incorrectly.

The voltage displayed can be misleading due to the way that Variable Channels manage voltage. The TIU assumes that the voltage input to a Variable Channel is always 22 volts. This assumption is a natural one since many MTH transformers have a maximum output of 22 volts.

Track voltage increases when the + button on the Track Control Screen is tapped and decreases when the - button is tapped. The voltage displayed on the Track Control Screen increases by 1/2 volt for each click above 5 volts. However, the actual voltage that reaches the tracks controlled by the TIU Track may be different because of the way that the TIU manages voltage. For each 1 volt displayed on the Track Control Screen, DCS increases the voltage at the TIU channel output terminals by 1/22 of the input voltage to the TIU channel. If the input voltage is 22 volts, the display on the Track Control Screen will always correspond to the actual voltage being output by the TIU channel. If the display reads 18 volts, the actual voltage at the output terminals of the TIU channel will be: 22 volts input X 18/22 = 18 volts.

However, if the input voltage is lower, the actual output voltage will be less than the display indicates. For example, if the input voltage to the TIU channel is 18 volts and the display reads 18 volts, the actual voltage at the output terminals of the TIU channel will be: 18 volts input X 18/22 = 14.73 volts.

One other important item to note is the method that the Variable Channels actually use to vary the input voltage when power is increased or decreased. Since the maximum voltage that may be output to the tracks can be no larger than the input voltage, unless the Track Control Screen is set to the maximum displayed value of 22 volts, the input voltage is always being lowered. The TIU does this by using a process of chopping the sine wave. While this is not a bad thing to do, it is also the way that some modern transformers vary voltage themselves. The combination of a transformer that chops the sine wave and a second chopping of the sine wave inside the TIU, however, is a bad thing and should be avoided. There are a few ways to avoid the problem.

If using a brick-type transformer as an input to a TIU Track, connect the brick directly to the TIU channel, bypassing any included power controller. It's the power controller that actually chops the sine wave. One of the biggest offenders in this regard is the Z-Controller that often accompanies the MTH brick-type transformers. MTH sells a connecting cable (item #50-1017) that is used to connect an MTH brick directly to the TIU channel input terminals. Omitting any controller also ensures that the TIU channel receives the maximum output from the brick itself.

If using a modern transformer that chops the sine wave to vary voltage, adjust the transformer's throttle to its maximum voltage setting. This will typically bypass any chopping of the sine wave and also ensure that the TIU channel receives the maximum output from the transformer itself.

4. Operating Command & Conventional Engines on the Same Track

It is possible using DCS to operate command control and conventional engines simultaneously on different, or the same, tracks. However, there are several challenges involved in doing so.

Command control engines are operated using the DCS Application's Engine Control Screen. Commands are sent that are only executed by the designated DCS, TMCC or Legacy engine. Command control engines completely ignore commands intended for other command control engines.

Conventional engines are operated using the DCS Application's Track Control Screen. Rather than executing specific commands, conventional engines react to changes in track voltage to speed up, slow down or reverse direction. Further, all conventional engines have a herd mentality - they all react the same way to track voltage changes and at the same time.

The differences between how command control and conventional engines operate creates several challenges for the DCS operator who desires to run both types of engines on the same layout. It becomes even more challenging if it is desired to run both kinds of engines on the same track loops.

The first challenge is the one faced by conventional operators every day. That is, keeping the conventional engines themselves from colliding with each other. Many, if not most, conventional engines lack speed control, and no two conventional engines can be assumed to run at the same speed given the same voltage. Keeping them apart can be a real chore. Most conventional operators simply assign conventional engines to operate on separate tracks.

Another challenge is switching between the Engine Control Screen to control command control engines, and the Track Control Screen to control conventional engines. This can require some degree of manual dexterity and organizational skills.

A third challenge is providing enough power to the command control engines for them to perform effectively while keeping the power low enough so that the conventional engines don't run away. A DCS engine requires a minimum of approximately 9-10 volts in order to properly operate the engine's electronics. At this voltage some conventional engines may run fast enough to depart the rails on curves. Further, each time the DIR button on the Track Control Screen is pressed to change the direction of a conventional engine, all the command control engines on the same TIU channel will momentarily lose power. Generally, PS3 engines, and PS2 engines with reasonably well-charged batteries, will continue to operate properly with no loss of sound and only, perhaps, a slight stutter in their movement. TMCC or Legacy command-controlled engines that lack a battery will momentarily lose sound and may also stutter in their movement.

Finally, if command control and conventional engines are operated on the same track, the issues associated with the previous challenges become quite a bit more difficult to manage. At this point, it becomes almost mandatory that the layout operator use two smart devices, each with its own DCS Application, to run the trains, where one DCS Application is dedicated to the Engine Control Screen for operating command control engines and the other is dedicated to the Track Control Screen for operating conventional engines. Additionally, if more than a handful of engines are being operated at once, a further suggestion is to have a separate operator for each DCS Application.

While simultaneous operation of command control and conventional engines is, indeed, possible, many operators find it less than satisfying.

Part XI - The DCS Application's More... Screen

The DCS application has a More... Screen that serves several purposes:

- It allows access to advanced DCS features. The various advanced features of the DCS Application are discussed in detail in Part IX - Advanced Features and Functions earlier in this book.
- It provides the capability to upgrade the free version of the DCS Application to the Standard or Premium versions of the application.
- It allows contacting MTH through the DCS Application, resetting the DCS Application's settings and learning the DCS Applications software version.
- It provides a path, through the Internet, to several of MTH's websites.

The last three of the above functions of the More... Screen are discussed in the following section of this book.

The DCS Application's More... Screen is shown below.

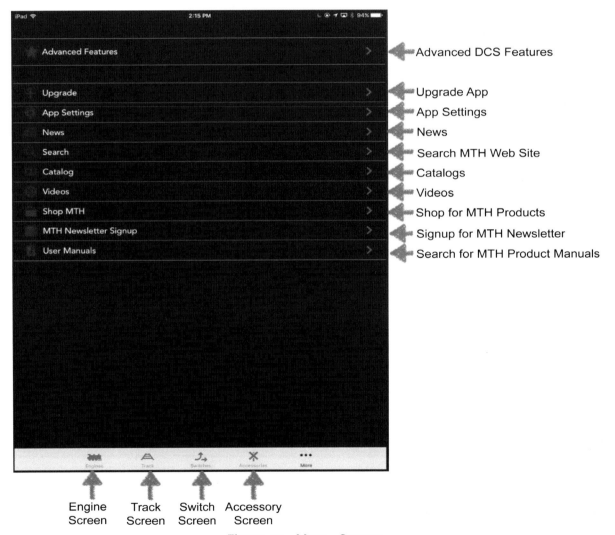

Figure 55 - More... Screen

How to access the More... Screen, as well as a description of its functions, is described in the table below.

More... Screen	
PURPOSE:	Allows access to advanced DCS features, DCS Application settings, MTH's website, and DCS Application upgrades.
HOW TO GET IT:	Tap the More... button on any screen where it appears.
INFORMATION DISPLAYED:	A list of available DCS Application features and functions.
BUTTONS:	Tap Advanced Features to transfer to the Advanced Features Screen.
	Tap Upgrade App for the opportunity to upgrade the DCS Application to the Standard or Premium version.
	Tap App Settings to change the DCS Application's settings.
	Tap News to transfer control to the MTH News website.
	Tap Search to transfer control to the Internet to search MTH's website.
	Tap Catalogs to transfer control to the Internet to view MTH's catalogs.
	Tap Videos to transfer control to the Internet to view MTH's videos.
	Tap Shop MTH to transfer control to the Internet to access MTH's online product store.
	Tap MTH Newsletter Signup for the opportunity to receive MTH's E-mail newsletters.
	Tap Engine Screen to transfer control to the Engine Control Screen.
	Tap Track Screen to transfer control to the Track Control Screen.
	Tap Switch Screen to transfer control to the Switch Track Control Screen.
	Tap Accessory Screen to transfer control to the Accessory Control Screen.

1. Upgrading the DCS Application

The DCS Application, when initially downloaded from the Apple iTunes Store or Google Play, is a free application that is very limited in its functionality. In order to realize the full potential of the DCS Application, it's necessary to upgrade it to one or the other of the application's Standard or Premium version.

The Standard version of the DCS Application allows complete control and operation of all of your DCS engines as individuals. The Premium version of the DCS Application adds functionality to operate lashups, switch tracks, accessories, and all of the other DCS features and functions.

To upgrade to either the Standard or Premium version of the DCS Application, it's necessary to do what's known as an "in-app" purchase. This is accomplished as follows:

- Navigate the DCS Application to the More... Screen. This screen can be accessed by tapping the More... button at the bottom of any screen where it appears. The More... button can be found at the bottom of the Engine Control Screen, Track Control Screen, Switch Control Screen, and Accessory Control Screen.
- Tap the Upgrade App button at the top of the More... Screen. The Upgrade Application Screen will be displayed.

How to access the Upgrade Application Screen, as well as a description of its functions, is described in the following table.

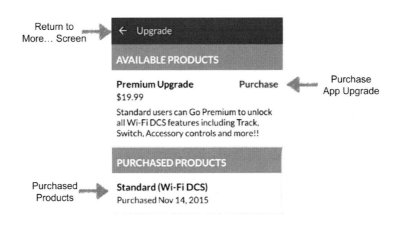

Figure 56 - Upgrade Application Screen

Upgrade Application Screen	
PURPOSE:	Upgrade DCS Application.
HOW TO GET IT:	Tap the Upgrade App button on the More… Screen.
INFORMATION DISPLAYED:	Current version of the DCS application and any available upgrades.
BUTTONS:	Tap the Return to More… Screen button to return to the More… Screen.
	Tap Purchase to purchase an upgrade to the indicated version of the DCS Application.

The Upgrade Screen displays which products are available as upgrades from the purchased product. If the purchased product is the free version of the DCS Application, then both the Standard and Premium versions will be shown as available for purchase. If the purchased product is the Standard version, only the Premium version will be shown as available. If the purchased product is the Premium version, there will not be any products available for purchase.

To upgrade from the purchased product, tap on Purchase to the right of the desired upgrade product. You will be led through the purchase process and your Apple iTunes or Google Play account will be charged. After the purchase, your copy of the DCS Application will be upgraded to the version just purchased and the Upgrade Screen will reflect the updated version.

Note that in order to upgrade additional copies of the DCS Application on other smart devices, it's necessary to go though the in-app purchase process with each of the smart devices where you desire to upgrade the DCS Application. However, there is not any additional charge to do so. You are only charged once for each version of the DCS application to which you upgrade.

Further, if you upgrade first to the Standard version and subsequently upgrade to the Premium version, when you upgrade to the Premium version you are only charged the difference between the price of the Standard and premium versions of the application.

Lastly, if you change your mind after completing the in-app purchase process, it is not possible to "downgrade" the version of the DCS Application in order to receive a refund of the price of the upgrade.

2. DCS Application Settings Screen

The DCS Application's App Settings Screen allows you to reset the settings of the DCS Application itself, obtain information regarding the DCS Application, and contact support for both the DCS Application and other MTH products.

How to access the App Settings Screen, as well as a description of its functions, is described in the following table.

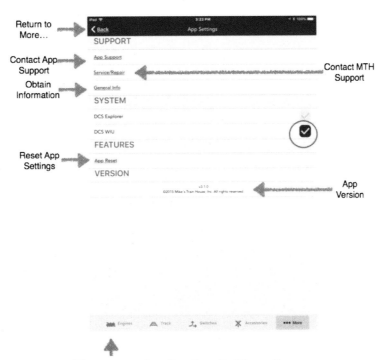

Figure 57 - Application Settings Screen

Application Settings Screen			
PURPOSE:	View or Change the DCS Application's Settings.
HOW TO GET IT:	Tap the App Settings button on the More… Screen.
INFORMATION DISPLAYED:	MTH Contact Information, DCS Application Reset, and the DCS Application's firmware version.
BUTTONS:	Tap the Return to More… button to return to the More… Screen.
	Tap the Contact App Support to send information to MTH Application Support.
	Tap the Contact MTH Service button to send information to MTH Service.
	Tap the Obtain Information button to obtain information from MTH.
	Tap the Reset App Settings button to reset the DCS Application to its original settings.
	System indicates if the DCS Application is connected to a DCS Explorer or a WIU.
	App Version indicates the version of the DCS Application.

To Contact MTH DCS Application Support with questions or issues regarding the DCS Application, tap on the Contact App Support button on the DCS Application's App Settings Screen. Complete the form to provide feedback to MTH regarding the DCS Application.

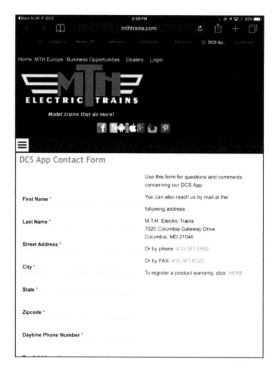

Figure 58 - DCS Application Contact Form

To Contact MTH Service with questions or issues regarding the operation of any MTH products, tap on the Contact MTH Service button. Complete the form to provide feedback to MTH regarding the DCS Application.

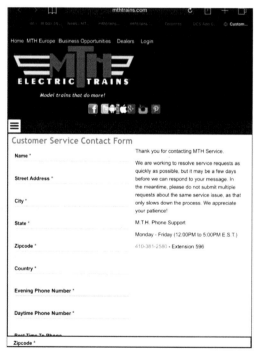

Figure 59 - Contact MTH Service Form

To obtain general information about MTH products or services, tap on General Info.

To reset all of the DCS Applications Settings to their original, factory defaults, tap on App Reset.

Main Contact Form

Your Name *

Please enter your name

Figure 60 - General Information Form

The software version of this copy of the DCS Application is indicated at the bottom of the Application Settings Screen.

3. MTH Website Access

The remainder of the functions of the More... Screen allows the DCS Application to connect to several MTH webs sites. However, in order to do so, the MTH WIU must be in Home network mode and the smart device must be connected to the Internet. How to accomplish this is described earlier in this book in Part VI - DCS WiFi Interface Unit, 2. Setup and Configuration for Using the DCS Application, Connecting to the WiFi Interface Unit in Home WiFi Network Mode.

Further, in order to access one of these websites, the DCS Application will transfer control to the smart device's default Web browser, which will then make the actual connection to the requested MTH website.

Each website that may be accessed is discussed below.

MTH News Website

To access the MTH News website, tap on News on the DCS Application's More… Screen. On the News website will be current MTH news articles.

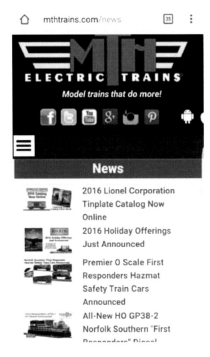

Figure 61 - MTH News

MTH Search Website

To access the MTH Search website, tap on Search on the DCS Application's More… Screen. On the Search website will be a text box where you can enter search criteria, such as an MTH product number or item description.

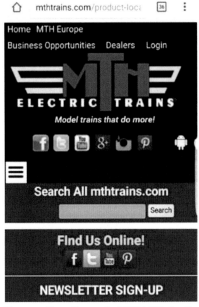

Figure 62 - Search MTH Website

MTH Online Catalogs Website

To access the MTH Online Catalogs website, tap on Catalog on the DCS Application's More... Screen. On the Catalog website, tap on an MTH product line to view its available catalogs.

Figure 63 - Online Catalogs Website

MTH Online Videos Website

To access the MTH Online Videos website, tap on Videos on the DCS Application's More... Screen. On the Videos website, tap on an MTH video to view it.

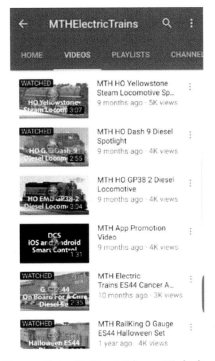

Figure 64 - Online Videos Website

MTH Online Store Website

To access the MTH Online Store website, tap on Shop MTH on the DCS Application's More… Screen. On the Store website, view and purchase MTH products.

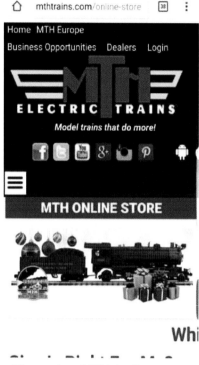

Figure 65 - MTH Online Store

MTH Newsletter Signup Form

To access the MTH Newsletter Signup Form, tap on MTH Newsletter Signup on the DCS Application's More… Screen. Complete the form and submit it to subscribe to the MTH newsletters of your choice.

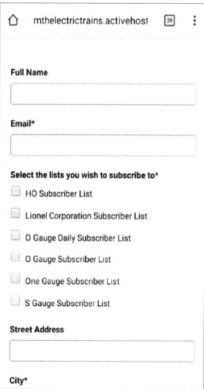

Figure 66 - MTH Newsletter Signup Form

MTH DCS User Manuals

To access MTH DCS product user manuals, tap on User Manuals on the DCS Application's More… Screen. The User Manuals Screen will be displayed.

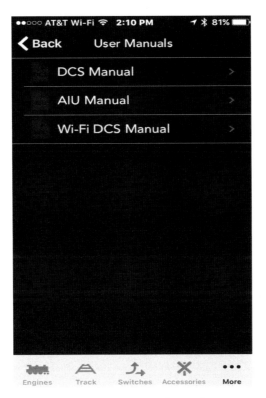

Figure 67 - User Manuals

From this screen, the following DCS manuals may be accessed via the smart device's web browser:

- Tap DCS Manual to access the latest version of the DCS Operator's Manual.
- Tap AIU Manual to access the latest version of the DCS Operator's Manual.
- Tap Wi-Fi DCS Manual to access the latest version of the full WiFi DCS User's Guide.

Part XII - DCS Upgrading and Remote Backup/Restore

1. DCS is a Software-Defined System

DCS is a software-defined system. That means that the DCS Remote, TIU and WIU, and all DCS engines contain computers that require software to operate. This software contains all the instructions that are executed each time that a command is issued by the DCS Remote. Unlike other command control systems that can only be upgraded by either replacing their actual components with newer components or using memory modules that must be acquired from the manufacturer of the command control system, the DCS system can be upgraded simply by replacing the software in the DCS Remote, TIU, WIU or DCS engines with newer software downloaded from MTH's website. Upgrading the software in the DCS Remote and TIU, and DCS engines requires a personal computer with the Microsoft Windows operating system. Upgrading the firmware in the WIU can be done on almost any personal computer that has a web browser. The only additional one-time expense is for a few inexpensive cables to connect the PC to the DCS devices being updated. The AIU is not a computer and does not contain software so it does not ever need to be upgraded.

DCS upgrades are in the form of software releases that are available as free downloads from MTH's website. These software releases include new DCS features and functions, and corrections to problems discovered in previous releases. The ability to provide software releases for DCS ensures that even the earliest versions of the DCS Remote and TIU can stay current with new DCS versions that include new features and functions.

Each DCS engine has a sound file that is tailored to the operating characteristics and sound effects for that particular engine. In addition, each PS3 engine also has a chain file that allows modification of additional engine operating characteristics that could not be modified in PS2 engines. The latest versions of these files are also available for download from MTH's website at no charge. The ability to provide sound files for PS2 engines, and both sound and chain files for PS3 engines, allows older models of newer engines to be upgraded with newer sound files. This allows corrections to errors in original sound files for these engines, as well as inclusion of new or different sound effects or features.

and TIU software upgrades, and engine sound file upgrades are accomplished by using the DCS Loader Program running on a personal computer with the Microsoft Windows operating system. DCS WIU upgrades may be done on almost any personal computer type using a web browser.

In addition, the DCS operator can save copies of the contents of the DCS Remote to a personal computer, and restore these copies to the same or different DCS Remote, from the personal computer. The saved data includes everything in the DCS Remote that was loaded into it by the operator. It does not include the DCS software itself. The contents of the DCS Remote that are saved on the personal computer may be later reloaded into the same DCS Remote if necessary after the DCS Remote has either been reset, clearing out all of the operators information, or if information must be restored for some other reason. The same information can also be loaded into another DCS Remote or the DCS Application running on a smart device to make an exact copy of the data in the original DCS Remote.

2. DCS Loader Program

The DCS Loader Program runs on a personal computer under the Microsoft Windows operating system. It is used to transfer new software releases of DCS into the DCS Remote and TIU, and new versions of DCS engine sound and chain files into DCS engines. The Loader Program comes in two versions.

The Consumer version allows upgrading the software in the DCS Remote and the TIU, uploading sound files from DCS engines to a personal computer, and downloading sound and chain files from a computer to a DCS engine. It also allows backing up and restoring the contents of the DCS Remote. The Dealer Loader Program does all the functions of the Consumer Loader Program. However, it also includes functions to initialize a DCS engines electronics with a serial number, and to read and write other information.

The remainder of this section is in regards to the Consumer version of the program. The latest version of the Consumer DCS Loader Program, as well as instructions for its use, are always available as free downloads on MTH's Protosound 2 website at www.protosound2.com.

3. Personal Computer Requirements

Generally, the requirement for running the DCS Consumer Loader Program is any personal computer that runs under the Microsoft Windows operating system, version 95 or later. Personal computers that operate under an earlier version of the Microsoft Windows operating system, the Apple Macintosh operating system, UNIX, Linux, or any other operating system cannot run the DCS Loader Program directly.

While it may be possible to run the DCS Loader Program on a non-Intel personal computer using some form of Microsoft Windows emulation, it is not recommended. However, the author has had great success running the DCS Loader Program on an Intel Macintosh computer using either Apple's Boot Camp or a Parallels virtual computer running Windows. For tips regarding using an Intel Macintosh to perform DCS upgrades on TIUs and DCS Remotes, refer to section 5. Upgrading DCS Component Software, Upgrading the Software in the DCS Remote and TIU, Using a Windows Environment on a Mac, later in this section.

A serial port or USB port is required to communicate with the TIU during all operations. If a Rev. L TIU is used, either a serial port or a USB port may be used. If any earlier TIU is used and if the computer does not have a serial port, a USB port with a suitable adapter may be used instead.

4. Required Cables and Connectors

As previously discussed, the DCS Consumer Loader Program has several functions:

- Upgrading software in the TIU
- Upgrading software in the DCS Remote
- Uploading sound files from DCS engines
- Downloading sound and chain files to DCS engines
- Backing up and restoring the contents of the DCS Remote.

Based upon the personal computer being used and the function being performed, different cables may be required.

One cable that is always required is a 9-conductor serial cable or, for the Rev. L TIU only, a USB cable that has a Type B USB connector on one end and a connector that fits the PC's USB port on the other end. These cables connect the personal computer and the TIU, and one of them is required to perform any of the DCS Loader Program functions. The serial cable is known by various names, including RS232 cable,

RS232C cable, keyboard extension cable or modem cable (but not a null modem cable), and is generally available from computer and office supply stores. The cable should be long enough to reach from the personal computer to the TIU. One end of the serial cable must have a 9-pin male connector to plug into the TIU's serial port and the other end must have a connector that connects with the connector on the serial COM port of the personal computer. If the personal computer lacks a serial COM port but has a USB port, there are two approaches to connecting a non-Rev. L TIU to the personal computer.

MTH recommends two methods for connecting a personal computer without a serial COM port to the TIU. One method recommended by MTH is, if the personal computer has an available slot for a PC card, to install a PC serial port card in that slot. MTH has reported success using the SIIG, Inc. model JJ-PCM02 card. This card should be available from computer supply stores.

The other method recommended by MTH is for computers that lack a serial COM port and do not have an available slot for a PC card, but do have an available PCMCIA port. This would include most laptop and notebook computers. In this case, the E-Link RoHS PCMCIA card or the SIIG, Inc. Single-Serial PC card should be used. These cards should be available from computer supply stores.

If the personal computer does not have an available slot for a PC card or a PCMCIA card slot, then a USB to Serial Adapter may be used. The author has obtained excellent results using an Insignia USB to RS-232 Serial adapter NS-PU99501 purchased for $20. This cable comes with Windows software drivers that should be installed before using the cable for the first time.

A 4-conductor telephone handset cable is required to upgrade the DCS Remote software or to perform backup or restore of the user-entered contents of the DCS Remote. This is the cable that connects a telephone handset to a telephone base and has smaller connectors than the cable that connects the telephone base to the wall. This cable should be available from Radio Shack, computer supply stores, or office supply stores, and need only be long enough to connect the DCS Remote to the Remote Input port on the TIU.

A 1/8" to 1/8" stereo patch cable is required to upgrade TIU software. The cable must be a stereo cable, not a monaural cable, and is available from MTH (item #50-1009 6' Mini-to-Mini Cable), Radio Shack, or audio/video stores. This cable need only be one foot in length. Inserting the cable prior to powering-up the TIU is what puts the TIU into program mode. When a TIU is powered-up with the cable in place, the red LED doesn't blink, rather, it just comes on steady as soon as power is applied.

Upgrading the firmware in the WIU requires the same USB cable that would be used to connect a Rev. L TIU's USB port to a PC.

5. Upgrading DCS Component Software

As previously discussed, there are DCS software upgrade files for both the TIU and the DCS Remote. Although there are separate upgrade files for each component they are downloaded as one file. The latest versions of the upgrade files are always available as a free download on MTH's Protosound 2 website at www.protosound2.com. New upgrade files for the DCS Remote and TIU are both published at the same time.

If a Rev. L TIU is connected to the PC using a USB cable, the TIU will obtain power for itself via the PC's USB port. It will not be necessary to provide power for the TIU itself from any other source.

DCS NEWS

- --------------------Revised DCS Wiring Schemes - May 1, 2002
- DCS Track Signal Quality Improvements - May 1, 2002
- PS1 Engine Transformer Issues - June 12, 2002
- AIU Revised Operating Track Section Wiring(PDF Format) - July 1, 2002
- DCS Patent (PDF format) - Dec. 6, 2002
- DCS Speed Control Patent (PDF Format) - Dec 1, 2003
- DCS Syncronization Patent (PDF Format) - Dec 3, 2003
- AIU To LGB Switch Wiring Diagram (PDF Format) - Jan 22 2004
- AIU Tortise Switch Wiring(PDF Format) - Feb 25, 2004
- DCS Tips & Techniques Articles - June 6, 2007
- DCS Loader Support For Windows Vista - June 27, 2007
- DCS Loader Tutorial Article - December 26, 2007
- DCS 4.0 Manual Addendum - March 13, 2008
- New DCS Loader Released - September 3, 2008
- Digital DCS O Gauge Companion 2nd Edition E-Book Released - December 1, 2010
- DCS Rev "L" TIU News & Notes - December 20, 2010
- New DCS Software Release Notes - December 23, 2010
- DCS Rev L TIU Update - March 15, 2011
- Determing Your PC's Version of .NET Before Installing The DCS Consumer Loader (Version 2.30) - August 19, 2011
- Windows USB Drivers For DCS Loader Program - March 24, 2015
- DCS Loader Program Installation/Operating Instructions - March 26, 2013
- New Version 5.0 DCS Software and DCS Consumer Loader Program Available For Download - November 5, 2015

DCS Software Updates:

Date	File Name	Description (Click for Description)	Release Date
1/12/2011	V1.40	DCS Commander	Download NOW!
11/05/2015	V5.00	DCS Version 5.00	Download NOW!
11/05/2015	V5.00	DCS Consumer Loader Program	Download NOW!
	Production Ps2 or Ps3 Locomotive Sound Files	Search for locomotives on the MTH Electric Trains website to download their Production PS2 sound file	Production Sound Sets
	PS2 Upgrade kit sound files	Find Sound Files for PS2 upgrade kit installations	Upgrade Kit Sound Sets

See DCS in action at a DCS demonstration presented by a local train club:

DCS Show Near You

Figure 68 - MTH Protosound 2 Website

Downloading DCS Remote and TU Software Upgrade Files

Download the DCS Loader Program

Before upgrading DCS components, it's always a good idea to first download the latest version of the DCS Loader Program. The procedure for downloading this file is as follows:

- On a personal computer, use a web browser to connect to MTH's Protosound 2 website, www.protosound2.com
- On the web page, locate the DCS Loader Program. The version posted will always be the latest one available for general use. MTH does not post pre-release or beta copies of software on their websites. Click on the Download NOW! link to the right to download the DCS Loader Program to the personal computer.
- Complete the required fields and follow the on-screen prompts.
- When prompted, click on the download link and choose the location in the personal computer to save the file. Make sure that the file is downloaded someplace on the personal computer where it can be easily later found, such as on the Desktop.

The DCS Loader Program only needs to be downloaded once, not each time it is desired to upgrade DCS components or DCS engine software, unless a newer version of the DCS Loader Program becomes available. Always use the latest version of the DCS Loader Program that is available on MTH's Protosound 2 website.

Download the Latest Version of the DCS Software

Download the latest version of the DCS software as follows:

- On a personal computer, use a web browser to connect to MTH's Protosound 2 website, www.protosound2.com
- On the web page, locate the DCS software. The version posted will always be the latest one available for general use. MTH does not post pre-release or beta copies of software on their websites.
- Click on the Download NOW! link to the right to download the DCS software to the computer
- Complete the required fields and follow the on screen prompts.
- When prompted, click on the download link and choose the location in the personal computer to save the file. Make sure that the file is downloaded someplace on the personal computer where it can be easily later found, such as on the Desktop.

The DCS software only needs to downloaded once, not each time it is desired to upgrade a DCS component, unless a newer version of the DCS software becomes available.

Installing the Downloaded Files

Before the upgrade files may be used to upgrade the software in the TIU and DCS Remote, they and the DCS Loader Program must be installed.

Installing the DCS Loader Program

Before installing a newer version of the DCS Loader Program, any older versions of the program should first be deleted. Follow the instructions to remove an application program as provided with your version of Microsoft Windows.

To begin the installation of the DCS Loader Program, double-click on the DCS Loader Program icon and proceed as follows:

- To continue, it is necessary to agree with the disclaimer. Click on "Agree", and then click "Next" at the bottom of the screen
- Read the instructions for installing the DCS Loader Program, then click on "Next"

- Leave the displayed Destination Location" as its default to place a folder on the personal computer's C:\drive, unless there is another place you would rather install the program. In that case, click on Browse to navigate to the preferred install location. Click Next.
- Once the DCS Loader Program is installed, click on Finish. An MTH DCS Consumer Loader icon will appear on the Desktop. This is a Microsoft Windows shortcut to the actual DCS Loader Program.
- To run the DCS Loader Program, simply double-click on this icon.

Preparing the DCS Remote and TIU Upgrade Software

To begin the installation of the DCS software upgrade, locate the file where it was saved on the personal computer and double-click on its icon. Then proceed as follows:

- Click on "OK" to allow the Windows self-extractor program to unzip the file
- When the next dialog box appears click Unzip. The file will be saved in a folder on the personal computer's hard drive named My MTH files. If you wish to save it somewhere else, click Browse and navigate to the preferred location
- The DCS software upgrade will be expanded and made ready to be installed. The DCS Remote and TIU software upgrades are now ready for uploading to the DCS Remote and TIU.

Upgrading the Software in the DCS Remote and TIU

Performing DCS Upgrades Using a Macintosh Computer

As previously mentioned, it's possible to perform DCS software upgrades from the TIU and DCS Remote using a modern (Intel-based) Macintosh computer in one of two ways. Both methods require a licensed copy of Microsoft Windows to be installed on the Macintosh computer.

The first method is to establish a Boot Camp environment using the Boot Camp Assistant program included as part of the Mac OS. This program may be found in the Utilities Folder within the Applications folder on the Macintoshes boot drive. Follow the program's prompts to establish a separate hard drive partition with a copy of Microsoft Windows installed.

The advantage of this method is that the resulting partition will look and operate exactly like a Windows PC. The only disadvantage is that it will be necessary to reboot the Macintosh into this partition any time it is desired to update DCS software.

The second method utilizes a Macintosh program, such as Parallels or VMware Fusion. These programs run as native Macintosh applications and run Windows as a virtual machine (VM) under their control. The instructions for installing the VM software and Windows on a Macintosh are included with each company's product.

The advantage to the VM approach is that the Windows environment is always available on the Macintosh and there's no need to reboot the computer in order for it to be accessed. The disadvantage to this approach is that there is additional expense required to purchase the Parallels or VMware Fusion software. Details regarding each product are available on the product's respective web sites:

- Parallels: http://www.parallels.com
- VMware Fusion: http://www.vmware.com

Based on the author's experiences with regularly using a Parallels virtual machine to upgrade DCS components, it's worth noting one item that, if not understood, can create problems that prevent DCS components from being recognized by Windows. That item is that the Macintosh will typically default USB port assignments to the native Macintosh environment, thereby making them unavailable to the Windows environment. When this occurs, the DCS Loader Program will report that it cannot find a TIU because there aren't any communication ports available.

Fortunately, there is a simple solution to this problem. The following discussion involves using the Parallels virtual machine, however, the solution for VMware Fusions should be similar.

What's required is that when the Windows virtual machine is launched, the USB port to which the USB to USB cable (Rev. L TIU or newer only), or Serial to USB cable (older TIUs), is connected, must be assigned to the Windows virtual machine. After the Windows VM environment has been created and Windows has been launched, before attempting to upgrade DCS software, perform the following steps (these steps are for Parallels. The steps for VMware Fusion should be similar):

- Launch the virtual machine application, Parallels or VMware Fusion.
- Launch the Windows virtual machine.
- Launch the Loader Program (latest version).
- Connect a TIU to the Macintosh.
- At the top of the Windows virtual machine's screen, click on the Devices drop-down menu, External Devices, Configure as shown in the first figure below.
- The Devices panel will be displayed as shown in the second figure below.
- Click the box for Connect it to the active virtual machine.
- Click the red button at the top-left of the box to close it.

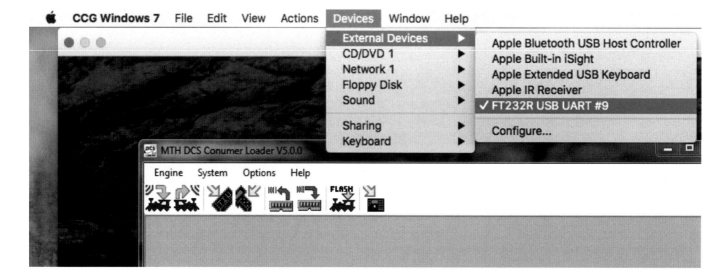

Figure 69 - Parallels Devices Menu

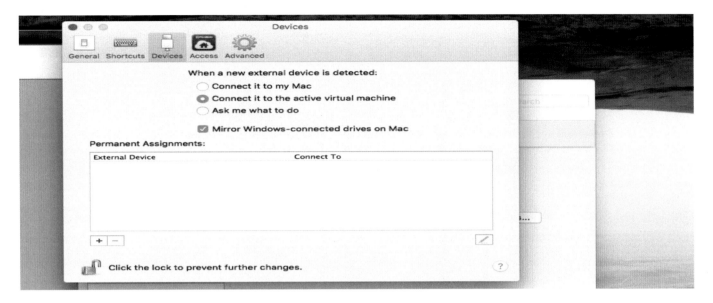

Figure 70 - Parallels Devices Dialog Box

The USB port will now be connected to the virtual machine. Once the USB port has been connected to the virtual machine, the software upgrade process proceeds exactly as it would on any regular Windows personal computer.

Installing the DCS Remote and TIU Upgrade Software

Before performing any upgrades using the Loader Program, it's a good idea to tell the Loader Program exactly where to find the TIU. This is accomplished by clicking on the Options Menu at the top of the

Figure 71 - DCS Consumer Loader Program

Loader Program's window, and selecting Serial Port and then Auto Search for TIU to have the Loader Program locate the TIU.

If it becomes necessary to cancel an upgrade to the TIU or DCS Remote, or a transfer of a DCS engine's sound or chain file, click on the Cancel button. To exit the program, click on the X in the top right corner of the Loader Program's window.

If the DCS software in the TIU or DCS Remote is being upgraded from any version of DCS 2.x to any version of DCS 3.x or newer, or to any other version that requires that the component being upgraded be reset prior to upgrading, perform a Factory Reset of the TIU (refer to section Part IX - Advanced Features and Functions,9. System Settings, TIU Settings Screen earlier in this book) or a reset of the DCS Remote. This will erase everything in the affected DCS component and reset its DCS ID# to 1. Be sure to later change the TIU's DCS ID# back to whatever it was before the reset. If the version of DCS currently in the DCS component lacks a menu entry for reset, skip this step.

Power for the TIU During Software Upgrades, and Remote Backup and Restore

Although the TIU is able to obtain power for itself via a USB cable connected between the computer's USB port and the TIU's USB port, this power is sufficient only to upgrade software in the DCS Remote and the TIU. Backup and restore of DCS Remote contents, as well as uploading and downloading of sound files, requires that the TIU receive power from either the TIU's Aux. Power port or Fixed Channel #1 input.

Upgrading the TIU

Sometimes, TIU placement makes it inconvenient to remove a TIU from the layout to upgrade the TIU's DCS software, particularly if the TIUs are placed under the layout, as are mine. To get around this inconvenience, you can connect extension cables to each TIU's serial, ProtoCast and ProtoDispatch ports to bring them out from under the table. I also have a long serial ribbon cable that goes from the PC in the train room work area, around the layout to where the TIUs are located.

When it's DCS upgrade time, I connect the serial cable from the train room to the serial port jumper cable connected to the TIU. I also jumper together the extension cables connected to the ProtoCast and ProtoDispatch ports. Then I can upgrade the TIUs in place, since a little known fact is that it's not necessary to unhook anything other than the serial, USB, ProtoCast, and ProtoDispatch ports when upgrading a TIU's DCS software.

To begin upgrading the software in the TIU, first close all other programs running on the personal computer. This includes virus protection software, PDA software, telecommunications programs, and any other programs that use the serial COM port. Next, click on the TIU icon (3rd from left) at the top of the Consumer Program Loader window and follow the on-screen prompts exactly as shown in the Figure below, with one exception.

If upgrading the software in a Rev. L (or newer) TIU that has a USB port, and if that USB port is being used to provide power the TIU, be sure to connect the 1/8" to 1/8" stereo patch cable between the TIU's ProtoCast and ProtoDispatch ports before connecting the USB cable to the TIU,

Then, click the "START" button at the bottom left of the window.

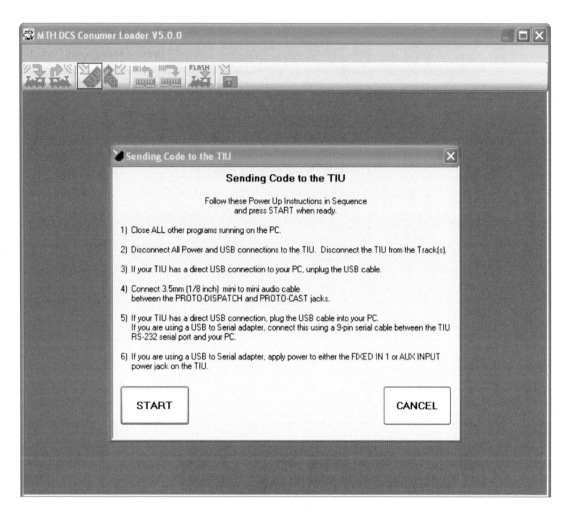

Figure 72 - Upgrade TIU Code

Next, navigate to where the DCS upgrade software was saved when it was downloaded and unzipped. If the default location was used the software should be in a folder named My MTH files. Select the TIU upgrade file listed and click on OK.

The software upgrade for the TIU should take less than 2 minutes. Upon completion of the software upgrade, remove the 1/8" stereo jumper cable, turn off the TIU's power and then turn it back on again.

If the TIU software was upgraded from version 2.x to version 3.x or newer, or to any other version that required that the TIU be reset, perform a Factory Reset of the TIU (refer to section Part IX - Advanced Features and Functions, 9. System Settings, TIU Settings Screen earlier in this book). This will erase everything in the TIU and reset its DCS ID# to 1. Then, change the TIU's DCS ID# back to whatever it was before the reset (refer to Part IX - Advanced Features and Functions, 9. System Settings, TIU Settings Screen earlier in this book).

To begin upgrading the software in the DCS Remote, first close all other programs running on the personal computer. This includes virus protection software, PDA software, telecommunications programs, and any other programs that use the serial COM port. Next, click on the DCS Remote icon (4th from left) at the top of the Consumer Program Loader window and follow the on screen prompts exactly as shown in the Figure above. Then, click the START button at the bottom left of the window.

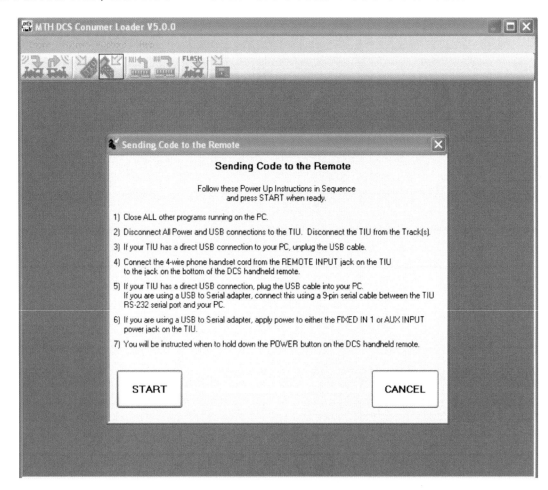

Figure 73 - Upgrade DCS Remote Code

Next, navigate to where the DCS upgrade software was saved when it was downloaded and unzipped. If the default location was used the software should be in a folder named My MTH files. Select the DCS Remote upgrade file listed and click on OK.

While upgrading the software in the DCS Remote and when prompted by the Loader Program to do so, hold down the power button on the DCS Remote until the upgrade process is complete. Ensure that the DCS Remote's LCD screen remains blank and that the DCS Remote does not power on during the process. Note that it is possible that the on-screen prompts may indicate that the power button should be pressed and released more than once. Be sure to follow all of the prompts exactly as instructed.

If the DCS Remote does power on, cancel the upgrade process and inspect the handset cable to ensure that it has 4 conductors, and inspect the jacks on the TIU and the DCS Remote to ensure that no pins are touching or bent. Re-initiate the upgrade process from the beginning.

The software upgrade for the DCS Remote should take approximately 5 minutes. Upon completion of the software upgrade, remove the telephone handset cable from the base of the DCS Remote before turning on the DCS Remote's power. Cycle the TIU's power by turning it off and then back on again.

If the DCS Remote software was upgraded from version 2.x to version 3.x or newer, or to any other version that required that the DCS Remote be reset, perform a Remote Reset of the DCS Remote. This will erase everything in the DCS Remote and reset its DCS ID# to 0. Change the DCS Remote's DCS ID# back to whatever it was before the reset.

6. Changing DCS Engine Sound and Chain Files

Every DCS engine has a set of operating characteristics and sounds that make it different from other DCS engines. These operating characteristics and sounds are contained in the DCS engine's Sound and Chain Files.

These files contains all of the engine's sound effects, including bell, whistle or horn, freight yard, passenger station or transit announcement sounds, cab chatter, idle sounds, train wreck sounds, and other accent sounds. In addition to sound effects, these files contains the following:

- All of the DCS engine's soft keys for manual control of sounds, lighting and other engine features and functions.
- The DCS engine's name.
- Speed control parameters, including gear ratios, wheel size and other parameters that are used to control speed in scale miles per hour (SMPH).

Sound Files may be copied out of DCS engines using the DCS Loader Program into a personal computer. This process is called uploading. Sound and Chain Files may also be copied from a personal computer into DCS engines using the DCS Loader Program. This process is called downloading. Additionally, these files for most DCS engines may be found on MTH's website, on the web page devoted to the particular DCS engine. These files, when present on the website, may be downloaded from the website to a personal computer, then further downloaded to the DCS engine.

There are three versions of Sound Files. Older PS2 engines have PS2 boards that required a 5 volt DC input for the board to operate, while newer, current production PS2 engines have PS2 boards that require a 3 volt DC input. Sound Files also come in 5 volt and 3 volt versions for both versions of PS2 engines. A 5 volt PS2 Sound File cannot be downloaded into a PS2 engine that has 3 volt PS2 board and a 3 volt PS2 Sound File cannot be downloaded into a PS2 engine that has a 5 volt PS2 board.

PS3 engines have Sound Files that are different, and larger than those of PS2 engines. Further, PS3 engines have Chain Files while PS2 engines do not.

The rules for which sound files may be loaded into which DCS engines are as follows:

- A PS2 5 volt Sound File may only be loaded into a 5 volt PS2 engine.
- A PS2 3 volt Sound File may be loaded into a 3 volt PS2 engine or a PS3 engine.
- A PS3 Sound File may only be loaded into a PS3 engine.

Additionally, there are various types of 5 volt PS2 boards. One is the standard 5 volt board that can handle most diesel, electric and steam 5 volt sound files. Another type of 5 volt board can handle all of the above 5 volt sound files, as well as the expanded 5 volt sound files for subways, trolleys and articulated steamers. If one attempts to load a 5 volt sound file for a subway, trolley or articulated steamer into a standard, non-subway/trolley/articulated 5 volt board, it will load. However, the transit station announcements or articulated chuffing sounds will not play, although all other sounds will work.

Uploading a DCS Sound File From a DCS Engine

When planning to download a different Sound File into a DCS engine, it's always a good idea to first save the Sound File already present in the engine by uploading it to the personal computer.

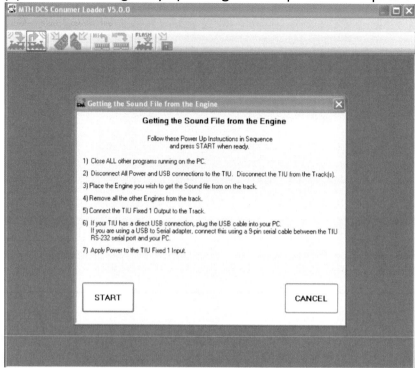

Figure 74 - Uploading a DCS Sound File From a DCS Engine

Downloading a new Sound File to the DCS engine will overwrite the existing Sound File already in the DCS engine. If it is determined that the new Sound File is less desirable than the one that was previously in the DCS engine, it would be good to be able to restore the original Sound File.

To upload the DCS engine's existing Sound File to the personal computer, proceed as follows.

If the DCS Loader Program is not already running, double-click on the DCS Loader Program icon on the Desktop to run it now. Next, click on the Engine to PC icon (2nd from left) at the top of the Consumer Loader Program window and follow the on screen prompts exactly as shown in the Figure above. Then, click the START button at the bottom left of the window.

Next, navigate to where the DCS engine's Sound File is to be saved. A good place would be the My MTH files folder. Input a name for the Sound File and click on Save.

Uploading the Sound File from the DCS engine to the personal computer should take approximately 18-36 minutes. Upon completion of the upload process, turn off power to the DCS engine, turn the TIU off and then back on again, provide power to the DCS engine, and press Start Up on the DCS Application to operate the DCS engine.

Updating the Sound or Chain Files in DCS Engines

PS2 and PS3 engines differ in terms of where information regarding engine features are stored, as well as what information may be updated by the DCS operator. Further, the format and handling of PS2 and PS3 download files is different. Therefore, updating information for PS2 and PS3 engines will be presented separately, with PS2 presented first and then followed by PS3.

Downloading a PS2 Sound File From MTH's Website

When MTH makes improvements to PS2 engine sound files, the updated sound file is posted on the MTH web page for that particular PS2 engine. If a sound file is posted on the engine's web page, it will appear as a clickable icon on the page.

In order to download a sound file into a PS2 engine, the sound file must be the same type, 3 volt or 5 volt, as the engine's PS2 board. Further, if the sound file is for a 3 volt PS2 engine, it may be a 1 Megabyte file or a 2 Megabyte file. If it's a 2 Megabyte file, it can not be loaded into a 3 volt PS2 engine that has a 1 Megabyte memory chip. Additionally, it is possible to download a 3 volt PS2 sound file of either size into a PS3 engine, and the PS3 engine continues to use its own speed control parameters.

To download the sound file, simply click on the icon. The file will be downloaded to the personal computer. Note where the download is placed on the personal computer so that it may be easily located for downloading to the PS2 engine.

Downloading a PS2 Sound File to a PS2 Engine

As previously discussed, before downloading a sound file to a PS2 engine, it is strongly recommended to upload the existing sound file from the PS2 engine to the personal computer. If the current engine sound file is not first uploaded, it will be overwritten during the downloading process and lost. To download a PS2 sound file to a PS2 engine, proceed as follows.

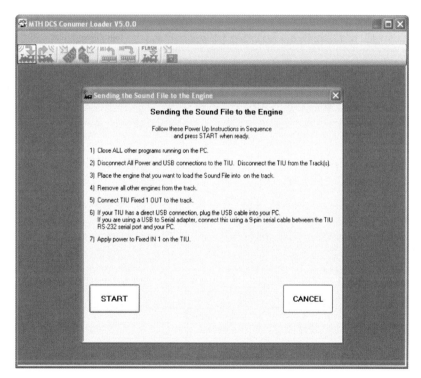

Figure 75 - Downloading a PS2 Sound File to a PS2 Engine

If the DCS Loader Program is not already running, double-click on the DCS Loader Program icon on the Desktop to run it now. Next, click on the Engine From PC icon (1st from left) at the top of the Consumer Program Loader window and follow the on screen prompts exactly as shown in the Figure above. Then, click the START button at the bottom left of the window.

Next, navigate to where the PS2 engine's new sound file was saved. A good place to save PS2 engine sound files would be the My MTH files folder. Select the sound file and click on Open.

Downloading the sound file from the personal computer to the PS2 engine should take approximately 10-20 minutes. Upon completion of the download process, turn off power to the PS2 engine, and turn the TIU off and then back on again. Next, delete the PS2 engine from all DCS Applications and re-add it to each. This is necessary because the DCS Loader Program does a Factory Reset of the PS2 engine as the last step in the sound file download process. Then press Start Up on the DCS Application to operate the PS2 engine.

Downloading a PS3 Engine's Sound File and Chain File From MTH's Website

When MTH makes improvements to PS3 engine sound files or chain files, the updated files are posted on the MTH web page for that particular PS3 engine. If a sound file or chain file is posted on the web page, it will appear as a single clickable icon on the page. If the icon is greyed-out, neither a sound file nor a chain file is available for this PS3 engine. Note that it is possible to download a 3 volt PS2 sound file into a PS3 engine and the PS3 engine will continue to use its own speed control parameters. This is because PS3 speed control parameters are not stored in the PS3 engine's sound file, rather, they are instead stored in the PS3 engine's chain file.

To download a PS3 engine's sound file or chain file to the personal computer, simply click on the icon. A single file will be downloaded to the personal computer. Note where the file is placed on the personal computer so that it may be easily located for further downloading to the PS3 engine.

Clicking on the sound icon on the PS3 engine's web page will download a single file that contains both the engine's sound file and chain file. Typically, this file will have a .zip suffix and is known as an archive. Double-clicking on this archive file will cause two additional files to be unarchived and created. One will have a suffix of .mth. This is the PS3 engine's sound file. The other file will be another archive with a chain.zip suffix. This is the PS3 engine's chain file and should not be further unarchived.

At times, rather than downloading a .zip archive file, a .mth file will be downloaded instead. This indicates that a chain file for this PS3 engine is unavailable and only the engine's sound file was downloaded. Nothing further should be done to this .mth file prior to actually loading it into a PS3 engine.

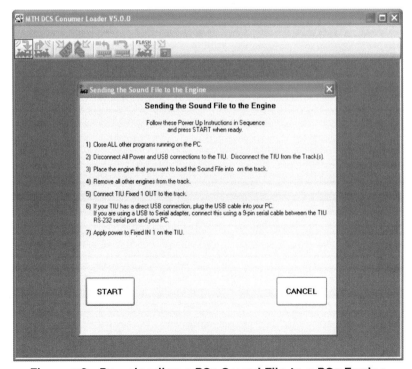

Figure 76 - Downloading a PS3 Sound File to a PS3 Engine

Downloading a PS3 Sound File to a PS3 Engine

Before downloading a sound file into a PS3 engine, it is strongly recommended to upload the existing sound file from the PS3 engine to the personal computer. If the current engine sound file is not first uploaded, it will be overwritten during the downloading process and lost. To upload a PS3 sound file from a PS3 engine, refer to Part XII - DCS Upgrading and Remote Backup/Restore, 6. Changing DCS Engine Sound and Chain Files, Uploading a DCS Sound File From a DCS Engine, earlier in his book. To download a PS2 sound file to a PS2 engine, proceed as follows.

If the DCS Loader Program is not already running, double-click on the DCS Loader Program icon on the Desktop to run it now. Next, click on the Engine From PC icon (1st from left) at the top of the Consumer Program Loader window and follow the on screen prompts exactly as shown in the Figure above. Then, click the START button at the bottom left of the window.

Next, navigate to where the PS3 engine's new sound file was saved. A good place to save PS3 engine sound files would be the My MTH files folder. Select the sound file and click on Open.

Downloading the sound file from the personal computer to the PS2 engine should take approximately 10-20 minutes. Upon completion of the download process, turn off power to the PS3 engine, and turn the TIU off and then back on again. Next, delete the PS3 engine from all DCS Applications and re-add it to each. This is necessary because the DCS Loader Program does a Factory Reset of the PS3 engine as the last step in the sound file download process. Then press Start Up on the DCS Application to operate the PS3 engine.

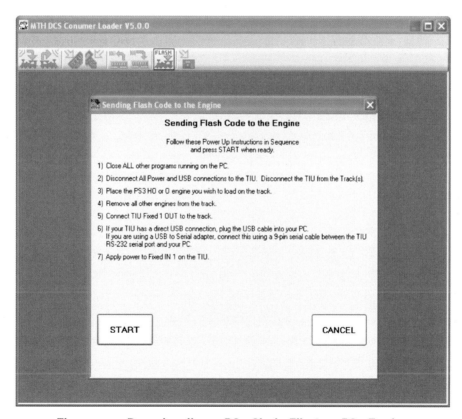

Figure 77 - Downloading a PS3 Chain File to a PS3 Engine

Downloading a PS3 Chain File to a PS3 Engine

If the DCS Loader Program is not already running, double-click on the DCS Loader Program icon on the Desktop to run it now. Next, click on the Flash icon (last from left) at the top of the Consumer Program Loader window and follow the on screen prompts exactly as shown in the Figure above. Then, click the

START button at the bottom left of the window. Next, navigate to where the PS3 engine's new Chain File was saved. A good place to save PS3 engine Chain Files would be the My MTH files folder. Select the Chain File and click on Open.

Downloading the chain file from the personal computer to the PS3 engine should take approximately 20 minutes. Upon completion of the download process, turn off power to the PS3 engine, and turn the TIU off and then back on again. Next, delete the PS3 engine from all DCS Applications and re-add it to each. This is necessary because the DCS Loader Program does a Factory Reset of the PS3 engine as the last step in the chain file download process. Then press Start Up on the DCS Application to operate the PS3 engine.

Unusual Sounds After Chain File Update

Newer PS3 diesel replacement boards may come from the factory with special software installed. If the software is present on the PS3 replacement board and this is the first time that the board's Chain File is being loaded, this software may cause an unusual series of beeps to sound, as follows:

- When the Chain File is finished loading, the engine will power up as usual.
- At this time, the engine may be added to the DCS Application and will operate correctly.
- However, the next time the engine is powered off and then back on, a series of short "beeps" followed by longer beeps, will sound for approx. 10-12 seconds, followed by a few seconds of silence.
- The engine will then automatically start up in conventional mode with normal sounds, and may then be selected from the DCS Application and operated normally.

If this situation occurs, it will only occur once for any replacement PS3 board.

7. Common Problems During DCS Remote and TIU, and DCS Engine Software Upgrades

Most problems encountered while upgrading DCS components or DCS engine files are due to issues with either the personal computer or Microsoft Windows. Additionally, problems may be encountered that are due to poor connections between the personal computer, the TIU and the DCS Remote, or to weak DCS signal strength.

Personal Computer Problems

One common problem occurs on personal computers that lack a serial COM port. As previously discussed (refer to art X - DCS Component Upgrading and Remote Backup/Restore, 4. Required Cables and Connectors earlier in this book), there are several possible remedies to this problem.

If the personal computer lacks an available serial COM port and either lacks a USB port as well, or a USB port cannot be made to work as previously discussed, the personal computer cannot be used to upgrade DCS components or DCS engines.

If the personal computer does not have a version of Microsoft Windows indicated above, the DCS Loader Program may not be used. The solution is to obtain and install a version of the Microsoft Windows operating system indicated above that the personal computer is capable of running.

Microsoft Windows Operating System Problems

If the version of the Microsoft Windows operating system installed on the personal computer is too old, the DCS loader Program will not run. If the personal computer can run Microsoft Windows 95 or later, the solution is to obtain and install a version of the Microsoft Windows operating system indicated above that the personal computer is capable of running. A very common problem is that there are other applications running on the personal computer that are controlling the serial COM port. Many programs on personal computers often contend for use of the COM ports, whether they are serial or USB ports. If one of these programs, such as virus protection software, telecommunications programs, or any other program that accesses the COM ports, does not or cannot relinquish control of the port to the DCS Loader Program, the DCS Loader Program will be unable to communicate with the TIU. When this occurs, the DCS Loader Program will continuously cycle through messages showing attempts to find a TIU on all COM ports until the Cancel button is clicked. Be sure to close all other programs running on the personal computer before running the DCS Loader Program.

DCS Loader Program Problems

During the TIU update, DCS Remote update or Sound File transfer processes, the Loader Program may encounter one or more error conditions and display an explanation of the error. At this time, the operator will have the option to Retry or Cancel by clicking on one of the two displayed buttons. It is suggested to make several attempts at retrying the failed operation before cancelling the process and starting it over from the beginning. If the TIU software upgrade fails as soon as it starts, check to be sure that the 1/8" stereo jumper cable is plugged into the ProtoCast and ProtoDispatch ports, and that it is, indeed, a stereo rather than a monaural cable.

If the power button on the DCS Remote is not held down during the entire software upgrade process, the upgrade will fail. Also, if the DCS Remote is turned on during the software upgrade process, the upgrade will fail. One solution to holding down the power button on the DCS Remote during the entire upgrade process is to obtain an inexpensive (approximately $1) spring-loaded plastic clamp from a home improvement or hardware store. They are ideal for holding down the DCS Remote's power button during the software upgrade process.

Sometimes when downloading Sound Files to a DCS engine it may be difficult to navigate to the desired Sound File. When uploading a Sound File from a DCS engine to a personal computer, or when downloading a Sound File from MTH's website, be sure to note where the Sound File is saved on the personal computer.

Uploading and downloading files from DCS engines are the most challenging processes within DCS. These processes require very strong DCS signal strength for the entire time that the process is in progress which, in the case of Sound File transfers, can be as long as 36 minutes. If the DCS signal strength isn't strong enough during the entire process, the process will fail. If the process fails for any reason, conduct a DCS signal strength test on the track where the engine was when the failed process took place. If DCS signal strength isn't 9 or 10, connect a short section of track directly to a TIU channel and test the DCS signal on that track. If DCS Signal strength is a 9 or 10, use that track to upload and download DCS engine Sound Files.

8. DCS Remote Backup and Restore

The DCS Remote backup and restore processes allow the DCS operator to make one or more copies, or clones, from a master DCS Remote by backing up one DCS Remote and restoring it into one or more additional DCS Remotes or DCS Applications. There are, however, two caveats regarding the backup and restore processes:

- The backup and restore processes require that DCS Release 4.0 or newer is installed on any DCS Remote that is to be backed up or restored. Previous releases of the DCS Remote's software do not include the functionality necessary to support these processes.
- The backup and restore process backs up only the data in the DCS Remote, not its software.

Backing Up the Contents of the DCS Remote

To begin the backup process, first close all other programs running on the personal computer. This includes virus protection software, PDA software, telecommunications programs, and any other programs that use the serial COM port. Then proceed as follows below.

When the process is completed a message is displayed on the personal computer. Cycle power to the TIU and the DCS Remote by turning them off and on again.

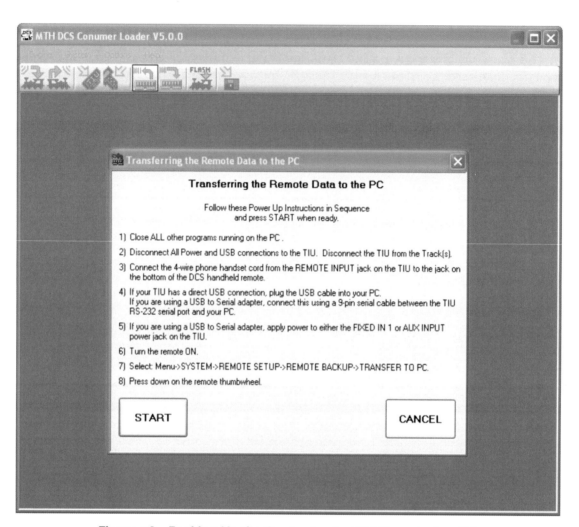

Figure 78 - Backing Up the Contents of a DCS Remote to a PC

If the DCS Loader Program is not already running, double-click on the DCS Loader Program icon on the Desktop to run it now. Next, click on the DCS Remote to PC icon (5th from left) at the top of the Consumer Program Loader window and follow the on screen prompts exactly as shown in the Figure below. Then, click the START button at the bottom left of the window.

Next, navigate to where the copy of the contents of the DCS Remote is to be saved. A good place to save copies of the contents of the DCS Remote's would be the My MTH files folder. Name the file and click on Save.

When the process is completed a message is displayed on the personal computer. Cycle power to the TIU and the DCS Remote by turning them off and on again.

Restoring the Contents of the DCS Remote

To begin the restore process, first close all other programs running on the personal computer. This includes virus protection software, PDA software, telecommunications programs, and any other programs that use the serial COM port. Then proceed as follows.

If the DCS Loader Program is not already running, double-click on the DCS Loader Program icon on the Desktop to run it now. Next, click on the PC to DCS Remote icon (6th from left) at the top of the Consumer Loader Program window and follow the on-screen prompts exactly as shown in the Figure below. Then, click the START button at the bottom left of the window.

Next, navigate to where the copy of the contents of the DCS Remote were previously saved. A good place to save copies of the contents of the DCS Remote would be the My MTH files folder. Select the file and click on Open.

When the process is completed a message is displayed on the personal computer. Cycle power to the TIU and the DCS Remote by turning them off and on again.

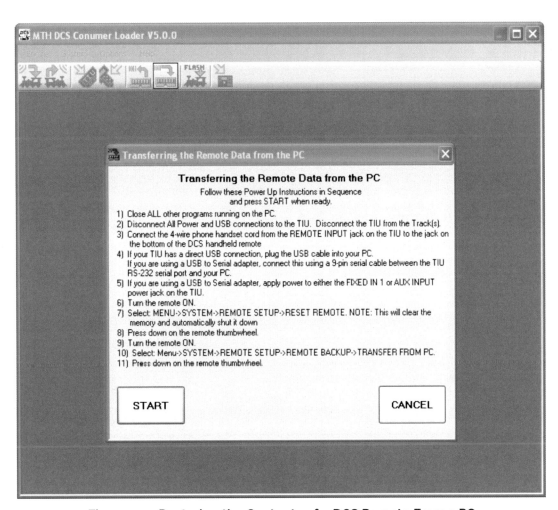

Figure 79 - Restoring the Contents of a DCS Remote From a PC

9. Updating the Firmware in the WIU

The latest version of the WIU update file is always available as a free download on MTH's Protosound 2 website.

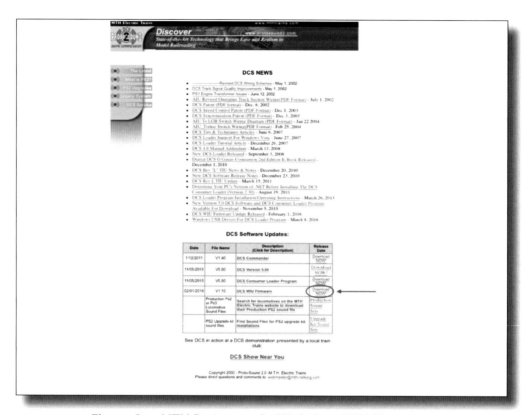

Figure 80 - MTH Protosound 2 Website - WIU Firmware

Downloading a WIU Firmware Update File

The following procedure applies to personal computers, Android tablets and smartphones, and iOS tablets, smartphones and iPods that are using iOS 11.x or later. The procedure for downloading a WIU firmware update file is as follows:

- Use a web browser to connect to MTH's Protosound 2 website, www.protosound2.com
- On the web page, locate the link for DCS WIU Firmware. The version posted will always be the latest one available for general use. MTH does not post pre-release or beta copies of software on their websites. Click on the Download NOW! link to the right to download the DCS WIU firmware update file to the personal computer, tablet or smartphone.
- Complete the required fields and follow the on-screen prompts.
- When prompted, click on the download link and choose a location in the personal computer, tablet or smartphone to save the file. Make sure that the file is downloaded someplace that is actually on the computer, tablet or smartphone so that it can be easily found later. If you place the file in cloud storage, such as by saving it to Dropbox, when later downloading to the WIU it will be necessary to be connected to the Internet, rather than directly to the WIU. It's suggested to download to the Desktop for personal computers and to Files/Textedit for iOS devices. For Android devices, simply choose DOWNLOAD to download the file to the Documents folder on the device.

Installing the Downloaded File

The following procedure applies to personal computers, Android tablets and smartphones, and iOS tablets, smartphones and iPods that are using iOS 11.x or later. In order to update the software in the WIU, it's necessary to use the LuCI program that is built-into the WIU.

LuCI is a web interface for the WIU that provides a custom web page used exclusively to access advanced setup functions and features in the WIU. Whenever MTH releases an update to the WIU firmware, it's necessary to use LuCI to install the update file, as follows:

- Set the WiFi Interface Unit's MTH/Home selector switch to MTH.
- Attach the included antenna, and plug the WiFi Interface Unit's power supply into an AC outlet and the power supply's cable into the PWR port on the WiFi Interface Unit. Wait a minute or two for the WiFi Interface Unit's PWR, Wi-Fi and TIU LEDs to light.
- As discussed above, using any computer, or an appropriate smart phone or tablet, with WiFi capability, navigate to see the available wireless networks and connect to the network named MTH_DCS-XXXX, where XXXX may be any 4 characters. This is the same network name that's printed on the bottom of the WIU.
- When prompted, enter the network password (network key) mthdcswifi in all lower case. The network key is also printed on the bottom of the WIU.
- Open a web browser and enter the following IP address in the url address line at the top of the browser's window: 192.168.143.1 This will display LuCI, the MTH DCS web interface.
- Enter the password mthdcs in all lower case and press the keyboard ENTER or RETURN key. Do not change the username from ROOT.
- Click on the SYSTEM tab at the top of the screen. Then, select BACK-UP/FLASH FIRMWARE from the drop-down menu.
- Scroll down the page to see FLASH NEW FIRMWARE IMAGE near the bottom of the page.
- Do not un-check the KEEP SETTINGS box. Doing so will cause LuCI to lose its network settings.
- Select CHOOSE FILE and navigate to where you previously saved the WIU's firmware upgrade file. For Android devices, choose the action "Documents", then select the WIU firmware upgrade file. When the file has been located, click OPEN.
- Wait until the file window closes (this could take as long as 15 seconds). Verify that the filename displayed next to the CHOOSE FILE button is the same as the one that was selected.
- Click on FLASH IMAGE...
- When the FLASH FIRMWARE - VERIFY page is displayed, click on the blue PROCEED button.
- The SYSTEM FLASHING SCREEN is displayed.
- Wait a full 3 minutes or until LuCI's login screen is once again displayed.

Verifying the Firmware Update

To confirm that a WIU firmware update was successful, after the update is completed log into LuCi, just as you did to perform the update. Then, scroll down the page about halfway to see the updated firmware version.

When you have verified that the update was successful, remove power from the WIU and reconnect it to your layout.

Part XIII - Troubleshooting Problems

DCS is a very powerful and very sophisticated operating system for your trains. For the most part, it is intuitive, and the information displayed by the DCS Application make DCS very easy to use. However, from time to time the DCS operator may encounter a problem when using DCS and, since every layout is different from others, the problem may be related to any number of factors.

This section attempts to present a way to address problems that the DCS operator may encounter by providing methodology aimed at solving problems; an explanation of error messages; and some specific types of problem solutions.

When attempting to troubleshoot an issue with the layout, it's best to first verify that the problem isn't due to an oversight on the part of the operator or some other basic item that's causing DCS to work differently than expected. In this regard, there are a few basic items that should be reviewed prior to beginning to troubleshoot a perceived DCS problem:

- Ensure that the DCS App is the latest version, currently 3.0.2.
- Ensure that the WIU firmware is the latest version, currently 1.1.
- Ensure that the DCS software is the latest version, currently DCS 6.1, and is installed in all of the layout's TIUs. Further, if any DCS Remotes are used with the layout, they should also be using the same level of DCS software.
- Be certain to wait long enough for all of the layout's WIUs to stabilize after being powered on. This can take several minutes, depending upon how you're connecting to the WIUs:

    The most lengthy wait is when the WIU is wirelessly connecting to your home router. This is subject to the reliability of your router, its distance from the WIU, whether you use a static IP or Bonjour connection, and other factors.

    Typically, a slightly shorter wait time is experienced if connecting wirelessly in MTH mode.

    The shortest wait time is experienced if connecting via wired Ethernet.
- Ensure that the connecting cable between the TIU and the WIU is the correct cable and is known to work properly.
- If a Rev. L TIU is connected to the WIU using a USB cable, ensure that there is not a serial cable connected to the TIU's serial port that isn't connected to another device.

1. General Approach

There are two basic ways to approach solving a DCS problem, the intuitive approach and the methodical approach.

Intuitive Approach

The intuitive approach makes the assumption that the problem has occurred due to some recent change in the train room. There are three questions that, if answered, will most likely yield the source of the problem. Using the intuitive approach can often quickly provide the answer to a troublesome problem. Even when the intuitive approach fails, it provides a thorough review and understanding of the problem.

The first question is, "What changed prior to the problem occurring?" If things were working fine and now a problem has developed, there's a good chance that something that changed in the layout has caused the problem. It's a good idea to think back over any recent wiring or track changes that were made, or other changes that might have caused a problem.

The second question to ask is, "What did I do prior to the problem occurring?" It's sometimes the case that something the operator did, perhaps unknowingly, caused the problem to occur. If the problem is an intermittent short circuit, perhaps adding a new passenger car with misaligned trucks is causing a problem when traversing a switch track. It may also be the case that, while modifying the track work a screw was dropped between the rails where the motion of a train is causing the screw to short circuit between control rails on an operating track. Again, a careful review of what transpired between the time that all was well and the current problem situation may yield the solution to the problem.

The third question to ask is, "Has it happened before and what was the solution?" There are some things that, due to the layout construction habits of the individual operator, may cause the same problem to occur from time to time. If possible, keeping a log of problem symptoms and resolutions can save a lot of time if a problem reoccurs.

Methodical Approach

The methodical approach makes no assumptions regarding what may be causing the problem. Using this approach, everything is suspect until proven otherwise. A process of elimination is utilized in a step-by-step procedure that works to reduce the number of possible causes of the problem until the culprit is found.

The first step is to rule out DCS component failures. This is most easily accomplished by temporarily replacing the DCS components with known, good ones. However, not everyone has the luxury of having an extra smartphone or tablet, DCS Remote, TIU, WIU, or AIU available. In this case, it may be possible to bring the questionable components to another layout at a friend's home or a hobby shop to test them there. It's also easy to simply swap TIU channels and see if the problem moves to the other channel or stays on the original channel. Either one tells the operator something new about the problem and can narrow down the issues.

The next step is to rule out problems with individual DCS engines by attempting to duplicate the problem using a different engine. If the problem persists, it's unlikely that a DCS engine is the source of the problem.

The third step is to eliminate wiring problems. This can be time consuming, however, if a logical process is used this will nearly always isolate the problem. The procedure is to work outwards, starting at the transformer. Check to ensure that the transformer is putting out the expected voltage. An inexpensive multimeter can be a big help in troubleshooting wiring problems. If one is not available, an 18 volt bulb in a holder connected to a pair of wires can be used to indicate if voltage is present. Measure the voltage at the TIU's channel's input terminals and then at the output terminals. Look for a blown fuse inside the TIU or in an external fuse holder.

Continue checking the voltage at the entry to the terminal block and at the exit point where the terminal block is connected to the tracks. Then check to see if voltage, and the DCS signal, is leaking between blocks that should have their center rails isolated.

Substitute transformers, DCS components, TIU channels, and wires wherever possible. At some point the cause of the problem will be discovered.

2. Error Messages

While the DCS Application display provides quite a bit of information regarding the operation of a DCS layout, it also displays several DCS error messages are not always specific to a particular problem. Although some error messages provide meaningful information, others may be quite ambiguous. Additionally, some error messages may have more than one possible reason. The following discussion provides some understanding of what DCS error messages that are displayed by the DCS Application are really attempting to report.

No TIUs Found

This error message is rather specific and appears whenever the DCS Application cannot find any TIUs that are connected to WIUs. This message may be displayed for a variety of reasons:

- The WIUs aren't powered up.
- The TIUs aren't powered up.
- The WIUs aren't connected to their TIUs.
- The smart device and the WIUs aren't on the same home network.
- The smart device isn't connected to any network.
- The smart device is connected to the home network and the WIUs are in MTH mode.
- Some other network related issue.

No Engine to Add

This error message is rather specific and only appears during a failed attempt to add an engine. When this error message appears, all powered tracks connected to all TIU channels were searched for a DCS engine to add and DCS could not find a DCS engine that was not already in the DCS Application.

Request Failed

This error message is displayed whenever the DCS Application sends a command to an engine that is the active engine on the Engine Control Screen and that engine cannot be found by the DCS Application.

This can occur when an engine that was currently running has lost power due to a derailment or for some other reason. To resolve the problem, remedy the issue that caused the error and tap Refresh in the error's dialog box.

Switch Command Failed

This error message is displayed whenever the DCS Application attempts to send a command to activate a switch track and the TIU or AIU to which the switch is connected cannot be found by the DCS Application.

This can occur when a TIU loses power for itself, such as when the TIU is being powered via Fixed Channel #1 input power and something, perhaps a derailment, has caused that power to be turned off. To resolve the problem, remedy the issue that caused the error and tap OK in the error's dialog box.

Accessory Command Failed

This error message is displayed whenever the DCS Application attempts to send a command to activate an accessory and the TIU or AIU to which the accessory is connected cannot be found by the DCS Application.

This can occur when a TIU loses power for itself, such as when the TIU is being powered via Fixed Channel #1 input power and something, perhaps a derailment, has caused that power to be turned off. To resolve the problem, remedy the issue that caused the error and tap OK in the error's dialog box.

Import Failed

This error message is displayed if the DCS Application attempts to import a DCS Remote backup file that was created from a DCS Remote whose contents were corrupted or that contained Z4K Tracks. In either case the file is not imported. The Z4K Tracks issue is expected to be corrected in a future release of the DCS Application so that any Z4K Tracks will be ignored if present in an import file.

At present, the workaround to avoid the error message is to import an uncorrupted DCS Remote backup file or remove the Z4K Tracks from the DCS Remote before creating the backup file.

3. Verifying Operation of DCS Components

One of the first things to do when applying the methodical approach previously discussed to problem solving is to rule out the DCS components by verifying that they are operating correctly. The following section describes the method to use in order to verify each component is operating correctly.

Diagnosing DCS Application Problems

If it appears that a DCS Application is misbehaving, the easiest way to determine if it is, or is not, having problems is to attempt the same command using another DCS Application on a different smart device, or using a DCS Remote. If the second DCS Application operating on a different smart device, or the DCS Remote, is able to perform the command correctly when the original DCS Application cannot, the problem may be in the configuration of the original DCS Application or the smart device itself.

On the other hand, if the second DCS Application, or the remote, also fails the attempted command, the issue is most likely not a problem with the DCS Application or the smart device. Rather, the problem lies elsewhere.

Diagnosing TIU Problems

The easiest way to verify that a TIU is operating properly is to swap it for a known, good TIU and see if the problem is resolved. If it is, the TIU was causing the problem. However, if another TIU is not readily available, there is a procedure that can determine if the existing TIU is or is not causing a problem.

Even if another TIU is available to substitute for the existing TIU and as a result the cause of the problem is determined to be the existing TIU, the following procedure can further isolate the problem to one of the existing TIU's channels. To verify operation of the TIU, proceed as follows:

- First, ensure that the TIU is powered up via either the Aux. Power port or Fixed Channel #1 IN and that the red LED blinks as many times as the TIU ID#. If the red LED does not come on, check the power source for the TIU, any external fuse in line with the TIU's power source, and the internal fuses of the TIU. If the LED blinks the wrong number of times, refer to Part IX - Advanced Features and Functions, 9. System Settings, TIU Settings Screen to correct the TIU ID#.
- Second, check power output from the TIU channel. If it's a Variable Channel, ensure that the Track Control Screen is used to dial up the voltage on the Variable Track.
- Third, use the DCS Application to ensure that the DCS signal is present on all TIU channels as described previously in Part IX - Advanced Features and Functions, 9. System Settings, TIU Settings Screen. Test to see if the problem persists. If it does not, the problem is solved. If it does, continue below.
- Fourth, swap the connections from the transformer to the TIU input terminals, and from the output terminals of the TIU channel, to a different TIU channel. Test to see if the problem remains on the original TIU channel or moves to the other TIU channel. If the problem does not move, the original TIU channel is most likely the cause of the problem. If the problem moves to the other TIU channel, the TIU is not the cause of the problem. Swap the connections back to the original TIU channel and continue below. While doing this test, make sure that the TIU still has power for itself by either connecting a power source to the TIU's Aux. Power port or to the inputs for Fixed Channel #1.
- Fifth, check the DCS signal strength from the TIU channel using a DCS engine. If the DCS signal strength is 7 or higher, the TIU is most likely operating properly. If the DCS signal strength is less than 7, repeat the test after first connecting the TIU channel's output terminals to a short piece of track. If the DCS signal strength remains low, the TIU channel may be defective.
- If all of the above does not rule out the TIU as the cause of the problem, perform a Feature Reset of the TIU as described in section Part IX - Advanced Features and Functions, 9. System Settings, TIU Settings Screen. If the problem persists, the TIU may well be the cause of the problem.

There is one TIU problem that the author has seen on one occasion that has also been reported by a few other DCS operators. In this instance, the TIU's DCS address becomes outside of the normal range, i.e., between 1 and 5. When this occurs, DCS Remotes will become unable to access the affected TIU. It is unknown, however, if the DCS Application is also unable to access the affected TIU since the author has not experienced this problem while using the DCS Application, and has not received reports from any other DCS Application users in this regard.

MTH has provided a resolution to the problem by modifying the DCS Loader Program 5.0 and later so that if this situation is encountered while attempting to load a TIU with DCS software, at the conclusion of the update the TIU is automatically reset to be TIU #1. Therefore, the problem solution is to reload the TIU's DCS software and then reset the TIU's DCS ID# to whatever address it had prior to the problem occurring.

Diagnosing AIU Problems

The easiest way to verify that an AIU is operating properly is to swap it for a known, good AIU and see if the problem is resolved. If it is, the AIU was causing the problem. However, if another AIU is not readily available, there is a procedure that can determine if the existing AIU is or is not causing a problem. First, check the AIU to TIU connecting cable that accompanied the AIU. It could be defective and cause the AIU to not operate at all. If the AIU cable, when laid flat, does not have the locking clips on both ends facing in the same direction, contact MTH for a replacement cable.

To verify operation of the AIU, proceed as follows:

- First, verify that all connections between the AIU and the TIU are correct. The connection should be between the TIU's AIU Input port and the AIU's TIU Input port. If the cable is mistakenly plugged into the AIU's AIU Connection port instead, serious damage to the AIU can result.
- If there's a problem throwing a switch track from the DCS Application, first ensure that the switch track is correctly programmed in the DCS Application. Then, check the continuity of the SW port on the AIU to which the switch track is connected by using a multimeter set to read resistance (ohms) as follows:
  1. Touch the meter's two test probes to terminals 1 and IN on the AIU's SW port while using the DCS Application to activate the associated switch track to switch straight. The meter should deflect momentarily.
  2. Touch the meter's two test probes to terminals 2 and IN on the AIU's SW port while using the DCS Application to activate the associated switch track to switch curved. The meter should deflect momentarily.
  3. If the above tests are successful and the switch track still will not throw, the problem is most likely in the wiring between the switch track and the AIU. If the tests are not successful, there most likely is a problem with the AIU itself.
- If there's a problem operating an accessory from the DCS Application, first ensure that the accessory is correctly programmed in the DCS Application. Then, check the continuity of the ACC port on the AIU to which the accessory is connected by using a multimeter set to read resistance (ohms) as follows:
  1. Touch the meter's two test probes to terminals 2 and IN on the AIU's ACC port. The meter should deflect as long as the probes are in place.
  2. Touch the meter's two test probes to terminals 1 and IN on the AIU's ACC port while using the DCS Application to activate the associated accessory. The meter should deflect while the accessory is turned on from the DCS Application.

If the above tests are successful and the accessory still will not operate, the problem is most likely in the wiring between the accessory and the AIU. If the tests are not successful, there most likely is a problem with the AIU itself.

4. General Problems

This section discusses some of the more general types of problems that may be encountered during construction or operation of a DCS layout. These general problems are further broken down into two groups:

- Low DCS signal strength problems
- Power problems.

Low DCS Signal Strength

There are two indications that DCS signal strength is too low to effectively operate the layout. Symptoms of low DCS signal strength include error messages that appear on the DCS Application when a command is issued. Another indication is a DCS signal strength reading of lower than 7 or error messages when conducting a DCS signal strength test using a DCS engine. When these symptoms occur, there are several possible reasons.

When encountering a low DCS signal strength, it's a good idea to attempt to rule out the TIU itself as the cause of the problem by connecting a different TIU channel to the affected tracks and see if the situation improves. If it does not, disconnect all wires to and from the TIU except for TIU and transformer power. Then, connect a short section of track to the TIU channel that exhibits low signal strength and connect the transformer to the TIU channel's inputs. Place a DCS engine on this short track section, power it up and conduct a DCS signal test. If DCS signal strength is not 9 or 10, it's possible that the TIU channel has a problem. Repeat the test for the remaining TIU channels. If the TIU channels test good, review all the other causes of low DCS signal strength discussed below.

Most often, the main reason for low DCS signal strength is not following the best practices for DCS when designing and constructing a layout. Common failures to follow the guidelines include:

- The wire size used for the DCS/power connections between the transformer and TIU, TIU and terminal blocks, and terminal blocks and the tracks, is too small. 16 gauge, stranded wire should be used. For wire runs longer than 40 feet, 14 gauge stranded wire is recommended.
- There are too many linear feet of track connected to one TIU channel. A single TIU channel can provide adequate DCS signal strength for up to 750 feet of track per channel, subject to other considerations.
- There are too many splits in the DCS signal. Ideally, the output from one TIU channel should be spilt into no more than 12 to 15 separate blocks. Further, the connection from the output of a TIU channel should not be split, rather, it should connect only to only one terminal block.
- A track block is too long. The maximum block size is calculated based on the number of track sections in the block. Whenever possible, a block should contain no more than 11 track sections.
- There are too many DCS feeds to a block. Each block should have one and only one DCS feed to prevent a DCS engine from receiving the same DCS command from more than one source. Ideally, the DCS feed should be situated in the center of the block where the center is the middle track section.
- Track blocks are not center-rail isolated from adjacent track blocks. Again, isolating track blocks helps prevent a DCS engine from receiving the same DCS command from more than one source.

Low DCS signal strength may also occur because the tracks or engine pickup rollers are dirty. This can also occur because of the blackening that is applied to the center rail of some manufacturers track systems. Gargraves and Ross track has a protective, oily coating on its center rail that must be removed before the track is used by cleaning the center rail with track cleaning solution; there's no need to remove the blackening itself. The blackening on the top of the center rail of MTH RealTrax, however, should be removed in its entirety. Currently, RealTrax is sold with the blackening on the center rail already removed. Any other track system should have the blackening removed from the center rail if the blackening comes off on engine and rolling stock pickup rollers.

Some, but not all, TMCC engines will degrade the DCS signal of any DCS engine with which they are in close proximity. This effect varies both by individual TMCC engine and by the distance between the TMCC and DCS engines. In many cases, an RF choke inserted in the Hot wire between the pickup rollers and the TMCC engine's circuit board will correct this problem.

Some lighted cabooses, most notably those manufactured by Atlas O, may degrade the DCS signal, as may some engines or passenger cars with constant voltage (CV) lighting boards. Again, an RF choke inserted in the Hot wire between the pickup rollers and the circuit board in these cars will generally correct this problem. Although a number of different RF chokes may be effective in reducing interference from CV boards, one that has an electrical value of 22uh (micro henries) is known to work well.

Lionel TMCC Direct Lockons can also degrade the DCS signal and should not be used with DCS layouts. There are two additional ways in which TMCC or Legacy may cause a degradation of the DCS signal.

The first is if the "one wire" from either the TMCC command base or Legacy command base is connected to a Common wire that subsequently is connected to a TIU channel input. While there isn't a lot of data collected in this regard, it makes sense that nothing good can come from passing the TMCC or Legacy signal through a TIU channel's DCS signal generator.

The second is that there have been reported cases where plugging a TMCC or Legacy command base into some surge protector power strips can cause, in addition to a degraded TMCC or Legacy signal, a degraded DCS signal, as well. Although the author has had no issues with the Legacy command base (or its predecessor TMCC command base) being plugged into a surge protector power strip, not all surge protector power strips are the same, and "your mileage may vary" from that of the author. Regardless, if a degraded DCS or TMCC/Legacy signal is an issue, ensuring that the command base is plugged directly into a 3-prong, grounded AC wall socket is suggested.

As previously discussed, DCS uses a transmission method known as differential signalling to provide improved data communications through the rails between the TIU and DCS engines. Information is transmitted electrically by two complementary signals sent on two separate wires. In the case of DCS, these wires are the Hot and Common wires between the TIU and the tracks. If there isn't a clear path on the Common wires between the engine and the TIU, because of things such as insulated track sections or switch track control rails, the Common path may then include engine or car axles that bridge dead rails. If the Common path through the outside rail is not reasonably direct, error messages on the DCS Application may occur. In addition to low DCS signal strength, other symptoms are that DCS engines may not respond to commands or may respond after a delay, or the DCS Application appears to freeze for 30-60 seconds, followed by an error message.

Many times the addition of a jumper from a dead section of outside rail to one that has a direct connection to Common, can alleviate a problem such as this.

Another cause of a loss of DCS signal strength can be due to the very small gauge jumper wires used to carry voltage on the center rail between the three legs of Atlas O switch tracks. Before installing Atlas O switch tracks on a layout, it's a good idea to replace these jumpers with 16 gauge wires. If the problem of low signal strength arises across an Atlas switch track that's already installed on the layout, solder 16 gauge jumper wires under-the-table between the center rails of the legs of the Atlas O switch tracks that need them.

Conducting a DCS Track Signal Test

If DCS signal strength is low, perform a DCS signal strength test as follows:

- Select the engine you want to use to perform a DCS track signal test in the Active Engine List and start it up. Make sure that the engine is powered on at the point of the layout where a problem is suspected, and that the engine is moving at a slow rate of speed. The recommended speed for a DCS track signal test is as slow as you can stand it. The most accurate track signal readings are obtained when the engine is standing still.

- Navigate to the engine's Soft Keys Screen, scroll down to the Functions soft keys and tap Track Signal Test. Engine sounds are muted and the track signal level is displayed as a number between 1 and 10. A value of 9 or 10 indicates a strong DCS signal. A value of 6-8 indicates an acceptable DCS signal. Values of 5 or less, or error messages, indicate layout areas that are candidates for improvement. Note what the signal level is at various spots on the layout.
- To end the test, tap Close. The test is ended and engine sounds are restored.

Power Problems

Modern transformers generally have fast-acting circuit breakers while many older, postwar transformers utilized bi-metallic circuit breakers or had no circuit protection at all. The bi-metallic circuit breakers in older transformers were slow acting when they were new, and after 50 years they generally become almost completely non-functional. Even if these older circuit breakers are repaired and made like new, they still will not act quickly enough to effectively protect the modern electronics in command control engines and other electronic devices.

Whenever possible, modern transformers should be used to power command control engines and the DCS TIU. Older transformers should be used only where power is required for switch tracks and accessories and, regardless of their role on the layout, should never be used unless they are outfitted with fast-blow fuses. Fuse size should be no greater than 15 amps if power demands placed on these transformers exceeds 10 amps. If the demands are more modest, 10 amp fast blow fuses should be used instead.

Circuit breakers may be used in place of fast-blow fuses, however, the operator should ensure that the circuit breakers will trip when the amperage drawn from the transformer reaches no more than 15 amps.

Some modern transformers regulate voltage by chopping the AC power sine wave. In and of itself, this is not a bad thing. While Fixed Channels are more tolerant of transformers that vary power by chopping the sine wave, Variable Channels are not. This is because Variable Channels themselves manage power by chopping the sine wave. They react badly to transformers that do the same to the input to the Variable Channels. The MTH Z4000 does not chop the sine wave to regulate voltage, and is an excellent choice as a power source for TIU channels, either fixed or variable. The smaller MTH transformers (Z500, Z750 and Z1000) each consist of a brick, as well as a control device, the Z-Controller. Since the Z-Controller regulates power by chopping the sine wave, it is strongly suggested that, when used to power TIU channels, the Z500, Z750 and Z1000 bricks be directly connected to the input of the TIU channels without the use of the Z-Controller. MTH provides a cable, #50-1017 TIU Barrel Jack Adapter Cable, for this purpose.

All TIUs have Transient Voltage Protectors (TVSs) on each channel to protect modern electronic engines against voltage spikes. TIU models Rev. H , I and L also contain 20 amp fast-blow, blade-type fuses to protect each TIU channel. These fuses should be considered a last resort and should not be relied upon to protect the TIU or the electronics in modern engines since replacing these fuses can be very inconvenient. Replacing the fuses inside the TIU requires taking the TIU off the layout and removing its cover to access the fuses.

Additionally, if the internal fuse for TIU Fixed Channel #1 were to blow, the following would occur:

- The TIU itself would become non-operational.
- There would be no power from the outputs of Fixed Channel #1, as well as either of the Variable Channels that were set to Variable Mode. All engines operating on tracks connected to those channels, whether command or conventional, would immediately cease operation.
- Power would continue to flow through Fixed Channel #2, as well as either of the Variable Channels that were set to Fixed Mode and all engines on tracks connected to those channels would continue to operate. However, none of the DCS Application on the layout would be able to send commands to DCS or TMCC engines on those tracks, or to regulate the power of those tracks to control conventional engines.

There are some common power-related problems that may occur that are easy to diagnose and correct.

The first is when power is off to all tracks that are connected to a single TIU channel. If the TIU is also powered off (no red LED visible), proceed as follows:

- Check if the power source for Aux. Power is providing power.
- If the TIU's red LED turns on when power is applied through the Aux. Power port, but not when power is applied through Fixed Channel #1 IN, it's possible that the micro switch in the Aux. Power port is stuck, causing the TIU to believe that a power supply is plugged into the Aux. Power port when one is not. This will cause the TIU to be unable to receive power from Fixed Channel #1 IN.
- Check if the power source for Fixed Channel #1 input is providing power.
- Check if the transformer circuit breaker for Fixed Channel #1 is tripped.
- Check if a fuse or circuit breaker between the transformer and the affected TIU channel is blown or tripped.
- Check if the fuse for Fixed Channel #1 inside the TIU is blown.

If TIU power is on (red LED is visible), proceed as follows:

- Check if a fuse or circuit breaker between the transformer and the affected TIU channel is blown or tripped.
- Check if the transformer circuit breaker for the affected TIU channel is tripped.

Once the point of failure has been identified, look for the cause of the blown fuse or tripped circuit breaker, e.g., derailment or other short circuit.

If power is off to all tracks connected to all TIU channels, check that the AC plugs for all transformers and the TIU are securely plugged in.

DCS Application Problems

This section addresses several possible issues regarding the DCS Application. These issues are almost entirely related to WiFi communications problems between the DCS Application and the WIU.

If the DCS Application cannot seem to communicate with TIUs, first tap Refresh on the DCS Application's Engine Control Screen. If the DCS Application fails to find the layout's TIUs or DCS engines, proceed as follows:

- Ensure that the WIU's WiFi LED is on solid and not blinking steadily.
- Ensure that the WIU is connected to the TIU and that the WIU's TIU LED is lit.
- If the WIU is in MTH mode, ensure that the DCS Application's smart device is connected to the WiFi network being broadcast by the WIU.
- If the WIU is in Home mode, ensure that the DCS Application's smart device is connected to the same WiFi network to which the WIU is connected.

5. DCS Engine Control Problems

Control problems that may occur when operating DCS engines are grouped into the following categories:

- Battery Related Problems
- Multiple DCS Application control problems
- Foreign DCS engine problems
- Incorrect settings
- Missing the watchdog signal
- Silent DCS engines
- Can't add engines problems

- Engine's DCS ID# is outside the normal range
- Identical engine problems
- Speed control problems
- Incorrect engine settings
- Physical problems
- Engine software problems.

Each of these types of problems are discussed in the following sections.

Battery Related Problems

Arguably, the predominant cause of problems with PS2 (not PS3) engines is when the engine's rechargeable battery is too weak to carry out its assigned tasks. Older PS2 engines with the original 5 volt PS2 boards have a rechargeable 8.4 volt Nickel-Cadmium (NiCad) battery. These engines have a round, barrel-type battery charging port on the bottom of the engine or tender, or no battery charging port at all. Newer PS2 engines have a rechargeable 2.4 volt NiCad battery. These engines have a rectangular, 2-pin charging port on the bottom of the engine or tender. Some diesels may have the charging port in another place, such as behind a door or under a removable part.

8.4 Volt Battery

2.4 Volt Battery

Figure 81 - PS2 Engine Batteries

8.4 volt battery Charging Port Engine

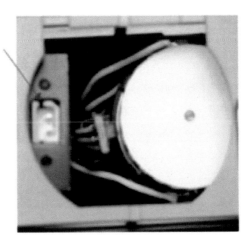

3 volt battery Charging Port Engine

Figure 82 - PS2 Engine Battery Charging Ports

Often, these batteries are referred to as 9 volt or 3 volt batteries. Regardless of the voltage of the battery, there are several things that the battery in a PS2 engine does that are very important:

- The battery allows a PS2 engine to continue making sounds even if power is momentarily interrupted when the engine crosses switch tracks or loses power momentarily for other reasons.
- The battery keeps a PS2 board operating even if power is momentarily interrupted so that the PS2 engine remains in DCS mode and continues to operate effectively.
- The battery is used to save settings in the PS2 engine's memory after power to the engine is turned off. One critical setting that is saved in this manner is the engine's DCS ID# after it is changed for any reason.
- In conventional mode, the battery is required to change a PS2 engine's direction. If the battery is too weak, a PS2 engine operating in conventional mode will not be able to get out of neutral.

The good news, however, is that unlike the battery in earlier PS1 engines from MTH, no damage will result to the PS2 engine's electronics in the event that the battery becomes discharged. For PS2 engines, all that's required to make things right is to recharge the battery.

PS3 engines have a super capacitor instead of a battery and so are not subject to weak battery issues.

It's important to note that, when a PS2 engine has its power turned off (not simply Shut Down), the battery must be strong enough to write all data to memory prior to power being turned off. If this happens successfully after an address change has been made, then the engine will retain its new address. The PS2 board has a pair of memory areas that it uses to save an engine's settings, including its DCS ID#, and it alternates between these two memory areas when it saves the engine's settings, when the engine is powered off.

However, if the battery was weak when the engine had power turned off, then there could be invalid data written into one of the memory areas on the PS2 board. If this happens, upon subsequent power up the engine would find the latest set of saved values to be unusable and would instead use the previous set of values, including the engine's previous DCS ID#. The above is true of all 5 volt and 3 volt PS2 boards. If the engine has its DCS ID number reset to its previous value, it will be necessary to delete it and re-add it to any DCS Remote to which it had been previously added.

For an explanation of how DCS assigns ID numbers to PS2 engines, refer to Appendix B: The Truth About DCS Engine ID Numbers, later in this book.

Battery Substitutes
In the past few years, several battery substitutes have come on the market that are intended to replace the batteries in all O gauge engines that require batteries. The device that replaces the 8.4 volt NiCad battery is commonly known as a BCR and the device that is a replacement for the 3 volt battery is commonly referred to as a BCR2. The BCR and BCR2 are both capacitor devices that require 30 to 60 seconds to fully charge. They then operate exactly as a battery during an operating session, and can hold their charge for several hours after power to the engine is removed.

The life of these devices is much longer than a conventional rechargeable battery, and they are considered by many operators to be the last battery ever needed for a PS2 engine. However, these devices require that the PS2 engine sit idle for 30-60 seconds after being powered on and before being operated to allow the capacitors in the devices to fully charge. Operating a PS2 engine with a BCR or BCR2 installed before it is fully charged can cause erratic engine operation. While there are many operators of PS2 engines that regularly replace the batteries in their engines with BCR-type devices when the batteries reach the end of their useful life, there are many other operators that continue to use rechargeable batteries.

Another replacement for the rechargeable NiCad battery in a PS2 engine is a Nickel Metal Hydride (NiMH) battery. These batteries will generally have a longer life than a NiCad battery (although not nearly as long as a BCR) and they don't suffer from the memory effect that can cause NiCad batteries to not accept a full charge.

However, NiMH batteries will not hold a charge as long as will NiCad batteries. MTH recommends that NiCad's be used in PS2 engines that are operated infrequently while NiMH batteries be used in PS2 engines that are operated more often.

Weak Battery Issues

A weak or completely discharged battery can cause several different problems. The most common such issue occurs when a PS2 engine is added to a DCS Application for the first time. The symptom is that the PS2 engine will add to the DCS Application, operate properly until power is turned off and then not be found by the DCS Application on subsequent power-up.

The reason this occurs starts with the fact that every PS2 engine comes from the factory with the same DCS ID# (call it 1 for now). When a PS2 engine is added to a DCS Application, DCS will attempt to keep whatever DCS ID# is present in the engine. However, if the DCS Application already contains a PS2 or TMCC engine with that DCS ID#, the DCS Application will assign the lowest available (unused) DCS ID# to the PS2 engine that's being added. Once it's been added to the DCS Application, the PS2 engine will respond to commands issued by the DCS Application for the engine number that it was assigned.

When track power to the engine is turned off, the DCS ID# is written into the engine's on-board memory using power from the engine's battery. If the battery is not sufficiently charged, the DCS ID# is not written into the engine's memory and the engine retains whatever DCS ID# it had prior to being added. The next time the engine is powered up and selected from the DCS Application's Engine List, the DCS Application looks for it using the DCS ID# that the engine was assigned when it was added to the DCS Application. Since the PS2 engine has its original DCS ID# rather than the one assigned by the DCS Application, the DCS Application will be unable to find the engine and will display an error message.

Other PS2 engine problems may also be encountered due to a weak or fully discharged battery. These include:

- Since the battery is used to save a variety of PS2 engine settings for sound effects and other engine features when track power is turned off, changed PS2 engine settings may appear to be saved and operate properly until power is turned off and back on. They will then revert to the previous settings.
- The PS2 engine may briefly lose sounds, stop and drop into conventional mode while operating under DCS if the engine encounters a momentary loss of power or short circuit and the battery is not strong enough to maintain power to the PS2 electronics during the momentary power outage.
- Engine sounds may be low or garbled. Note that while this may indicate a battery problem, this symptom may indicate other problems such as a defective engine speaker, an intermittent break in a wire, a defect in PS2 engine's sound file or a problem with the PS2 board's audio amplifier.
- If a PS2 engine momentarily loses power while conducting a Track Signal test, the battery may be strong enough that the engine does not drop into conventional mode (see above), however, it may be too weak to keep the PS2 board operating effectively. When this occurs, the DCS Application may display a low DCS signal strength reading even though DCS signal strength is high.

It's important to note that a broken, loose or intermittent connection inside the PS2 engine between the battery and the PS2 board can show the same symptoms as a discharged battery.

Checking the Battery

The DCS soft key command Battery Check (refer to Part VII - Engine Operation Using the DCS Application, 1. DCS Application Engine Operation Screens, DCS Application Engine Soft Keys Screen - DCS Engines earlier in this book) provides a readout which indicates the status of a DCS engine's battery as being "OK", "LOW" or "HI." This can mean different things based upon the nature of the battery, or battery substitute, in the DCS engine.

A PS2 engine with a battery will read "OK" when the battery is sufficiently charged and the circuit is trickle charging.

It will read "Low" when the battery is less than fully-charged and the charging circuit is charging the battery normally. A reading of "High" indicates that the battery's voltage is higher than expected, and the charging circuit is inactive and not charging at all. A "High" reading may simply be due to the normal variation of a few tenths of a volt among batteries, and typically is not indicative of a problem. However, if an engine has been in storage for several months and consistently has a "High" readout, its battery should be considered suspect.

PS3 engines with super capacitors and PS2 engines with a BCR should always read "OK" as soon as the super capacitor or BCR is fully charged. This typically takes 1-20 seconds for a PS3 engine's super **capacitor**s or 20-60 seconds for a PS2 engine with a BCR, after the engine starts receiving power. When using DCS, it is not necessary to wait for a PS3 engine's super capacitor to be fully charged before operating the engine.

The most effective battery check for a battery that's installed in a PS2 engine is to first start the engine up making sounds, in either DCS or conventional mode. Then, immediately turn off power to the tracks. If engine sounds do not continue for 6-7 seconds after power is turned off, the battery needs to be charged.

Another test of the battery is to attempt to operate the engine conventionally. If the PS2 engine remains in neutral in conventional mode and sounds cut out when the direction button on the transformer is pressed, the battery needs to be charged.

A PS2 engine's suspect battery can be confirmed by changing the engine's horn or bell sound level via the DCS Sound menu (refer to Part VII - Engine Operation Using the DCS Application, 1. DCS Application Engine Operation Screens, DCS Application Engine Soft Keys Screen - DCS Engines earlier in this book), turning track power off and then back on after 30 seconds, and noting if the lowered volume is still present. If it is, the battery or its related wiring is most likely the issue.

The battery may be charged in three different ways. If the PS2 engine has a battery charging port, the most convenient way is to use the MTH Battery Charger (item # 50-1019). This charger will charge both 8.4 volt or 2.4 volt batteries, either NiCad or NiMH. If the PS2 engine lacks a battery charging port, the second method is to place the engine on a track with voltage set at 10 to 12 volts to charge the battery. The least desirable method is to open the engine, remove the battery and place it in an external battery charger. Recharging the battery can take as long as 8 hours if the battery is fully discharged. If an 8 hour charge does not restore the battery, it should be replaced with a fresh, fully-charged NiCad or NiMH rechargeable battery.

Figure 83 - PS2 Engine Battery Charger

The DCS WIFI Companion

Multiple DCS Application Problems

Adding a DCS Engine to a Second DCS Application

Every time an engine is added to a DCS Application, the DCS Application will attempt to use the engine's existing DCS ID#. If a DCS engine is added to more than one DCS Application and the DCS engine's DCS ID# that was assigned by the first DCS Application is unavailable in the second DCS Application, the engine's DCS ID# will be changed to the lowest available number in the second DCS Application.

This will cause any DCS Applications which assigned the DCS engine a different DCS ID# to be unable to locate or control the engine. To avoid this problem, it is good practice that when adding engines to multiple DCS Applications, they are added to each DCS Application during the same session. This will ensure that all DCS Applications on the layout know each DCS engine by the same DCS ID#.

Foreign DCS Engine Problems

The DCS Application knows a DCS engine only by its DCS ID#, and each DCS Application ensures that only one engine with the same ID# may be entered into its Engine List. However, there are no guarantees that two DCS Applications will have the same DCS ID# for the same engine. It's also possible that two DCS Applications may have the same DCS ID# for two different DCS engines.

When the first of these situations arises, only the DCS Application that knows the DCS engine by the DCS ID# that is in the DCS engine's memory can control the DCS engine. In the second situation, operating a DCS engine in one DCS Application may operate another engine that has the same DCS ID# in another DCS Application, as well.

A relatively straightforward solution to prevent either of these two conditions from arising among DCS Applications that are all used on the same layout is simply by always adding an engine to all of the layout's DCS Applications when the engine is added to any DCS Application. This will ensure that all DCS Applications know all of the layout's DCS engines by their proper DCS ID# and that there is no duplication of DCS ID#s within the layout's engines. However, the problem can become very serious when DCS operators bring their engines and DCS Applications to another layout, such as a train club, for an operating session.

When train club members bring their own DCS Application to operate their engines on a club layout, there is the potential for real operating confusion. When a DCS Application starts up an engine, it does so by engine ID#. It doesn't look for a particular engine with that ID#, rather, any one with that ID# will do. If more than one engine on the tracks has the same DCS ID#, as when two club members bring their own engines and DCS Applications to a club operating session, multiple DCS engines may start up together since different DCS Applications may have different engines with the same DCS ID#. For example, if two remotes have an engine #12 in their Engine Lists, when one DCS Application attempts to start up its engine #12, there's no telling which engine, or engines, with #12 will start up.

It's worth noting that this problem is not restricted to DCS. This same problem exists with other command control systems, as well.

Fortunately, the problem may be entirely avoided if simple rules are followed. It's just a matter of not adding foreign engines to the club layout indiscriminately.

If someone wants to control a DCS engine on the layout that belongs to someone else, they should first ensure that there is an open DCS ID# with that engine's current DCS ID# in their own DCS Application. Otherwise, when the DCS engine is added to their DCS Application, its ID# will be changed, and any DCS Application in which it was previously entered will be unable to find it. If there is not an open slot with that ID#, one must be made available in their own DCS Application before attempting to add the engine.

If someone wants to operate their own personal DCS engine on the layout, they must first ensure that the engine's ID# is not already in use by a club DCS engine. If it is, a separate programming track should be used to change their engine's DCS ID# to one that's not in use. It would be a good idea to have a group of guest engine ID#s that are never used for club engines, available for this purpose.

The rules for effective operation of foreign DCS engines and DCS Applications can be summarized as follows:

- Each DCS engine that will participate in the club operating session must have a unique DCS ID#
- Once the DCS engine DCS ID#'s are made to be different from each other, each DCS Application that will control an engine during the operating session must have that engine added according to its now unique DCS ID#
- Each DCS Application should have a unique DCS ID# that is different from all other DCS Applications being used.
- A separate programming track that is powered on while all other tracks are powered off can be a big help. First, determine unique DCS ID#s for all the engines that will participate in the session. Then, each member uses their own DCS Application to change the DCS ID# of their own engine to its assigned number while it's on the programming track.
- Members should move any DCS engines they are not operating to the Inactive Engine List in their DCS Application.
- Operators should ensure that only those DCS engines that are to participate in the operating session are on the tracks.

If the club has few enough members that own DCS engines, it's a good idea to assign each of them a few DCS ID#s for their DCS engines in advance. That way, they can pre-set the DCS ID#s of their DCS engines and DCS Application prior to arriving for the operating session.

Incorrect Settings

Often, situations that may appear at first glance to be DCS engine problems are actually caused by incorrect settings for a DCS engine's features. This can be caused by a child or visitor to the layout inadvertently pressing a key while using a DCS Application to operate a DCS engine where an errant button tap may have changed one of the engine's settings. It could also happen as a result of the operator experimenting and trying something new. Regardless, it's a good idea to review the DCS engine's settings as the first step in troubleshooting the issue.

It's important to note that there are three aspects of a DCS engine that are not a consideration when troubleshooting DCS engine problems while in DCS mode of operation. The following controls on the bottom of the DCS engine are not active while running under DCS: the volume adjustment (potentiometer), the smoke on/off switch and on newer DCS engines, the smoke level adjustment (potentiometer). Changing the settings of the volume adjustment or the smoke level adjustment will have no effect on the sound volume or smoke volume when operating under DCS. Turning the smoke on/off switch to on or off will only cause the default for the engine to be that setting when operating under DCS.

Many newer DCS engines are equipped to run on either 3-rail or 2-rail track. These engines have a 2-Rail/3-Rail switch to select the mode of operation. If this switch is in the 2-rail position, a DCS engine will not operate on 3-rail track. Consult the operator's manual that accompanied the engine to determine if the engine is so equipped and, if it is, locate the switch and ensure that it is in the 3-rail position.

In addition to having a 2-Rail/3-Rail switch, PS3 (not PS2) Premier and early Rail King engines also have a DCS/DCC switch to allow the PS3 engine to operate on either DCS or DCC controlled layouts. Later Rail King PS3 engines have an internal jumper instead of a switch. If the switch is set in the DCC position or the jumper is removed, the DCS Application will be unable to detect the PS3 engine.

Next, check the following DCS Application Engine Features Screen functions:

- Tap the Smoke button if smoke is turned off to turn it back on.
- Tap the Engine Sound button if engine sounds are off to turn them back on.
- Adjust the master volume slider if sound is too high or too low.
- Tap the Headlight button if the headlight is turned off to turn it back on.
- Tap the ProtoCast button to turn ProtoCast on or off.
- Tap the Doppler button if the engine may be in Doppler mode to turn Doppler off.

Next, check the following DCS Application Engine Settings Screen functions:

- Set Clikity-Clack mode correctly. This will turn off all other engine sounds when set to Auto and engine runs at or greater than 30 SMPH (approx.) for 30 seconds.
- Set Chuff Rate correctly.
- Check if Proto Chuff is turned off. This will inhibit synchronized chuffing in steam engines.
- Check the volume settings of Bell, Horn/Whistle, Engine Sounds, and Accent Sounds.
- Set Cab Chatter correctly.
- Set Brake Sound correctly.
- Check if ProtoCast is turned on. This will inhibit all engine sounds.
- Set Smoke Volume correctly.
- Set Ditch Lights mode correctly.
- Set Max Speed correctly. Engine will not exceed this speed when operated from this DCS Application.
- Set Acceleration and Deceleration rates correctly.
- Set Labored Smoke correctly.
- Set Direction Lock Correctly.

Next, check any other of the DCS engine's settings since many DCS engines lack the ability to change other engine feature settings and therefore the engine's behavior.

Many settings act like software toggle switches. This means that tapping a setting, such as Firebox Light Glow On/Off, will first turn the setting on. Tapping it again will turn the setting off. Be sure to wait a second for the screen to respond before tapping again.

If none of the above resolve the issue with the DCS engine, it's possible that resetting the DCS engine will. There are two types of DCS engine resets available from the Engine Settings Screen, Feature Reset and Factory Reset.

Performing a Feature Reset of a DCS engine will reset all of the DCS engine's settings to their original, factory default values with two exceptions. The DCS engine ID# and the Custom Name, if any, will not be affected. A Feature Reset will generally restore sound, lighting and other settings that may have been unintentionally changed.

A Factory Reset will do everything that a Feature Reset will do. Additionally, it will also change the engine's DCS ID# back to its factory default, remove any Custom Name that was entered for the engine, and delete the DCS engine from the DCS Application. Once a DCS engine is Factory Reset, it should also be deleted from any other DCS Applications in which it resides before being added back to each DCS Application in turn.

If the DCS engine appears to not acknowledge the Feature or Factory Reset, or if the reset has no effect as regards resolving the problem, it may be because either the DCS engine's electronics are not recognizing the DCS reset commands or because the issue is due to a previously-issued conventional command, such as locking the engine into either neutral or a direction.

Regardless, if the DCS reset commands have no effect, it's possible to perform a Feature Reset using the transformer Bell and Whistle/Horn buttons. Although this is very similar to a DCS Feature Reset, the difference is not just the message, it's also the medium. The conventional reset from the transformer presents the reset command in the more basic language of bell and horn/whistle DC voltage fluctuations. The reset command from the transformer may be more easily understood by a DCS board that has temporarily lost its ability to understand DCS commands.

Missing the Watchdog Signal

As discussed earlier, DCS engines know that they are in a DCS environment when they detect the watchdog signal. The watchdog signal is only issued for a short time when the voltage at the output of a TIU channel changes from zero to any other value. In order for the DCS engine to detect the watchdog signal, the track voltage must be high enough that the engine's DCS electronics have enough power to function. Although this voltage requirement varies a bit from DCS engine to DCS engine, 10 volts is generally high enough for the DCS electronics to sense the watchdog signal.

If the voltage is increased too slowly, as when the voltage of a TIU Track is increased using the DCS Application's slider, the watchdog signal may expire before the operating voltage necessary for the DCS engine to see the signal is reached. Further, if power to a siding is turned on, as with a toggle switch, sometime after power to the tracks has been turned on, any DCS engines on the siding will miss seeing the watchdog signal. When this happens, DCS engines will always power on in conventional mode with lights and sounds. Fortunately, this situation is easily corrected.

If a DCS engine comes up in conventional mode for any reason, all that's required is to select the DCS engine using the Engine Control Screen and press the Start Up key. If the engine is not to be operated immediately, it may then be put into DCS stealth mode, dark and silent, by tapping Shut Down.

DCS engine lashups, however, are the exception to this rule. If a lashup misses seeing the watchdog signal, tapping Start Up has no effect. For DCS lashups to come up in DCS mode, it's necessary to power off the TIU channel to which the tracks where the lashup resides are connected. Then, if there's a toggle switch that controls the siding or track block where the lashup resides, this switch must be turned on before turning on power to the TIU channel to which the tracks are connected. Then, power to the TIU channel's input must then be turned on so that the lashup sees the watchdog signal.

As previously stated, this can present problems when power to TIU Tracks is increased using the slider on the DCS Application. One way to avoid this problem is by setting the minimum starting voltage for a TIU Track to a voltage high enough that track voltage can be raised to that voltage by one click of the thumbwheel when scrolling up power. This will ensure that all DCS engines that are on the track being powered up will see the watchdog signal.

If the wires between a TIU channel output and the track become reversed, such that the TIU's red output terminal is connected to an outside rail and the TIU's black output terminal is connected to the center rail, the watchdog signal will not be generated and any DCS engines will come on in conventional mode. To remedy this, simply reverse the pair of wires either at the TIU's output terminals or at the track, but not both.

If the DCS signal has been turned off for a TIU channel or channels, the watchdog signal will not be generated and any DCS engines will come on in conventional mode. To remedy this, turn the DCS signal back on using the DCS Application as described in Part IX - Advanced Features and Functions, 9. System Settings, TIU Settings Screen.

Silent DCS Engine

Occasionally, a DCS engine may start up in DCS mode with lights but without any sounds. This may occur either after a derailment or other problem that resulted in a short circuit, or after completing a DCS signal strength test where the DCS track signal was low, or for some other reason. There are four ways to correct this problem.

First, check if ProtoCast Chuff is turned on. This will inhibit all engine sounds.

Second, be sure that the silent DCS engine is the active engine and is displayed on the Engine Control Screen. If the operator is not concerned about losing any of the DCS engine's settings, then a Feature Reset of the engine is the easiest way to restore sounds. The DCS engine's DCS ID# and any Custom Name previously assigned to the engine are retained.

A third method is to use the volume slider on the DCS Application's Engine Features Screen to increase the engine's sound volume until sound returns to the desired level.

A fourth method is to check the engine's settings. In the DCS Application's Engine Settings Screen:

- Set Clickety-Clack mode correctly. This will turn off all other engine sounds when set to Auto and engine runs at or greater than 30 SMPH (approx.) for 30 seconds.
- Set Chuff Rate correctly.
- Check if Proto Chuff is turned off. This will inhibit synchronized chuffing in steam engines.
- Check the volume settings of Bell, Horn/Whistle, Engine Sounds, and Accent Sounds.
- Set Cab Chatter correctly.
- Set Brake Sound correctly.
- Set Chuff Rate correctly.

Can't Add Engine Problems

When the DCS Application cannot find an engine to add that isn't already in either of the Active or Inactive Engine Lists, and such an engine is most definitely on a powered track, one common reason is that the DCS signal strength is low on the track section where the engine is residing when attempting to add it. The command to add a DCS engine is the most DCS signal-intensive of all DCS commands. If the DCS signal is not strong enough, one of two things may occur.

Either the engine will not add and the message "No engine to add" will be displayed or the engine will add, however, it may not have a proper name or settings. If the engine adds with an improper name or settings, proceed as follows:

- Delete any occurrences of the engine from the DCS Application.
- Disconnect all wires from the TIU.
- Connect a pair of wires directly from transformer Hot and Common to TIU Fixed Channel #1 Input.
- Connect a pair of wires from Fixed Channel #1 Output to a short section of track.
- Place the DCS engine to be added on the short section of track and provide power to the track.
- Attempt to add the DCS engine.

If the DCS engine still does not add correctly and other DCS engines do add correctly, the problem is most likely with the DCS engine itself. In this case, the last thing to attempt is to reset the DCS engine. Since the DCS engine must be present in the DCS Application in order to use either the Factory Reset or Feature Reset DCS commands, the reset must be accomplished using the transformer horn and bell buttons. This transformer reset is the equivalent of the DCS Feature Reset. The DCS engine's ID# will remain unchanged and its Custom Name, if any, will be preserved. Ensure that the DCS engine is on a powered track and then press the horn button once followed by pressing the bell button 5 times. Each press should be 1/2 second in duration with 1/2 second pauses between button presses. If the reset is successful, the DCS engine will respond with two short blasts of its horn or whistle. The timing of button presses is important and it may take several attempts before the reset is successful. Once the DCS engine has been reset, attempt to add it again.

If the DCS engine still does not add to the DCS Application, proceed as discussed in the next section, Identical Engine Problems.

It's also possible that a DCS engine will appear to add normally with all the correct soft keys, however, the DCS engine's name will be blank. This will occur if the board was never initialized. Replacement boards that were never initialized by MTH and boards from DCS Upgrade Kits may add in this manner. The solution is to use the DCS Application's Engine Settings Screen to assign a Custom Name to the DCS engine as follows:

- Navigate to the DCS Application's Engine Roster Screen.
- Make the engine with the blank name the Active Engine in the Engine Control Screen.
- Navigate to the DCS Application's Engine Settings Screen.
- Enter a Custom Name in the engine's Engine Name field.
- The engine's name is changed in the DCS Application.
- To change the DCS engine's name in other DCS Application, it is necessary to delete and add the engine in the other DCS Applications.

Engine ID# Outside Normal Range

If a DCS engine's DCS ID# becomes set outside of the normal range (refer to Appendix B: The Truth About DCS Engine ID Numbers, for an explanation of DCS ID#s), it will not respond to any command from the DCS Application. Fortunately, there's a method to recover such engines.

To reset a DCS engine with a DCS ID# that is outside of the normal range, proceed as follows:

- Set the engine on a track connected to a TIU with a strong DCS signal and provide power to the track. You should not have any other engines powered up on any track connected to that TIU while attempting to recover an engine
- Navigate to the DCS Application's Recover Engines Screen.
- Tap on the TIU that is connected to the track upon which the engine to be recovered resides.
- Tap the Recover button. The DCS Application will display that it is attempting recovery of a lost engine.
- If the DCS Application is able to recover the engine it will display Engine Recovered. The newly recovered engine will be automatically Factory Reset by the DCS Application.
- The engine may now be added to the DCS Application as described in Part VII - Engine Operation Using the DCS Application, 1. DCS Application Engine Control Screens, DCS App Add Engine Screens earlier in this book.
- If the DCS Application is unable to recover the engine it will display No Engine Recovered. If this occurs, then there may be an issue with this particular engine. Contact your local service center or MTH for service options.

Identical Engine Problems

In general, the DCS Application identifies DCS engines solely by their DCS Engine ID#. However, when attempting to add a new engine to the DCS Application, DCS must first determine if the DCS engine is already present in the DCS Application. In order to do so, it stands to reason that some other criteria than DCS ID# must be used to differentiate engines because an engine to be added may have the same DCS ID# as one already present in the DCS Application. If two engines look alike to the DCS Application, i.e., an engine to be added appears to be the same as an engine already in the DCS Application, it's conceivable that DCS can mistake them for being one and the same DCS engine. In this case the engine is not added to the DCS Application. Fortunately, there's a way around this problem. Proceed as follows:

- Delete from the DCS Application all occurrences of any engines that DCS may suspect are identical to an engine to be added.
- Add the first of these DCS engines to the DCS Application and then do a Factory Reset on it. This will also delete it from the DCS Application.
- Repeat the previous step for all of the other DCS engines that DCS may consider to be identical to the first one.
- Add the first of the DCS engines again. Regardless of what DCS ID# the DCS engine is assigned when it adds, change the DCS ID# to something else.
- Repeat the previous step for all of the other DCS engines.

If one of the identical DCS engines still refuses to add to the DCS Application, the problem may be with the DCS engine itself.

Speed Control Problems

One of the most important features of DCS engines is their ability to run at speed settings measured in scale miles per hour (SMPH). This ensures that all DCS engines will run at the same speed when set to the same SMPH with the DCS Application. Although MTH guarantees that every DCS engine will run smoothly at a speed setting of 5 SMPH or higher, it has been the author's experience that most DCS engines will run smoothly at a speed as low as 2 SMPH.

In a sample measurement of approximately 100 DCS engines of different product lines (Premier and Rail King) and different engine types (steamers, diesels, electrics, subways, and trolleys) around a measured route, the author found the speed variation of all of the engines, from the fastest to the slowest, was no more than approximately 4% when running at 30 SMPH:

- The fastest engine ran at 30.67 SMPH.
- The slowest engine ran at 29.40 SMPH.
- The average speed was 30.00 SMPH.

In all cases each engine's speed was close enough to the others so that any of these DCS engines could operate effectively in a lashup with any other.

When a DCS engine runs considerably faster or slower than the above parameters indicate, or does not run smoothly at 5 SMPH or faster, it's generally indicative of some kind of an anomaly with the DCS engine. If this occurs, there are a number of possible culprits. They can be grouped into incorrect engine settings, physical problems or engine software problems.

Incorrect Engine Settings

When encountering a speed-related problem, the first thing to do is to check the DCS engine's settings, including:

- In the Engine Settings Screen, the engine's Maximum Speed should be set to the fastest speed at which the DCS engine will be required to operate, or to the default of 120 SMPH.
- In the Engine Settings Screen, Speed Control Mode should be set to Command.

Physical Problems

If changing the above settings does not resolve the problem, the next thing to look for is a physical problem:

- Traction tires: if a traction tire is missing the DCS engine may run slower than intended due to wheel slippage. If a traction tire has come off it may have become jammed in the gears and cause the engine to run in a jerky fashion or not at all. In either case, the traction tire should be replaced according to the instructions in the DCS engine's user guide.
- Steam engine linkage: bent, binding or loose linkage in a steam engine's drive assembly can cause a variety of speed problems. Inspect steam engine linkage and straighten or tighten as necessary.
- Motor bottoming in the truck assembly: if a motor has a screw gear that is just slightly too long, it can bind in the bottom of the truck assembly. This can cause the engine to run in a jerky fashion at slow speeds. The solution to this problem should only be attempted by an authorized MTH service center or an individual who is extremely knowledgeable of DCS engine operation.
- Timing tape: the speed control mechanism in DCS engines utilizes a tach reader that counts alternating black and white stripes on a timing tape that is wrapped around the flywheel of one of the motors in a DCS engine. If this timing tape becomes damaged in any way (torn or faded) the engine's speed will be adversely affected. One way that the timing tape may become damaged is if smoke fluid is added while the smoke unit is operating. The smoke unit fan may blow fluid onto the tape causing the black stripes to fade to gray and the tach reader to incorrectly count the stripes. The solution is to replace the timing tape with a new one. There are different timing tapes for different DCS engines, all of which may be obtained from MTH or an MTH authorized service center.
- Painted timing stripes: some newer DCS engines have a flywheel that has black and white stripes painted on rather than a timing tape. Occasionally, the paint on the flywheel may be too porous for the tach reader to accurately distinguish between black and white stripes. The solution is to cover the painted flywheel with a timing tape. There are different timing tapes for different DCS engines, all of which may be obtained from MTH or an MTH authorized service center.
- Tach Reader: the distance between the tach reader and the flywheel must be within a specific range that is approximately the thickness of a dime. If it is not, the distance may be adjusted slightly by carefully bending the tach reader closer or further away from the flywheel.

Engine Software Problems

If adjusting settings and checking for mechanical problems does not resolve the speed control issue, the problem may be due to an error in the DCS engine's sound or chain file. Each DCS PS2 engine has a Sound file that is tailored to the operating characteristics and sound effects for that particular engine. PS3 engines also have a Chain file. These files also contain information about the engine that DCS uses to control the engine's speed. This information includes gear ratios, wheel size and other information that is used to control speed in scale miles per hour (SMPH).

If the Sound or Chain file is a possible source of the speed anomaly, contact MTH to learn if a corrected sound file exists. If so, refer to Part XII - DCS Upgrading and Remote Backup/Restore earlier in this book to download a new sound file from MTH's website to replace the sound file in the DCS engine.

6. Switch Track Control Problems

The following discusses the most common issues associated with operating switch tracks through the DCS AIU:

- Activating a switch track through the DCS Application doesn't work.
- The switch track throws the wrong way when activated through the DCS Application.
- The switch track's automatic non-derailing mechanism doesn't work.

Switch Track Doesn't Activate

There are only three reasons that a switch track will not work properly when activated by the AIU:

- The AIU is incorrectly connected to the TIU or another AIU.
- The switch track is incorrectly connected to the AIU.
- The switch track is incorrectly programmed into the DCS Application.

If none of the switch tracks connected to the AIU operate when activated from the DCS Application, the first thing to check is that the AIU is properly connected to the TIU or the previous AIU that is correctly connected to the TIU. Using the cable that was provided with the AIU, plug one end of the cable into the AIU Input port on the TIU or the previous AIU, and the other end into the TIU Input port on the AIU.

If this cable is incorrectly connected serious damage to the AIU can result!

If a switch track that is connected to an AIU SW port is wired so that it may be activated from the control panel as well, ensure that the switch track operates from the control panel. If it does not, carefully check the wiring from the switch track to the control panel. If necessary, temporarily disconnect the switch track from the AIU. Once the switch track operates correctly from the control panel, reconnect it to the AIU.

If a switch track connected to an AIU port does not operate correctly from the DCS Application, check the wiring between the switch motor and the AIU SW port. Most switch tracks connect to the AIU in one of two ways.

Switch tracks with separate motors, such as Gargraves, Ross and Atlas O switch tracks, have three terminals or wires and typically are wired to the AIU SW port as follows:

- The center wire on the switch motor is connected to transformer Hot.
- The other two wires are connected to AIU SW port terminals 1 and 2.
- The AIU SW port terminal IN is connected to transformer Common.

Switch tracks with built-in motors, such as MTH RealTrax, Lionel O and Lionel Super O have 3 terminals that normally connect to their manual switch controllers. These three terminals are connected to the AIU as follows:

- One terminal is a Common terminal such that when one of the other two wires is connected to it, the switch track will throw in one direction. This wire is connected to the AIU SW port terminal IN.
- The other two wires are connected to AIU SW port terminals 1 and 2.

If the switch track still does not operate when activated from the DCS Application after the wiring connections have been checked, the programming of the switch track into the DCS Application should be verified. Re-enter the switch track into the DCS Application, being careful to enter the correct TIU ID#, AIU ID#, and SW port number.

If, after verifying that the AIU to TIU connections, the switch track connections to the AIU SW port and the programming of the switch track into the DCS Application are all correct, it's possible that the AIU may be defective. Refer to Part XIII - Troubleshooting Problems, Application, Diagnosing AIU Problems earlier in this book to perform basic hardware tests of the AIU's operation.

Wrong Switch Track Activates

If, when activating a switch track connected to the AIU from the DCS Application, a different switch track activates instead, delete the entry for the switch track in the AIU and re-enter it, ensuring that the TIU ID#, AIU ID#, and AIU SW port entered match where the switch track is connected.

Switch Track Throws the Wrong Way

If, after connecting a switch track to the AIU, it operates correctly except that it throws reversed when activated from the DCS Application (for example, straight instead of curved), simply reverse the wires connected to the 1 and 2 terminals of the AIU SW port.

Automatic Non-derailing Mechanism Doesn't Work

The switch track operates correctly when activated from the DCS Application, however, the switch track's automatic non-derailing mechanism does not activate. If this occurs, the first thing to check is that the automatic non-derailing feature is correctly wired.

Generally, switch tracks with built-in switch motors, such as MTH RealTrax and all Lionel switch tracks, are internally pre-wired for automatic non-derailing operation. Other switch tracks, such as those from Gargraves and Ross, need to be wired externally for automatic non-derailing operation according to the instructions that accompanied the switch track.

If the switch track receives power from a different transformer than the one used for track power the Common terminals of the track power and switch track power transformers must be connected to each other. However, before connecting these transformers it is necessary to ensure that they are in phase with each other, to eliminate the possibility of inadvertently creating dangerously high voltages. This can occur when locomotives or passenger cars with dual pickup rollers bridge two sections of track powered by different transformers, or when a transformer other than a track power transformer is used to power switch motors wired for non-derailing operation.

To ensure that two transformers are in phase:

- Start by plugging the two transformers into AC outlets.
- Turn on both transformers and set the output of each transformer to zero.
- Connect a wire from any Common terminal of one transformer to any Common terminal of the other transformer.
- Connect two wires, one to a Hot terminal of one transformer and one to a Hot terminal of the other transformer.
- Set both transformers to as close to the same voltage as possible, at or above 10 volts.
- Select one of the following three ways to now test to see if two transformers are in phase or not:
- Briefly touch the wires connected to the two Hot terminals to each other. If a spark results the transformers are not in phase. If there is no spark, they are in phase.
- Using a voltmeter, measure the AC voltage between the two wires connected to the Hot terminals. If it is approximately twice the value of the voltage to which the transformers are set, they are not in phase. If it's less than a few volts, they are in phase.
- Place an 18 volt light bulb between the two wires connected to the Hot terminals of the two transformers. If the bulb is bright the transformers are not in phase. If the bulb is dim or does not light at all, the transformers are in phase.

If the transformers are not in phase, reverse the AC plug of one of them in the outlet and repeat the test. This may be difficult if the transformer has a plug where one blade is broader than the other. After ensuring that the two transformers are in phase, connect a Common terminal of the switch track power transformer to a Common terminal of the track power transformer to enable automatic non-derailing operation for the switch track.

7. Accessory Control Problems

The following section discusses the most common issues associated with operating accessories through the DCS AIU. They are:

- Activating an accessory through the DCS Application doesn't work.
- Activating an accessory through the DCS Application causes the wrong accessory to activate.
- Concerns regarding connecting uncoupling tracks to the AIU.

Accessory Doesn't Activate

There are only three reasons that an accessory will not work properly when activated by the AIU:

- The AIU is incorrectly connected to the TIU or another AIU.
- The accessory is incorrectly connected to the AIU.
- The accessory is incorrectly programmed into the DCS Application.

If none of the accessories connected to the AIU operate when activated from the DCS Application, the first thing to check is that the AIU is properly connected to the TIU or the previous AIU that is correctly connected to the TIU. Using the cable that was provided with the AIU, plug one end of the cable into the AIU Input port on the TIU or the previous AIU, and the other end into the TIU Input port on the AIU.

If this cable is incorrectly connected serious damage to the AIU can result!

If an accessory that is connected to an AIU ACC port is wired so that it may be activated from the control panel as well, ensure that the accessory operates from the control panel. If it does not, carefully check the wiring from the accessory to the control panel. If necessary, temporarily disconnect the accessory from the AIU. Once the accessory operates correctly from the control panel, reconnect it to the AIU.

If an accessory connected to an AIU port does not operate correctly when activated from the DCS Application, check the wiring between the accessory and the AIU ACC port. If the accessory still does not operate when activated from the DCS Application after the wiring connections have been checked, the programming of the accessory into the DCS Application should be verified. Re-enter the accessory into the DCS Application, being extremely careful to enter the correct TIU ID#, AIU ID#, and ACC port. If, after verifying that the AIU to TIU connections, the accessory connections to the AIU ACC port and the programming of the accessory into the DCS Application are all correct, it's possible that the AIU may be defective. Refer to Part XIII - Troubleshooting Problems, Application, Diagnosing AIU Problems earlier in this book to perform basic hardware tests of the AIU's operation.

Wrong Accessory Activates

If, when activating an accessory connected to the AIU from the DCS Application, a different accessory activates instead, delete the entry for the accessory in the AIU and re-enter it, ensuring that the TIU ID#, AIU ID#, and AIU ACC port entered match where the accessory is connected.

Concerns Regarding Connecting Uncoupling Tracks to the AIU

Connecting Uncoupling Tracks to an AIU ACC Port

Although uncoupling tracks may be connected to an AIU ACC port, great care must be taken when they are activated from the DCS Application.

Once an accessory is connected to an AIU ACC port, it can be activated either by tapping its On button or its Activate button. If the On button is tapped, the accessory will activate and continue to operate until the Off button is pressed. If the Activate button is tapped, the accessory will activate and operate only as long as the Activate button is kept depressed.

If an uncoupling track, connected to an AIU ACC port, is activated by tapping its On button rather than its Activate button, neglecting to quickly tap its Off button will cause the uncoupling track magnet to continue to be energized. This in turn can cause the plastic surrounding the uncoupling track's magnet to melt, destroying the uncoupling track and possibly even starting a fire on the layout. When connected to AIU ACC ports, it is suggested that uncoupling tracks should always be operated using only the Activate button.

Connecting Uncoupling Tracks to an AIU SW Port

Another way to connect uncoupling tracks to the AIU is to use SW (switch track) ports instead of ACC (accessory) ports. This ensures that any activation of the uncoupling track is always momentary, preventing a magnet from possibly overheating and burning out the uncoupling track. Further, each SW port can control up to two uncoupling tracks.

The first uncoupling track is connected to the AIU as follows:

- One terminal of the uncoupling track is connected to SW port terminal 1.
- SW port terminal IN is connected to transformer Hot.
- If the uncoupling track has a second terminal, it is connected to transformer Common.

To connect a second uncoupling track to the same AIU SW port, proceed as follows:

- One terminal of the uncoupling track is connected to SW port terminal 2.
- If the uncoupling track has a second terminal, it is connected to transformer Common.

The AIU SW port is programmed as described in Part VIII - Accessory and Switch Track Control, 3. Operating Switch Tracks Using the DCS Application, Programming Switch Tracks Into the DCS Application earlier in this book.

Operating the first uncoupling track that's connected to an AIU SW port is accomplished by selecting the switch track entered for the SW port to which the uncoupling track is connected and tapping the straight arrow. If a second uncoupling track is connected to the same AIU SW port, it is activated by tapping the curved arrow.

8. TMCC and Legacy Control Problems

This section discusses issues that may arise when TMCC is added to a DCS O gauge layout. It is not intended to discuss all aspects of troubleshooting TMCC engine problems. It only discusses issues that are particular to operating TMCC on a DCS layout using the DCS Application.

Troubleshooting TMCC and Legacy Engine Control Problems

The DCS Application emulates Lionel TMCC and Legacy engine commands. Once an engine is entered into a DCS Application, it may be started up and operated just like a DCS engine. Most of the controls of the DCS Application operate TMCC and Legacy engine features the same way they operate DCS engine features, e.g., the headlight, smoke, bell, whistle/horn, and direction keys are the same for both TMCC and DCS engines. Additional TMCC engine commands are performed using a set of soft keys that appear in the DCS Application's Engine Control Screen, Engine Settings Screen and Engine Soft keys Screen when a TMCC or Legacy engine is selected. These soft keys allow control of most, if not all, other TMCC and Legacy engine functions. The DCS Application allows creation and operation of TMCC and Legacy lash-ups, as well as operation of just about all other TMCC and Legacy commands.

At times, a TMCC or Legacy engine may not respond to a command from the DCS Application. The way to address this is as follows:

- First, while sending a TMCC or Legacy engine a command from the DCS Application, observe the Lionel command base. If the red LED on the command base does not blink at least once when the command is sent, there is a connection problem between the TIU and the command base. If this is the case, ensure that the cable between the TIU and the command base is tightly connected to both devices, that the correct end (both ends are labeled) is plugged into each device, and that it is the correct cable for the command base to which the TIU is connected. If it is not the correct cable it should be replaced.

- Another reason why the TMCC command base's red LED may not blink when sending a command from the DCS Application, to the TMCC or Legacy engine, could be because the wrong TIU address was entered when the TMCC or Legacy engine was added to the DCS Application. The TIU address entered must be for the TIU to which the TMCC command base is connected.

- If the red LED on the command base does blink when the DCS Application sends a TMCC or Legacy command, the problem may be that the TMCC or Legacy command is not reaching the engine. Ensure that the TMCC or Legacy engine is on a powered track that is connected to one of the TIU's output channels.

- If the engine still does not receive the command, it's possible that the wire connecting the command base to the outside rails is not getting to the track upon which the TMCC engine resides. This may be because the outside rails are not all connected either through the rails themselves or through the transformer Common wiring if more than one transformer is providing track power. To ensure that TMCC and Legacy signals reach all of the TMCC and Legacy engines on the layout all of the time, connect a Common terminal from the command bases' one wire to all of the layout's TIU's output channels together after ensuring that all the layout's transformers are in phase as discussed in Part XIII - Troubleshooting Problems, 6. Switch Track Control Problems, Automatic Non-derailing Mechanism Doesn't Work earlier in this book.

If the TMCC or Legacy engine still does not respond to commands from the DCS Application, it's possible that the TMCC or Legacy engine has a TMCC/Legacy ID# that is different from what was entered into the DCS Application when the engine was added. In that case, change the TMCC or Legacy engine's TMCC/Legacy ID# to some other number as described in Part VII - Engine Operation Using the DCS Application, DCS App Engine Settings Screen - TMCC or Legacy Engines earlier in this book. Then attempt to control the TMCC or Legacy engine again using the changed TMCC/Legacy ID#. If it still does not respond the TMCC or Legacy engine itself may be the problem.

Part XIV - The DCS Explorer

1. DCS Explorer Purpose and Function

This section of the book discusses capabilities, installation, configuration, and use of the DCS Explorer.

What the DCS Explorer Does

The DCS Explorer is an entry-level, DCS control device that provides basic DCS functions. It is intended to be used by someone who is entering the world of DCS for the first time. It has a limited feature set and is not intended to be used in large DCS layouts. The DCS Explorer began to be included in MTH's Ready to Run train sets in late 2017.

The DCS Application communicates the DCS Explorer in the same way as it does with a WIU. However, there are several differences between the DCS Explorer and the WIU:

- The DCS Explorer doesn't connect to a TIU. Rather, it connects directly to the layout's tracks.
- The DCS Explorer has a single TIU channel built-in to where the WIU connects to 4 TIU channels in a single TIU.
- Unlike the WIU, which has connects to a separate power supply only for itself, the DCS Explorer requires a single power input that serves for its own power and also track power. The DCS Explorer cannot be used in conjunction with any other track power supply. Further, it can only provide 6 amps of power to the track.
- The WIU, through the TIU, can control AIUs and the DCS Explorer cannot.
- The DCS Application has only a limited set of commands available for use with the DCS Explorer, regardless of the version of the DCS Application (free, Standard or Premium).
- The DCS Application, when used with the DCS Explorer, can have no more than 3 DCS engines in its engine roster at any time. To add an additional engine requires removing one existing engine.
- While a DCS Application can access multiple WIUs, it can only access one DCS Explorer.

Like the WIU, there are two ways to install and wirelessly connect the DCS Application to the DCS Explorer. The first method, connecting to the DCS Explorer, is very simple. The second method, connecting to the DCS Explorer via a local area network (LAN), while more involved, has several advantages. Both methods will be discussed below. Note that if any of the following instructions conflict with the manual that accompanies the MTH DCS Explorer, the manual's instructions should be followed instead.

Figure 84 - DCS Explorer

2. Setup and Configuration for Using the DCS Application

Connecting to the DCS Explorer in MTH WiFi Network Mode

If you don't already have a local area network (LAN) in place, this is the suggested method to use to wirelessly connect the DCS Application to the DCS Explorer.

This method takes advantage of the mini-WiFi network generated by the DCS Explorer to wirelessly and directly connect the DCS Application on the smart device to the DCS Explorer. You should be aware, however, that although this is very easy to setup, it has two disadvantages.

The smart device is unable to access any other wireless devices, such as the Lionel iCab or LCS applications that allow control of TMCC and Legacy engines, without switching to the mini-networks that are generated by those application's Legacy command base-interfacing hardware. If there are no other WiFi applications present, this is not relevant.

An Internet connection is not possible using this method, precluding use of the DCS Application's ancillary News, Search, and Catalog functions.

To connect the DCS Application to the DCS Explorer in MTH WiFi Network Mode, proceed as follows:

- Set the DCS Explorer MTH/Home selector switch to MTH.
- Attach the included antenna, and plug a power supply for the DCS Explorer into an AC outlet and the power supply's cable into the POWER IN port on the DCS Explorer. Wait a minute or two for the DCS Explorer PWR, Wi-Fi and TRACK LEDs to light.
- On the smart device, open the device's settings.
- Select the MTH DCS network from the smart device's list of wireless networks
- Enter the MTH DCS network password: mthdcswifi
- The smart device should indicate that it is connected to the DCS Explorer mini WiFi network.

Connecting to the DCS Explorer in Home WiFi Network Mode

This method connects the DCS Explorer to the DCS Application by connecting the smart device to a wireless local area network (LAN). If you already have a local area network in place or are knowledgeable enough to set one up, this is the preferred method to connect the DCS Application to the DCS Explorer. This method has two distinct advantages.

The smart device is able to access other wireless devices, such as the Lionel iCab or LCS applications that allow control of TMCC and Legacy engines, simultaneously without switching wireless networks, assuming that these applications are also connected to the Legacy command base-interfacing hardware via the same local are network as is the DCS Application. If there are no other WiFi applications present, this is not relevant.

An Internet connection is possible using this method, allowing use of the DCS Application's ancillary News, Search and Catalog functions.

Connecting to the DCS Explorer Using a Router With a WPS Button

If your router has a "WPS" button, use this procedure to connect the DCS Application to the DCS Explorer in Home WiFi Network Mode:

- Set the DCS Explorer's MTH/Home selector switch to Home.
- Attach the included antenna, and plug a power supply for the DCS Explorer into an AC outlet and the power supply's cable into the POWER IN port on the DCS Explorer. Wait a minute or two for the DCS Explorer PWR, Wi-Fi and TRACK LEDs to light.
- On your network router, press the WPS button and then the WPS button on the DCS Explorer.

- Wait for the white WPS LED on the DCS Explorer to come on steadily, and then turn off.
- Select and open WiFi settings on the smart device.
- Choose the desired WiFi local area network from the smart device's list of wireless networks.
- The smart device should indicate that it is connected to the desired WiFi local area network.

Connecting to the DCS Explorer Using a Router Without a WPS Button

If the router does not have a WPS button, proceed as follows to connect the DCS Application to the DCS Explorer in Home WiFi Network Mode:

- Set the DCS Explorer's MTH/Home selector switch to MTH.
- Attach the included antenna, and plug a power supply for the DCS Explorer into an AC outlet and the power supply's cable into the POWER IN port on the DCS Explorer. Wait a minute or two for the DCS Explorer PWR, Wi-Fi and TRACK LEDs to light.
- Using any computer with WiFi capability, navigate to see the available wireless networks and connect to the network named MTH_DCS-XXXX, where XXXX may be any 4 characters. This is the same network name that's printed on the bottom of the WIU.
- When prompted, enter the network password (network key) mthdcswifi in all lower case. The network key is also printed on the bottom of the WIU.
- Open a web browser and enter the following IP address in the url address line at the top of the browser's window: 192.168.143.1 This will open LuCI, the MTH DCS web interface.
- Enter the password mthdcs in all lower case and press the keyboard ENTER or RETURN key. Do not change the username from ROOT.
- Click on the STATION MODE tab at the top of the screen
- Select WIRELESS from the drop-down menu.
- Locate the ESSID field and enter the home network name (SSID) to which the WIU is to be connected. This is the same network to which your smart device is to be connected.
- If your network requires a password, select the network's encryption type from the drop down menu. If the encryption type is not known, select the last choice in the list, mixed mode. If that doesn't work, obtain the encryption type from your router.
- Enter your home network password in the KEY field. Then, click the SAVE AND APPLY button on the lower-right of the screen.
- Remove power from the DCS Explorer and close the browser.
- Set the DCS Explorer's "MTH/Home" selector switch to "Home".
- Plug a power supply for the DCS Explorer into an AC outlet and the power supply's cable into the POWER IN port on the DCS Explorer. Wait a minute or two for the DCS Explorer PWR, Wi-Fi and TRACK LEDs to light.
- The DCS Explorer will now automatically connect to your home network each time it is powered up.

Connecting to the DCS Explorer Using Wired Ethernet

Connecting to a home network using a wired Ethernet connection requires a USB to Ethernet adapter. MTH recommends the Cable Matters 202023 USB 2.0 to 10/100 Fast Ethernet Network Adapter.

To connect with the home network using a wired Ethernet connection:

- Connect the DCS Explorer's USB port to a USB to Ethernet Adapter cable and then connect the network router to the adapter cable using a standard Ethernet cable.
- Set the DCS Explorer's MTH/Home selector switch to MTH.
- Attach the included antenna, and plug a power supply for the DCS Explorer into an AC outlet and the power supply's cable into the POWER IN port on the DCS Explorer. Wait a minute or two for the DCS Explorer PWR, Wi-Fi and TRACK LEDs to light.

- Select and open WiFi settings on your smart device.
- Choose the desired WiFi local area network from the smart device's list of wireless networks. If requested, enter the password for the desired WiFi local area network.
- The smart device should indicate that it is connected to the desired WiFi local area network.

If the Smart Device Loses its WiFi Connection to the DCS Explorer

If the smart device is connected to the DCS Explorer in MTH mode and the smart device's network connection often spontaneously changes to the home network connection, the DCS Application will report that it cannot find any TIUs. If this happens, use the smart device's WiFi network settings to "forget" the home network. Going forward, the smart device will not to attempt to join the home network unless specifically told to do so.

On an iOS device, this is accomplished by doing the following:

- Turn off the "Ask to Join Networks" option in WiFi settings
- Tap on the home network's entry in the list of available networks and then tap on the "Forget This Network" option.

Android users should do the equivalent of the above on their smart devices.

This should prevent the smart device from spontaneously switching from the WIU's network to the home network.

Resetting the DCS Explorer

If it becomes necessary at any time to reset the DCS Explorer to its initial factory settings, such as to deinstall and reinstall the DCS Explorer to move it to another layout or to depersonalize it before giving it to someone else, the process to reset the device is straightforward:

- Power-on the DCS Explorer normally and wait a minute or two for its PWR, Wi-Fi and TRACK LEDs to light
- Press the Reset button on the DCS Explorer for a full 10 seconds
- Unplug the DCS Explorer's power supply from its AC outlet.

The DCS Explorer has now been reset to the exact condition that it was in when it came from the factory.

Replacing the Fuse in the DCS Explorer

If the DCS Explorer suddenly causes track power to turn off and all of its LEDs turn off, as well, it's most likely because its fuse has blown. If this occurs, first determine and correct the issue that caused the fuse to blow. Next, disconnect power to the DCS Explorer and remove the blown fuse from the side of the DCS Explorer's case by pulling it straight out. It may be necessary to use a pliers with which to grip the fuse. Replace it with a 5 amp, fast-blow fuse of the exact same type. Replacement fuses can be found in hardware stores and auto parts stores, as well as from online retailers.

3. Using the DCS Application With the DCS Explorer

The very first time that the DCS Application is launched, it will ask if it is to be used with the DCS Explorer or with a WIU. Subsequent launches of the DCS Application will remember that selection. If it's necessary to change from using a WIU to using the DCS Explorer, navigate to the DCS Application's App Settings Screen and tap on the DCS Explorer box under System.

Then, return to the Engine Control Screen and tap the Refresh button. Once that has been accomplished, the DCS Application is ready to use the DCS Explorer.

It's important to note that the DCS Explorer will not send power to the track until the DCS Application actually connects to the DCS Explorer. This occurs when the DCS Application is launched and then the Refresh button is tapped. At this time, the track will become powered and a DCS watchdog signal will be sent to all engines on the track. The track will stay powered until the DCS Explorer is turned off.

When using the DCS Explorer, the DCS Application is very limited in scope. The following discusses which DCS Application features and functions are available for use with the DCS Explorer.

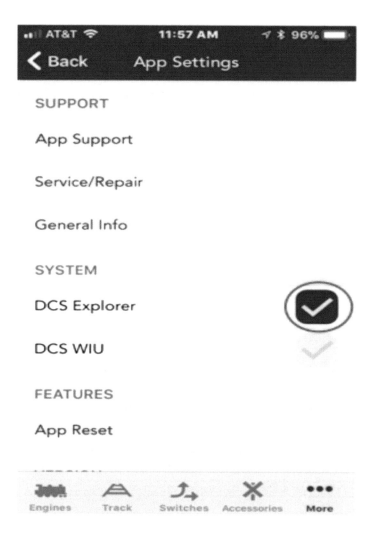

Figure 85 - DCS Explorer Application Settings Screen

DCS Application Functions Available Using the DCS Explorer

The DCS Application will always have available the Internet-related functions of the More… Screen, provided that an Internet connection is available. These functions include News, Search, Catalog, Videos, Shop MTH, MTH Newsletter Signup, and User Manuals.

Additionally, the More… Screen's Upgrade and App Settings functions are also available. The More… Screen's Advanced Features Screen also will allow use of System Settings to hide or show the E-Stop button, and to set engine speed lock.

The DCS Explorer will allow full use of the DCS Application's Engine Control Screen and limited use of the Engine Features Screen, as shown below.

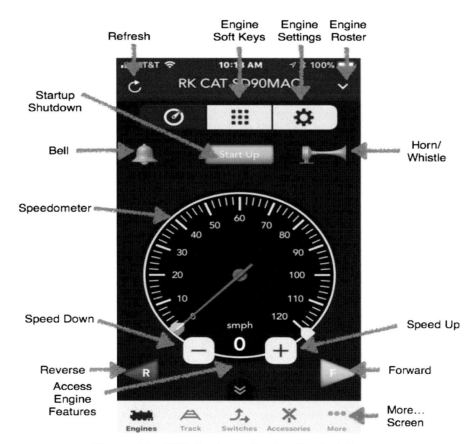

Figure 86 - DCS Explorer Engine Control Screen

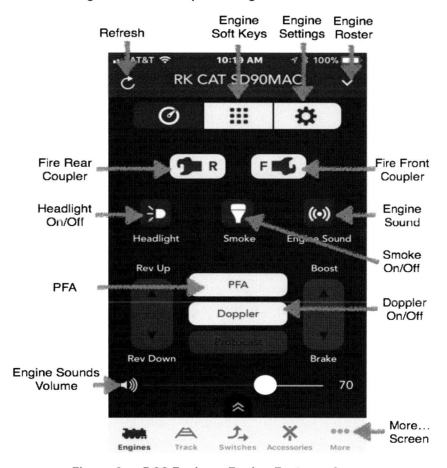

Figure 87 - DCS Explorer Engine Features Screen

The Engine Soft Keys Screen has no soft keys that can be used by the DCS Explorer and the Engine Settings Screen has only available the Engine Features Reset and Engine Factory Reset functions, as shown below.

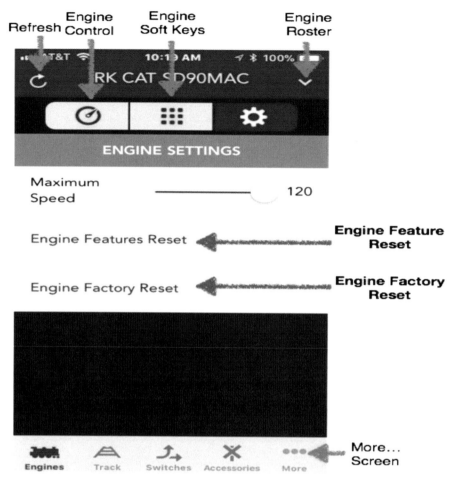

Figure 88 - DCS Explorer Engine Settings Screen

The DCS Application allows use of the More...Screen and all of its functions except the Upgrade function. Further, tapping the Advanced Features button brings allows access to only the System Settings function, as shown below.

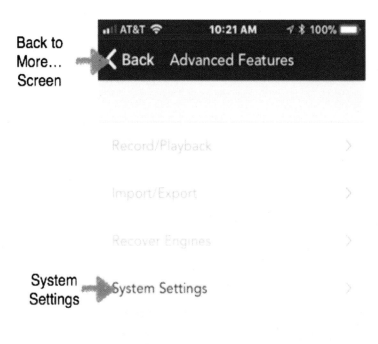

Figure 89 - DCS Explorer Advanced Features Screen

The only settings that may be modified using the DCS Explorer version of the DCS Application's System Settings Screen are Hide E-Stop Button and Max Engine Speed Lock, as shown below.

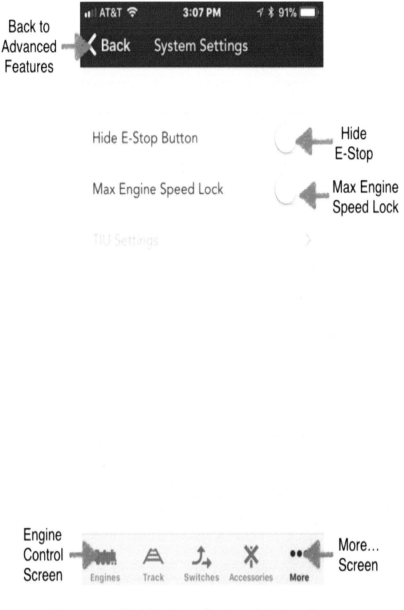

Figure 90 - DCS Explorer System Settings Screen

Both the Hide E-Stop Button and Max Engine Speed Lock each require the use of a password, just as they do when the DCS Application is being used with a WiFi Interface Unit (WIU) and TIU combination. Both functions use the same password and that password is the same for the DCS Application regardless of which device is being used. The settings for both functions will persist even if the DCS operator changes back and forth between using a WIU and a DCS Explorer.

While using the DCS Application with a DCS Explorer, it is not possible to upgrade the DCS Application to a higher level of functionality. This may only be accomplished when the DCS Application is set to WIU rather than to DCS Explorer. If the More... Screen's Upgrade button, or any other button that is not functional when using the DCS Application with the DCS Explore, is tapped while the DCS Application is set to DCS Explorer, the following message will be displayed.

Please Note!

The upgrades available for purchase unlock features that are not available in the DCS Explorer. If you would like to take advantage of the advanced features included in the Standard and Premium level apps, you must replace the DCS Explorer hardware with a DCS WIU and TIU.

More information about the full range of DCS products can be found online.

Figure 91 - DCS Explorer Hardware Upgrade Required Message

4. Updating the Firmware in the DCS Explorer

Updates to the DCS Explorer's firmware, when available, are found as a free download on MTH's Protosound 2 website.

Downloading a DCS Explorer Firmware Update File

The following procedure applies to personal computers, Android tablets and smartphones, and iOS tablets, smartphones and iPods that are using iOS 11.x or later. The procedure for downloading a DCS Explorer firmware update file is as follows:

- Use a web browser to connect to MTH's Protosound 2 website, www.protosound2.com
- On the web page, locate the link for DCS DCS Explorer Firmware. The version posted will always be the latest one available for general use. MTH does not post pre-release or beta copies of software on their websites. Click on the Download NOW! link to the right to download the DCS Explorer firmware update file to the personal computer, tablet or smartphone.
- Complete the required fields and follow the on-screen prompts.
- When prompted, click on the download link and choose a location in the personal computer, tablet or smartphone to save the file. Make sure that the file is downloaded someplace that is actually on the computer, tablet or smartphone so that it can be easily found later. If you place the file in cloud storage, such as by saving it to Dropbox, when later downloading to the DCS Explorer it will be necessary to be connected to the Internet, rather than directly to the DCS Explorer. It's suggested to download to the Desktop for personal computers and to Files/Textedit for iOS devices. For Android devices, simply choose DOWNLOAD to download the file to the Documents folder on the device.

Installing the Downloaded File

The following procedure applies to personal computers, Android tablets and smartphones, and iOS tablets, smartphones and iPods that are using iOS 11.x or later.

As previously discussed, when there are DCS software update files for the DCS Explorer, in order to update the software in the DCS Explorer, it's necessary to use the LuCI program that is built-into the DCS Explorer.

LuCI is a web interface for the DCS Explorer that provides a custom web page used exclusively to access advanced setup functions and features in the DCS Explorer. Whenever MTH releases an update to the DCS Explorer firmware, it's necessary to use LuCI to install the update file, as follows:

- Set the DCS Explorer's MTH/Home selector switch to MTH.
- Attach the included antenna, and plug a power supply for the DCS Explorer into an AC outlet and the power supply's cable into the POWER IN port on the DCS Explorer. Wait a minute or two for the DCS Explorer PWR, Wi-Fi and TRACK LEDs to light.
- As discussed above, using any computer, or an appropriate smart phone or tablet, with WiFi capability, navigate to see the available wireless networks and connect to the network named MTH_DCS-XXXX, where XXXX may be any 4 characters. This is the same network name that's printed on the bottom of the DCS Explorer.
- When prompted, enter the network password (network key) mthdcswifi in all lower case. The network key is also printed on the bottom of the DCS Explorer.
- Open a web browser and enter the following IP address in the url address line at the top of the browser's window: 192.168.143.1 This will open LuCI, the MTH DCS web interface.
- Enter the password mthdcs in all lower case and press the keyboard ENTER or RETURN key. Do not change the username from ROOT.
- Click on the SYSTEM tab at the top of the screen. Then, select BACK-UP/FLASH FIRMWARE from the drop-down menu.

- Scroll down the page to see FLASH NEW FIRMWARE IMAGE near the bottom of the page.
- Do not un-check the KEEP SETTINGS box. Doing so will cause LuCI to lose its network settings.
- Select CHOOSE FILE and navigate to where you previously saved the DCS Explorer's firmware upgrade file. For Android devices, choose the action "Documents", then select the DCS Explorer firmware upgrade file. When the file has been located, click OPEN.
- Wait until the file window closes (this could take as long as 15 seconds). Verify that the filename displayed next to the CHOOSE FILE button is the same as the one that was selected.
- Click on FLASH IMAGE...
- When the FLASH FIRMWARE - VERIFY page is displayed, click on the blue PROCEED button.
- The SYSTEM FLASHING SCREEN is displayed.
- Wait a full 3 minutes or until LuCI's Home login screen and is once again displayed. Then, remove power from the DCS Explorer and reconnect it to your layout.

Verifying the Firmware Update

To confirm that a DCS Explorer firmware update was successful, after the update log into LuCi, just as you did for the update. Then, scroll down the page about halfway to see the updated firmware version. When you have verified that the update was successful, remove power from the DCS Explorer and re-connect it to your layout.

5. Using Multiple DCS Explorers on the Same Layout

The DCS Explorer is meant to be used for small layouts. It has neither the capacity nor the functionality of its "big brother", the DCS WiFi Interface Unit (WIU). However, it is possible to use multiple DCS Explorers together on the same layout. There are three ways that this may be done.

Connecting Multiple DCS Applications to Different Explorers

The first way to use multiple DCS Explorers on a single layout is would have each DCS Explorer configured in MTH mode. Each DCS Explorer would be connected to a different loop of the layout's tracks, where each loop is isolated from all other loops of the layout's tracks. Then, each operator would use a DCS Application on their smartphone or tablet to connect to one of the layout's DCS Explorers. This would allow each operator to control trains running on one of the layout's track loops. Refer to Part XIV - The DCS Explorer, 2. Setup and Configuration for Using the DCS Application, Connecting to the DCS Explorer in MTH WiFi Network Mode earlier in this book to configure each DCS Explorer in MTH mode.

The major benefit from this method of operation is that it facilitates having multiple DCS operators, each using their own copy of the DCS Application, to operate three different DCS engines on a loop of a single layout. This, in a way, mitigates the DCS Explorer's three engine limit by allowing each operator to control three different DCS engines, using one DCS Explorer that is connected to one of the layout's loops.

An important caveat, however, is that each DCS engine is restricted to its own track loop and, if it should stray to a different loop, the operator would lose control of that engine until and unless the engine returned to the tracks of the DCS Explorer upon which it first was started up.

Connecting One DCS Application to Multiple DCS Explorers in MTH Network Mode

The second way to use multiple DCS Explorers on a single layout would have multiple DCS Explorers, each configured in Home mode, and each connected to the same home WiFi network. Each DCS Application connected to the home network would see multiple DCS Explorers and treat them as individual units. However, each DCS Application would still impose a limit of 3 DCS engines. Refer to Part XIV - The DCS Explorer, 2. Setup and Configuration for Using the DCS Application, Connecting to the DCS Explorer in Home WiFi Network Mode earlier in this book to configure each DCS Explorer in MTH mode.

The major benefit from this method of operation is that a single DCS operator can operate up to three different DCS engines spread across multiple loops of a single layout.

Again, an important caveat is that the DCS Explorers are operating in individual mode and each DCS engine is restricted to its own track loop. If it should stray to a different track loop, the operator would lose control of the engine until and unless the engine returned to the tracks of the DCS Explorer upon which it was first started up.

Connecting One DCS Application to Multiple DCS Explorers in Home Network Mode

The third way to use multiple DCS Explorers on a single layout would have multiple DCS Explorers with only one DCS Explorer configured in MTH mode. All additional DCS Explorers would be configured in Home mode. The DCS Explorer configured in MTH mode would act as a router with the other DCS Explorers, that were configured in Home mode, connected to it.

The first DCS Explorer would be configured in MTH mode as described in Part XIV - The DCS Explorer, 2. Setup and Configuration for Using the DCS Application, Connecting to the DCS Explorer in MTH WiFi Network Mode earlier in this book.

Additional DCS Explorers would be configured so that they are connected to the first DCS Explorer as if it was a router, as discussed below:

- Set the second DCS Explorer's MTH/Home selector switch to Home.
- Attach the included antenna, and plug a power supply for the DCS Explorer into an AC outlet and the power supply's cable into the POWER IN port on the DCS Explorer. Wait a minute or two for the DCS Explorer's PWR, Wi-Fi and TRACK LEDs to light.
- On the first (master) DCS Explorer, press the WPS button. The white WPS LED will begin flashing.
- Immediately press the WPS button on the second DCS Explorer. The WPS button must be pressed within 1 minute. The white WPS LED will begin flashing.
- Wait for the white WPS LED on the second DCS Explorer to come on steadily, and then turn off.
- Select and open WiFi settings on the smart device.
- Choose the MTH WiFi network from the smart device's list of wireless networks.
- The smart device should indicate that it is connected to the MTH WiFi network.
- Repeat the above steps for any additional DCS Explorers.

By using this method, these additional DCS Explorers will connect to the DCS Explorer that was set to MTH mode as if it was a router, thus allowing the DCS Application to connect to the additional DCS Explorers though the DCS Explorer that was set up in MTH mode.

Each DCS Application connected to the DCS Explorer in MTH mode would see multiple DCS Explorers as individual units. However, each DCS Application would still impose a limit of 3 DCS engines.

As with the previous method of accessing multiple DCS Explorers from one DCS Application, the major benefit from this method of operation is that a single DCS operator can operate up to three different DCS engines spread across multiple loops of a single layout.

Once again, an important caveat is that the DCS Explorers are in individual mode and each DCS engine is restricted to its own track loop. If the engine should stray to a different loop, the operator would lose control of it until the engine returns to the tracks of the DCS Explorer upon which it was first started up.

6. Using the DCS Explorer With Other DCS Devices

The DCS Explorer may be used in conjunction with a DCS Application; WIU and TIU combination; DCS Remote and TIU combination; DCS Commander; or DCS Remote Commander. It will interoperate with each of these different DCS control devices as long as certain rules are followed.

Operating the DCS Explorer and a WIU/TIU Combination on the Same Layout

The DCS Application on a smartphone or tablet must be set to either WIU or DCS Explorer mode, using the Application Settings screen, as discussed earlier in this section. Once the DCS Application is set to one of these device types, it can only communicate with that device type until the setting is changed.

If both the DCS Explorer and a WIU/TIU combination are to be used simultaneously on the same layout, the following rules must be followed:

- A smartphone or tablet may operate DCS engines via a DCS Explorer or a WIU, but not both, simultaneously.
- If a DCS engine has been added a DCS Application using a DCS Explorer and another DCS Application using a WIU/TIU combination, both DCS Applications may successfully send commands to the same DCS engine as long as the DCS engine is the active engine for both DCS Applications and the engine has the same DCS ID# in both DCS Applications.
- Any TIU channel connected to the same tracks as a DCS Explorer must be connected in Passive TIU Mode.

Operating the DCS Explorer and a DCS Remote/TIU Combination on the Same Layout

If both the DCS Explorer and a DCS Remote/TIU combination are to be used simultaneously on the same layout, the following rules must be followed:

- If a DCS engine has been added to a DCS Application using a DCS Explorer and to a DCS Remote using a TIU channel, both the DCS Application and the DCS Remote may successfully send commands to the same DCS engine as long as the DCS engine is the active engine for the DCS Application and for the DCS Remote, and the engine has the same DCS ID# in both the DCS Application and the DCS Remote.
- Any TIU channel connected to the same tracks as a DCS Explorer must be connected in Passive TIU Mode.

Operating the DCS Explorer and a DCS Commander on the Same Layout

If both the DCS Explorer and a DCS Commander are to be used simultaneously on the same layout, the following rules must be followed:

- If a DCS engine has been added to a DCS Application using a DCS Explorer and to a DCS Commander, both the DCS Application and the DCS Commander may successfully send commands to the same DCS engine as long as the engine is the active engine for the DCS Application and the DCS Commander, and the engines have the same DCS ID# in both the DCS Application and the DCS Commander.
- The DCS Application and the DCS Commander must be connected to different track loops, since both the DCS Explorer and the DCS Commander send power to the tracks, and neither may be connected to the tracks in Passive Mode.

Operating the DCS Explorer and a DCS Remote Commander on the Same Layout

If both the DCS Explorer and a DCS Remote Commander are to be used simultaneously on the same layout, the following rules must be followed:

- The DCS Explorer and the DCS Remote Commander cannot simultaneously operate the same DCS engine. The DCS Explorer can only operate DCS engines that have been added to the DCS Application and have a DCS ID# in the range of 1 to 99. The DCS Remote Commander can only operate engines that have a Factory Settings DCS ID#, which is outside of the range of 1 to 99.
- If any DCS engines are to be operated on the same track by both devices simultaneously, the DCS Remote Commander's receiver must be connected to the track in Passive Mode, without being connected to a power source.

7. Using the DCS Explorer With More Than 3 DCS Engine

The DCS Explorer is often described as being limited to operating no more than 3 DCS engines. However, it turns out that this is not *entirely* accurate.

While it is correct that no more than 3 DCS engines may be **added** to the DCS Explorer's engine roster, the DCS Explorer is fully capable of choosing an engine to operate from a list of as many as 99 DCS engines, numbered between 1 and 99. The "trick" is how to get those engines in the engine roster in the first place. This involves some manipulation and access to a TIU, and either a DCS Remote or a WIU.

The DCS Application is, when operating in WIU mode, capable of importing the contents of a DCS Remote or another DCS Application. This allows the for a procedure to load the DCS Application with as many as 99 DCS engines from which the operator may choose to make active, albeit no more than 3 at a time.

This is accomplished as follows:

1. First, gain access to a TIU and a DCS Remote, or a WIU connected to a TIU. It makes no difference if the TIU is used with a DCS Remote or a WIU.

2. Use DCS to load the DCS Remote or the DCS Application with all of the DCS engines that you would like to have available for use with the DCS Explorer. If using a DCS Application, ensure that the DCS Application is set to WIU mode in its Application Settings Screen, as described in Part XI - The DCS Application's More… Screen, 2. DCS Application Settings Screen, earlier in this book.

3. Launch the DCS Application that is to be used to operate the DCS Explorer. Navigate to its Applications Settings Screen and set its mode to WIU, as described in Part XI - The DCS Application's More… Screen, 2. DCS Application Settings Screen, earlier in this section of the book.

4. If the DCS Application that is to be used with the DCS Explorer is the same one that was used to store all of the DCS engines, skip to step 7.

5. Export the contents of the DCS Remote or the DCS Application, as described in Part IX - Advanced Features and Functions, 8. Import and Export of DCS Application Contents, earlier in this book.

6. Import the exported contents of the DCS Remote or DCS Application into the DCS Application that is to be used with the DCS Explorer, as described in Part IX - Advanced Features and Functions, 8. Import and Export of DCS Application Contents, earlier in this book.

7. Place **up to 3** DCS engines on the tracks. Ensure that these engines are on unpowered tracks that are connected to the DCS Explorer.

8. Power-on the DCS Explorer and connect it to the smartphone or tablet.

9. Launch the DCS Application to be used with the DCS Explorer. Navigate to the Applications Settings Screen and set its mode to DCS Explorer, as described earlier in this section of the book.

10. Navigate to the Engine Control Screen and tap the Refresh button. Then, tap on the Engine Roster button to view the engines that were previously imported. If the engines that you want to operate are in the Inactive Engine List, pull down on the Engine Roster Screen to refresh the engine list and move the engines that are on powered tracks to the Active Engine List.

Operate the DCS Explorer using those engines that are in the Active Engine List.

If you decide to operate other engines that are in the Inactive Engine List, turn off power to those that you won't be using, turn on power to those that you desire to use, and refresh the Engine Roster Screen. The engines on powered tracks will become active and those on unpowered tracks will become inactive.

No more than 3 engines should be powered on at any time that you refresh the DCS Application.

Appendix A: TIU Hardware Revisions

TIU Model	Indication	Processor	Differences
Rev. G	No indication	5 volt	Common (black) terminals of all TIU channels are internally connected
Rev. H	Label or heat stamp, H, possibly followed by a digit	5 volt	Common (black) terminals of all TIU channels are not internally connected Internal fuses for each channel Heavier traces Additional signal generator protection Requires DCS 3.1 or higher to operate
Rev. I	Label or heat stamp, I, possibly followed by a single digit or a digit and a letter	3 volt	Common (black) terminals of all TIU channels are not internally connected Internal fuses for each channel Heavier traces Additional signal generator protection Compatible with DCS 1.87 Loader program or newer
Rev. L	Label or heat stamp, L, possibly followed by a single digit or a digit and a letter	3 volt	Common (black) terminals of all TIU channels are not internally connected Internal fuses for each channel Heavier traces Additional signal generator protection Compatible with DCS 2.00 Loader program or newer Has an additional USB port Has an FPGA (Field Programmable Gate Array) chip rather than an ASIC (Application Specific Integrated Circuit) for much faster communication and improved DCS signal Strength

For those who want to purchase a new DCS set, or an additional TIU, and want to be sure to get a new Rev. L TIU, the only way to know the TIU's model is to look at the TIU itself. The new Type B female USB port is located on the short side of the TIU between the ProtoDispatch (MIC) port and the Proto-Cast port. There is also a sticker on the underside of the case that says Rev. L.

Appendix B: The Truth About DCS Engine ID Numbers

First, it's necessary to dispel a myth: there is no engine ID# of 0. DCS engines come from the factory with an internal ID# of 1 and a DCS Factory Reset changes the engine's ID# back to 1. The following explanation regarding the way in which DCS manipulates the engine ID# is provided for those readers who are interested in how DCS works, as might be said, "under the hood." The DCS engine numbering scheme works in the following way.

DCS always places an ID# in a DCS engine that is one greater than the ID# that it displays for the engine in the DCS Application, i.e., if one adds a DCS engine to a DCS Application and the engine adds as ID# 11, the number written into the DCS engine's memory is actually 12. This causes DCS ID#s that display in the DCS Application from 1-99 to actually be resident in DCS engines as 2-100. That's also why DCS ID# 99 is a special case - it's actually in the engine as 100, the only 3-digit internal DCS engine ID# number. This causes unique issues when using engines with DCS ID# 99.

First, at the present time DCS will not add a DCS engine to DCS ID#99, even if it is the only remaining DCS ID# available in the DCS Application. If, however, a DCS engine has its DCS ID# changed to 99 from some other DCS ID# by using the DCS Application's edit function, it will operate properly as DCS ID#99.

If, at some later time, that engine is deleted from the DCS Application, it will not be able to be added back into any DCS Application. In order to be able to re-add that engine to a DCS Application, either one of the following must be done.

If the original DCS Application that contained the engine with DCS ID# 99 was previously exported to a PC (refer to Part IX - Advanced Features and Functions, 7. Import and Export of DCS Application Contents, Exporting the DCS Application's Contents earlier in this book), then the backup file must be reloaded into the DCS Application and then used to do a Factory Reset of the engine. This will restore the DCS engine's DCS ID# to its Factory Default so that it may be re-added to a DCS Application.

If an export file of the DCS Application is not available, a different engine must be added to the DCS Application and edited to be DCS ID# 99. Then, the DCS Application must be exported to a PC. Next, the DCS Application can be used to perform a Factory Reset of the engine just changed to DCS ID#99. Finally, the procedure above can be used to restore the DCS Application's export file that contains DCS ID#99 into the DCS Application, and perform a Factory Reset of the original engine with DCS ID#99.

Further, this also explains why one cannot place a new DCS engine, or one that has just been Factory Reset, on the track and run it under DCS using an entry in the DCS Application for DCS ID# 1. In this case, the DCS Application is looking for an engine that has an internal ID# of 2.

Appendix C: DCS Engine Acceleration and Deceleration

Although an O gauge mile is actually 1/48 of an actual mile, or 110 feet, an actual minute and an actual second are the same in the real world as they are in the world of O gauge model railroading.

Velocity, or speed, is generally measured in miles per hour while acceleration and deceleration are measured as "miles per hour, per second." In the world of DCS, we substitute scale miles per hour for miles per hour. Therefore, DCS acceleration and deceleration are statements of the rate at which a DCS engine's speed, in scale miles per hour (SMPH), is changing each second.

Therefore, a train moving at 10 miles per hour that then decelerates at a rate of 2 miles per hour, per second, would behave as follows:

- After 1 second it would have slowed to 8 miles/hour
- After 2 seconds it would be moving at 6 miles per hour
- After 3 seconds it would be moving at 4 miles per hour
- After 4 seconds it would be moving at 2 miles per hour
- After 5 seconds it would be stopped

Similarly, a train at rest that accelerates at a speed of 2 miles per hour per second would behave as follows:

- After 1 second it would be moving at 2 mph
- After 2 seconds it would be moving at 4 mph
- After 3 seconds it would be moving at 6 mph
- After 4 seconds it would be moving at 8 mph
- After 5 seconds it would be moving at 10 mph

The same train at rest, if accelerated at 10 miles per hour, per second, would reach 30 mph after 3 seconds.

Appendix D: More Than 100 Command Control Engines

Although DCS is a full-featured system with a great many features, one of its limiting factors is that all commands control engines must have DCS ID numbers between 1 and 99. Further, even though TMCC and Legacy engines use a completely different numbering scheme for their engine addresses, they still occupy numbers in the same 1-99 range, further limiting the number of engines that may be present in a DCS Application's engine roster.

However, with the movement away from the DCS Remote to the DCS Application as a method for operating DCS engines comes an opportunity, due to the much greater resources of a smart device over the DCS Remote, to expand the range of numbers of DCS engines beyond the current 1-99 limit. However, in the mean time, the 99 engine limit remains.

The good news is that, using the DCS Application's import/export feature, there is now a workaround solution of sorts to allow increasing the number of engines that DCS can use.

The key to implementing this workaround solution is to have available, in the smart device, multiple sets of DCS engines. These engine sets can then be imported into the DCS Application in a matter of seconds, without the necessity of using a personal computer or any other device external to the device upon which the DCS Application is resident.

To implement this solution, first become familiar with the instructions in Part IX - Advanced Features and Functions, 8. Import and Export of DCS Application Contents, earlier in this book as regards importing and exporting DCS Application contents and DCS Remote backup files. Refer to this section as need while implanting the solution below.

Now, proceed as follows:

- Start by loading the DCS Application with items from the layout. This should include all of the layout's accessories, switch tracks, TIU Tracks, Routes, and Scenes, plus a group of uniquely-numbered DCS, TMCC and Legacy engines. It's suggested to keep DCS ID# 1 vacant for adding additional engines later on. Note that it's also permissible to import a previously saved backup file from a DCS Remote as the initial contents for the DCS Application.
- Then, following the instructions in Part IX of this book, export the contents of the DCS Application as an E-mail attachment. Make sure to send the E-mail using an E-mail address that can be received by the E-mail application on the smart device.
- Receive the E-mail on the smart device. However, do not attempt to open the attached export file.
- Next, delete some or all of the engines in the DCS Application. Leave present in the DCS Application's Engine Roster those engine that you most frequently operate. Refer to Part VII - Engine Operation Using the DCS Application, 1. DCS Application Engine Operation Screens, DCS Application Edit Engine Roster Screen earlier in this book. The engines deleted should be those that are less frequently selected for operation.
- Now, add additional DCS, TMCC, or Legacy engines to the DCS Application. These engines will reuse those DCS ID#'s that were made available in the previous step. Lashups may also be included.
- When you've added as many additional engines as desired, including any lashups, export the contents of the DCS Application once again.

Repeat the above steps as many times as necessary to create multiple export files, containing all of your command control engines, as attachments in the smart device's E-mail application. Further, multiple smart devices can all have, all of the same E-mails with different export files attached. This allows nearly unlimited flexibility of use of multiple smart devices.

It's recommended to use each smart device's E-mail application to create an E-mail folder, separate from the E-mail application's Inbox, as a place to store all of the E-mails with their attached DCS Application export and DCS Remote backup files.

When it's time to operate the layout, import whichever attached file from the several E-mail attachments present in the smart device's E-mail application, that has the engines and/or lashups that you desire to be operate. Note that all of the attached files will also contain all of the layout's accessories, switch tracks, TIU Tracks, Routes, and Scenes.

The only caveat is that each engine that is to be operated must be the only one with its DCS ID# that's on a powered track. Lashups must also consist of engines whose DCS ID#'s are not duplicated among engines that are receiving power.

Further, multiple smart devices can all have, all of the same E-mails with different export files attached. This allows nearly unlimited flexibility of use of multiple smart devices.

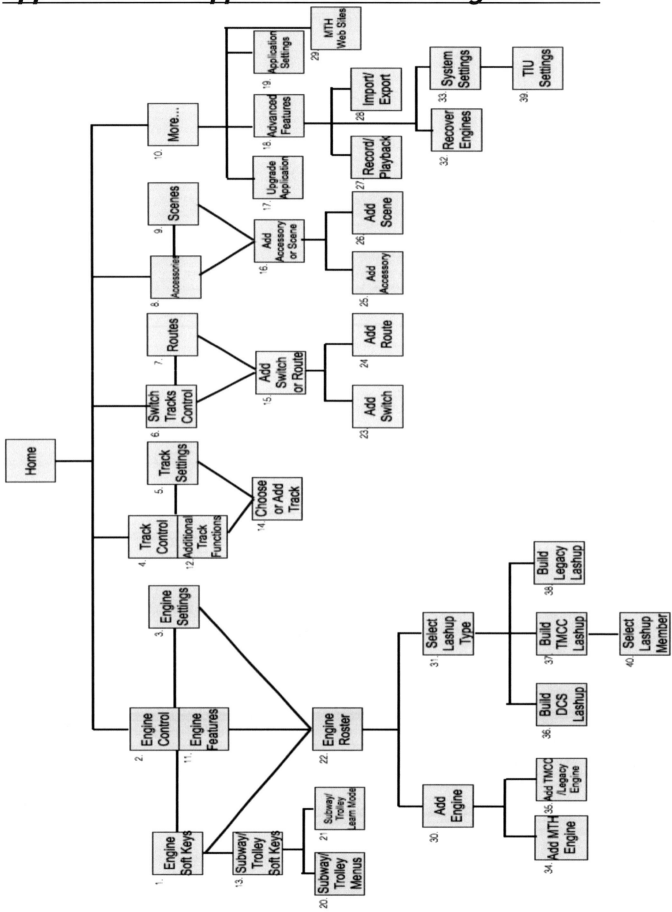

Use the following list of DCS Application screen names and each name's associated index number to locate the desired screen in the tree. It should then be evident how that screen may be accessed.

Screen Name	Index #
Accessories	8
Add Accessory	25
Add Accessory or Scene	16
Add Engine	30
Add MTH Engine	34
Add Route	24
Add Scene	26
Add Switch	23
Add Switch or Route	15
Add TMCC/Legacy Engine	35
Additional Track Functions	12
Advanced Features	18
Application Settings	19
Build DCS Lashup	36
Build Legacy Lashup	38
Build TMCC Lashup	37
Choose or Add Track	14
Engine Control	2
Engine Features	11
Engine Roster	22
Engine Settings	3
Engine Soft Keys	1
Import/Export	28
More...	10
MTH Web Sites	29
Record/Playback	27
Recover Engines	32
Routes	7
Scenes	9
Select Lashup Member	40
Select Lashup Type	31
Subway/Trolley Learn Mode	21
Subway/Trolley Menus	20
Subway/Trolley Soft Keys	13
Switch Track Control	6
System Settings	33
TIU Settings	39
Track Control	4
Track Settings	5
Upgrade Application	17

Appendix F: TMCC and Legacy

The DCS Remote has the ability to control TMCC engines, or Legacy engines in TMCC mode, provided that any Lionel command base is connected to one of the layout's TIUs. The Premium version of the DCS Application adds the ability to control Legacy engines in full Legacy mode.

The following discussion describes how to use the Premium version of MTH's DCS Application to control TMCC and Legacy engines, connect the required TMCC or Legacy components to a DCS layout, and some considerations regarding the DCS Application's ability to control TMCC and Legacy engines.

1. Adding Control of TMCC or Legacy Engines to DCS

DCS is a two-way data communications system where TIUs send commands consisting of data packets to DCS engines on the center (AC Hot) track rail and listen for acknowledgement data packets from the DCS engine on the outside (AC Common) track rails.

Lionel's Train Master Command Control (TMCC) and Legacy control systems are one-way communications systems that send commands to TMCC or Legacy engines by using the outside track rails as a transmitting radio antenna. Each TMCC or Legacy engine has a receiving antenna to accept commands.

Since these two schemes are very different in this and other ways, DCS and TMCC/Legacy control systems can easily coexist very well on the same layout. This allows O gauge layout operators to have the best of all possible worlds by operating DCS, TMCC and Legacy engines on the same layout.

TMCC or Legacy, when added to a DCS layout, can operate in one of two ways. The first is by using the Lionel TMCC Cab-1 or Legacy Cab-2 remote controls to control TMCC engines and Legacy engines. The second is by using the DCS Application to control TMCC and Legacy engines. Neither method precludes use of the other method.

Note that if it is desired to control Legacy engines, in Legacy mode, from the DCS Application, it is required that a that a Lionel Legacy command base and a Lionel SER2 module be installed. Refer to the following section, 2. Controlling Legacy Engines from the DCS Application, for instructions and connection diagrams.

Additional Devices Required for TMCC or Legacy Engine Operation

Since the DCS TIU does not contain the hardware components to communicate directly with a TMCC or Legacy engine, it's necessary that a Lionel TMCC command base, Base-1L or Legacy command base be added to the layout, regardless of which method of controlling TMCC or Legacy engines is selected.

If the Cab-1, Cab-1L or Cab-2 control method is selected, a Lionel Cab-1, Cab-1L or Cab-2 remote control is required in addition to the TMCC, Base-1L or Legacy command base. If the DCS Application control method is selected, an MTH cable is required to connect the TIU and the Lionel command base together. Depending upon which Lionel command base is being connected, the appropriate cable is required. To be useable, a Cab-1, Cab-1L or Cab-2 remote control requires the inclusion of its companion command base.

At the present time, there are three MTH cables that may be used to connect to a Lionel command base. The three cables are:

- #50-1018 TIU/TMCC 6' Connector Cable may be used only to connect the TIU to a Lionel TMCC command base.
- #50-1007 TIU/TMCC 6' Connector Cable may be used only to connect the TIU to a Lionel Legacy command base or a Lionel Cab-1L command base.
- #50-1032 TIU/TMCC-Legacy 6' Connector Cable may be used to connect the TIU to a Lionel TMCC command base, a Lionel Cab-1L command base or a Lionel Legacy command base.

For the following discussions in this Appendix, if there is a Lionel LCS module plugged into the Legacy command base's serial port, MTH cable #50-1007 or #50-1032 may not be plugged into the serial port. Instead, a Lionel SER2 module is required and the cable must be plugged into its serial port. Refer to the following section, 2. Controlling Legacy Engines from the DCS Application, for instructions and connection diagrams.

Further, when connecting a Rev. L TIU to a Lionel command base or SER2 module, the WIU is typically connected to the TIU using the USB cable supplied with the WIU. This leaves the TIU's serial port available for connecting with the command base or SER2 module. However, if a TIU other than a Rev. L is used, connect the TIU's serial port to both the WIU and the other device using a 9-pin, serial "Y" cable that has 1 male port and 2 female ports. This cable is inexpensive and should be available from any computer store or from Amazon.com.

Wiring for TMCC Engine Control (Only)

The following wiring methods allow control of TMCC engines, and Legacy engines that are configured as TMCC engines. If complete control of Legacy engines is desired, use the connection diagrams described in the following section 2. Controlling Legacy Engines from the DCS Application.

Regardless of the method of TMCC control chosen, a Lionel command base is wired by connecting its "one wire" to each loop of tracks upon which it is desired to operate TMCC or Legacy engines, as instructed in the command base's documentation.

Alternately, the command base's "one wire" can be attached to the Common connection of all of the TIU's channel's terminal blocks. If this method is used, it's important to note that only the original, Rev. G, TIU has the Common terminals of all channels connected internally and later revisions of the TIU do not. If a TIU other than a Rev. G is used, a Common connection of all of the TIU's channel's terminal blocks should be connected together, and to the command base, to ensure that the TMCC signal is present on all channels.

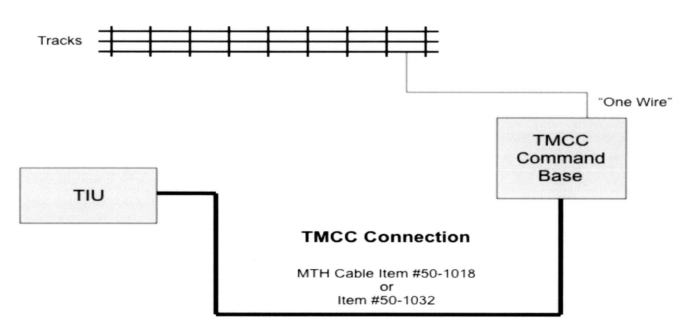

Figure F1 - Wiring for TMCC Operation Using a TMCC Command Base

Another alternative is to connect the command base's "one wire" to any one TIU's channel's terminal block, as long as all of the transformers that are providing power to TIU channels are in phase and have one of their Common terminals connected to a Common terminal of all other track power transformers.

It is not recommended that the "one wire" be connected directly to Common (black) terminal of a TIU input channel. This would pass the TMCC or Legacy signal directly through the TIU channel's DCS signal generator, and no good can possibly come from that.

If control of TMCC engines from the DCS Application is desired, the MTH cable is connected between the serial port on the TIU and the serial port on a Lionel command base. If both TMCC and Legacy command bases are to be connected to the layout, the TIU is connected to the Legacy command base.

Regardless, if the TMCC and Legacy command bases are both to be connected to a TIU, only the "one wire" from the Legacy command base should be connected as described above, and only one command base is ever connected to one DCS TIU.

Connecting DCS to a TMCC command base

If the DCS TIU is connected to only the TMCC command base, the MTH cable used is either MTH item #50-1018, TIU/TMCC 6' Connector Cable or #50-1032 TIU/TMCC-Legacy 6' Connector Cable. The above diagram illustrates how the DCS TIU is connected only to a TMCC command base.

When connected this way, with the Legacy Base "one wire" connected to an outside rail, the following operation is possible:

• The DCS Application will operate all DCS, TMCC and conventional engines in their respective modes, and will operate Legacy engines in TMCC mode. The Legacy engines must be configured in the DCS Application as TMCC engines.
• The Cab-1 will operate TMCC engines and Legacy engines in TMCC mode.

Connecting DCS to a Legacy command base

If the DCS TIU is connected to only the Legacy command base or the Base-1L command base, the MTH cable used is either MTH item #50-1007, TIU/TMCC 6' Connector Cable or #50-1032 TIU/TMCC-Legacy 6' Connector Cable. The following diagram illustrates how the DCS TIU is connected only to a Legacy command base.

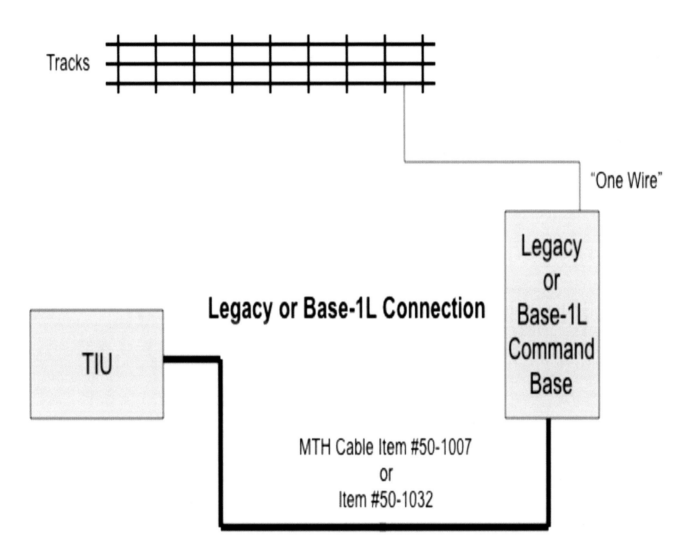

Figure F2 - Wiring for TMCC or Legacy Operation Using a Legacy or Base-1L Command Base

When connected this way, with the Legacy Base "one wire" connected to an outside rail, the following operation is possible:

- The DCS Application will operate all DCS, TMCC and conventional engines in their respective modes, and will operate Legacy engines in TMCC mode. The Legacy engines must be configured in the DCS Application as TMCC engines.
- The Cab-1 will operate TMCC engines and Legacy engines in TMCC mode.
- The Cab-1L will operate TMCC engines and Legacy engines in Legacy mode.

Connecting DCS to both TMCC and Legacy command bases

If the DCS TIU is connected to both the Legacy command base and also the TMCC command base, the MTH cable used is MTH item #50-1007 TIU/TMCC 6' Connector Cable or, preferably, MTH item #50-1032 TIU/TMCC-Legacy 6' Connector Cable, and the Legacy-supplied "Y" cable is also required. The following diagram illustrates how the DCS TIU is connected to a Legacy command base, and also a TMCC command base.

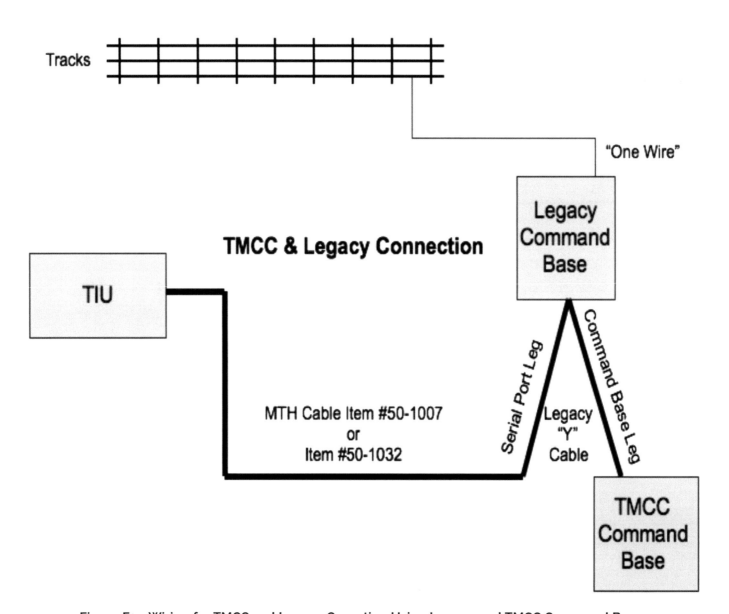

Figure F3 - Wiring for TMCC and Legacy Operation Using Legacy and TMCC Command Bases

When connected this way, with the Legacy Base "one wire" connected to an outside rail, the following operation is possible:

- The DCS Application will operate all DCS, TMCC and conventional engines in their respective modes, and will operate Legacy engines in TMCC mode. The Legacy engines must be configured in the DCS Application as TMCC engines.
- The Cab-1 or Cab-1L will operate TMCC engines and Legacy engines in TMCC mode.
- The Cab-2 will operate TMCC engines in TMCC mode and Legacy engines in Legacy mode.

The DCS WIFI Companion

2. *Controlling Legacy Engines from the DCS Application*

The Premium version of the DCS Application allows control of Lionel Legacy engines in Legacy mode with the use of all Legacy features. To do so, however, requires more than just connecting a TIU's serial port to the serial port of a Lionel Legacy command base.

While this simple connection allows operating TMCC engines in full TMCC modes, it will not allow full control of Legacy engines because the Legacy command base does not accept Legacy commands via the command base's serial port.

If the normal TIU to command base serial connection is utilized, only the following control of TMCC or Legacy engines is possible using the DCS Application:

- TMCC engines may be operated in full TMCC mode.
- Legacy engines defined as TMCC engines in the DCS Application may be operated as TMCC engines with full TMCC control.
- Legacy engines defined as Legacy engines may be added to the DCS Application and started up and shut down, and their basic, TMCC-like features and functions may be used. However, they will not accept commands to move forward or reverse, and some Legacy-only features, such as the quilling whistle, may not work.

This is because Legacy-specific commands are not accepted through the Legacy command base's serial port. This includes Legacy speed commands, which are different from TMCC speed commands. Fortunately, there is a solution to this problem.

There are two ways to implement full control of Legacy engines from the Premium version of the DCS Application. Which solution is appropriate depends upon whether or not Lionel's WiFi solution, LCS, has already been implemented on the layout.

The devices and cables involved in the solution may include any of the following:

- Always required is *either* an MTH #50-1007 TIU/TMCC 6' Connector Cable *or* an MTH #50-1032 TIU/TMCC-Legacy 6' Connector Cable, but not both, to connect the TIU to a Lionel Legacy command base. **The MTH #50-1032 is preferred.**
- If already present, a Lionel product 6-81325 LCS WiFi Module will be utilized.
- The Lionel product 6-81326 SER2 Module is always required.
- If not already present, a Lionel 6-81499 LCS DB-9 Cable With Power Supply will be required.
- If a Lionel 6-81325 LCS WiFi Module is already present, then a Lionel LCS PDI Cable will be required.

The components and cables described above are shown in the figures below.

Figure F4 - MTH #50-1032 TIU/TMCC-Legacy 6' Connector Cable

Figure F5 - Lionel 6-81325 LCS WiFi Module

Figure F6 - Lionel 6-81326 SER2 WiFi Module

The DCS WIFI Companion

Figure F7 - Lionel 6-81499 LCS DB-9 Cable With Power Supply

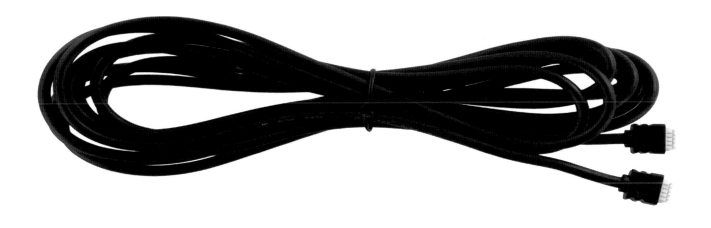

Figure F8 - Lionel PDI Cable

Implementing DCS Application Legacy Control if LCS is Installed

If LCS is already installed on the layout, the solution is to connect a Lionel product number 6-81326 SER2 Module to the existing Lionel product number 6-81325 LCS WiFi Module, using a Lionel LCS PDI cable. These PDI cables come in 1', 3' 10', and 20' lengths (product numbers 6-81500, 6-81501, 6-81502, and 6-81503, respectively), and the PDI cable only needs to be long enough to connect the LCS and SER2 modules.

The MTH #50-1032 cable then is connected between the TIU's serial port and the SER2's serial port.

The figure below describes exactly how the connections are made.

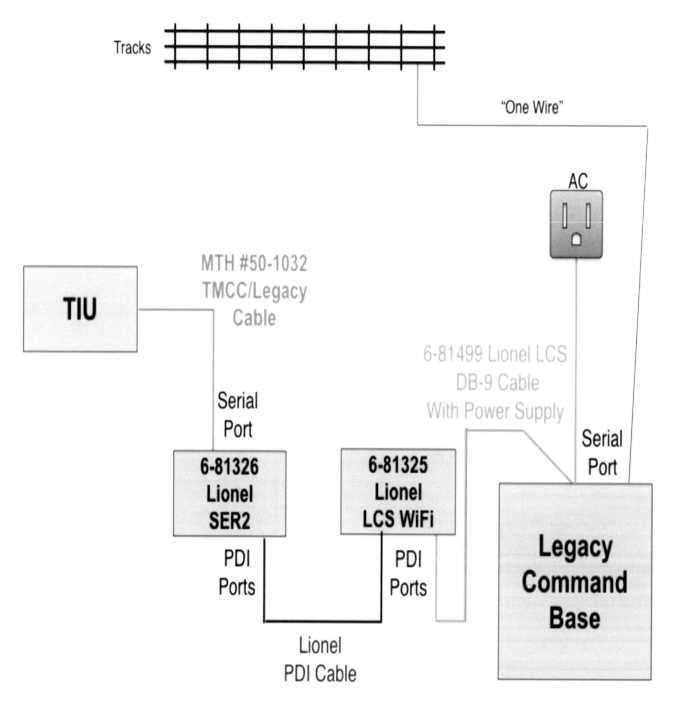

Figure F9 - Implementing DCS Application Legacy Control if LCS is Installed

Implementing DCS Application Legacy Control if LCS is Not Installed

If an LCS Module is not already installed on the layout and it isn't desired to install one, the solution is to connect a Lionel product 6-81326 SER2 Module directly to the Legacy command base using a Lionel 6-81499 LCS DB-9 Cable With Power Supply.

The MTH #50-1032 cable then is connected between the TIU's serial port and the SER2's serial port.

The figure below describes exactly how the connections are made.

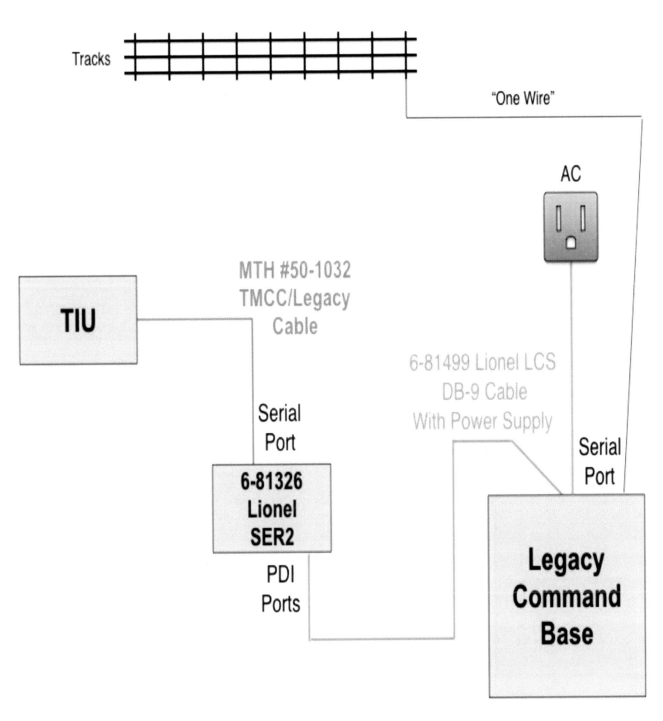

Figure F10 - Implementing DCS Application Legacy Control if LCS is Not Installed

3. Considerations for Control of TMCC and Legacy Engines Using the DCS Application

TMCC and Legacy engines are controlled in the same manner as DCS engines using the DCS Application. They are selected from the Active Engine List and operated from the Engine Control Screen. However, there are a few caveats of which the DCS operator should be aware.

Refreshing the Engine Roster

Whenever the Refresh button is tapped, or the Engine Roster Screen is pulled down, the DCS Application refreshes the Engine Roster by sorting all DCS, TMCC and Legacy engines according to the following rules:

- If a DCS engine is on a powered track, it will go into the Active Engine List.
- If a DCS engine is not on a powered track, it will go into the Inactive Engine List.
- All TMCC and Legacy engines, regardless of whether or not they are on powered tracks, will go into the Inactive Engine List.

This leads DCS Application operators to believe that, in order to operate a Legacy or TMCC engine that is in the Inactive Engine List, it's necessary to delete and re-add the engine. However, this is not the case at all. Rather, to operate a TMCC or Legacy engine that is in the Inactive Engine List, proceed as follows:

- Ensure that the TMCC or Legacy engine is on a powered track.
- Tap Edit at the top of the Engine Roster Screen.
- For iOS devices, move the parallel bars icon to the right of the engine's name, to move the engine up into the Active Engine List.
- For Android devices, tap the up-arrow icon to the right of the engine's name, to move the engine up into the Active Engine List.
- Tap Done at the top of the Engine Roster Screen.
- Return to the Engine Control Screen, where the TMCC or Legacy engine is now the Active Engine.

Importing Legacy Engines From a DCS Remote's Back File

When a DCS Remote's backup file is imported into the DCS Application, any Legacy engines that were present in the backup file are added to the Inactive Engine List, as are TMCC engines. However, since the DCS Remote is not capable of recognizing Legacy engines as being any different from TMCC engines, the Legacy engines are added to the DCS Application's Inactive Engine List as TMCC engines.

If these Legacy engines are to be operated as TMCC engines, nothing further is required. However, if the DCS operator desires to use the DCS Application to operate the Legacy engines in full Legacy mode, they must be deleted from the DCS Application and re-added as Legacy engines.

Refer to The DCS WiFi Companion 1st Edition, Part VII - Engine Operation Using the DCS Application, 1. DCS Application Engine Operation Screens, DCS Application Edit Engine Roster Screen and DCS Application Add Engine Screen, respectively, to delete and add the engines.

Changing a TMCC or Legacy Engine's DCS ID#

Although the Engine Settings Screen for TMCC or Legacy engines doesn't allow the DCS operator to change the DCS ID# of TMCC or Legacy engines, it is still possible to get a TMCC or Legacy engine into whatever DCS ID# in the DCS Application's engine roster that is desired, through a little planning before attempting to add the engine.

To get the TMCC or Legacy engine into a particular DCS ID#, proceed as follows:

- First, use the Engine Settings Screen for TMCC or Legacy engines (refer to The DCS WiFi Companion 1st Edition, Part VII - Engine Operation Using the DCS Application, 1. DCS Application Engine Operation Screens, DCS Application Add Engine Screen) to put "imaginary", nonexistent TMCC or Legacy engine entries into the DCS Application to act as placeholders and use up the space between the first open DCS ID#, which is where DCS wants to put the next TMCC or Legacy engine to be added, and the DCS ID# where the engine is actually desired to be placed.

- Enter the name of the imaginary engine as a fictitious engine name, such as "Imaginary # 1", "Imaginary # 2", etc.

- Enter the engine's TMCC address as "1". After adding enough imaginary engine entries to get to the desired DCS ID#, add the "real" TMCC or Legacy engine so that it gets into the next available DCS ID#.

- After you've added your "real" TMCC or Legacy engine, delete all of the imaginary engines (refer to The DCS WiFi Companion 1st Edition, Part VII - Engine Operation Using the DCS Application, 1. DCS Application Engine Operation Screens, DCS Application Edit Engine Roster Screen) to regain the DCS ID#'s that were temporarily used by the imaginary engine entries.

Appendix G: Power Control Tracks

The DCS Remote has the ability to control TMCC engines, or Legacy engines in TMCC mode, provided that any Lionel command base is connected to one of the layout's TIUs. The Premium version of the DCS Application adds the ability to control Legacy engines in full Legacy mode.

There's little argument that the DCS Application is more capable than the DCS Remote as regards its feature and functions set. However, there's one function that, regrettably, it cannot Implement. That function is Z4K Tracks. The reason that the DCS Application cannot implement Z4K Tracks is due to the differences between how the DCS Remote and smart devices communicate.

The DCS Remote communicates with TIUs using the 900 MHz frequency band. This is the same frequency that the Z4000 Remote Commander receiver uses to receive commands to adjust power in the Z4000 transformer. The DCS Application, however, communicates with WIUs at WiFi frequencies, i.e., 2.4 GHz. Therefore, the DCS Application cannot communicate directly with a Z4000 Remote Commander receiver. Unless and until MTH develops a new Z4000 receiver that can communicate at 2.4 GHz, or some other frequency conversion device, the DCS Application is unable to support the Implementation of Z4K Tracks.

If it's important to the DCS operator to be able to turn power on or off to one or more TIU channels from the DCS Application, there is a method by which this may be accomplished. However, it isn't complete channel power management since power can only be turned on or off and not adjusted up and down. Each track that is to be controlled in this manner will be called a Power Control Track.

1. Devices Required

This is an expensive workaround since it involves replacing the layout's Z4000 transformers with different fixed-voltage power supplies.

First, suitable power supplies must be obtained, two such power supplies for each Z4000 to be replaced. If the operator desires to have equivalent power available for each channel that was previously powered by one side of a Z4000, a 180 watt, 18 volt "brick" transformer is required. A good choice would be the Lionel 6-22983 180 Watt Powerhouse Power Supply. If a little less power is required, an MTH #40-1000A Brick could possibly suffice.

In addition to replacing the Z4000 transformers with "brick" transformers, it's also necessary to acquire one single or double pole, on/off relay that is capable to handling 10 amps of continuous power, as well as a power source for each relay.

Lastly, one AIU accessory port must be available for each TIU channel to be managed.

2. Connections

Connect the components as follows, one set for each Power Control Track:

- Connect the Hot output of the brick transformer to the input of the relay.
- Connect the output of the relay to the Hot input of a TIU channel.
- Connect the Common output of the brick transformer to the Common input of the same TIU channel.
- Connect the Hot output of the same TIU channel to the Hot input of a terminal block, or directly to the center rail of a track.
- Connect the Common output of the same TIU channel to the Common input of a terminal block, or directly to an outside rail of a track.
- Connect an AIU to the TIU.
- Connect the "I" terminal of an AIU's ACC port to one of the coil activation terminals of the relay.

- Connect the "IN" terminal of the same AIU's ACC port o the the other coil activation terminal of the relay.
- Connect the two terminals of the relay coil power to the two terminals for relay coil power on the relay.

The diagram below shows the wire connections.

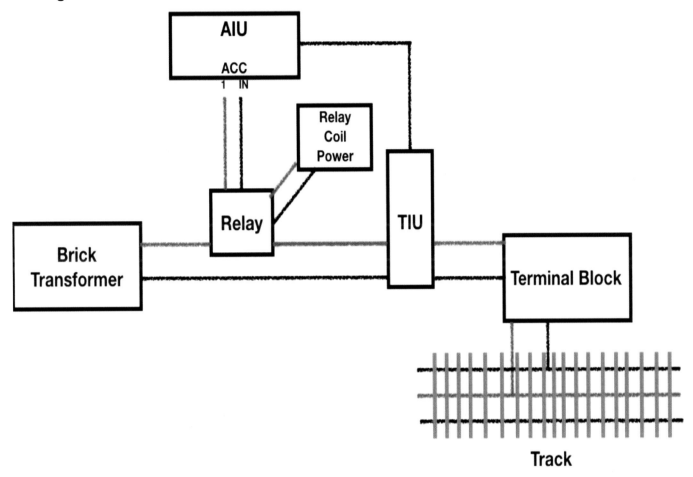

3. Create the Power Control Tracks

To implement a Power Control Track, create an accessory entry using the DCS Application's Accessory Control Screen. Refer to Part VIII - Accessory and Switch Track Control, 4. Adding and Controlling Accessories earlier in this book.

Repeat the above connectors and accessory entry for each additional Power Control Track.

If it's desired to turn on and off some or all of the Power Control Tracks as a group, create a Scene using the desired power Control Track accessory entries. Refer to Part IX - Advanced Features and Functions, 6. Scenes, Creating a Scene earlier in this book.

If it's desired to also use a DCS Remote to operate the layout, this can be accomplished by entering the accessories and Scenes into the DCS Remote.

4. Using the Power Control Tracks

To turn on power for a TIU channel where a Power Control Track has been created, navigate to the DCS Application's Accessory Control Screen, select the accessory that is the Power Control Track for that TIU channel and tap the On button. To turn power off for that TIU channel, tap the Off button.

Similarly, to turn on power for a group of TIU channels where Power Control Tracks have been created, navigate to the DCS Application's Scene Control Screen, select the Scene that is for the group of Power Control Tracks for those TIU channels and tap the On button. To turn power off for that group of TIU channels, tap the Off button.

Appendix H: DCS Application on a Kindle

A question that is asked frequently is "can the DCS Application be installed on a Kindle tablet?" The answer is "yes", however, there are a few caveats of which to be aware:

- *The installation of the DCS Application on a Kindle tablet is neither sanctioned nor supported by MTH. This means that, if you attempt the installation as described below and something goes awry, you're completely on your own.*
- *This process has not been tested on a small number of Kindle devices.*
- *There are no warranties or guarantees, expressed or implied, that the following process will work for you or your device in any way, shape or form.*
- *The author is not advocating this installation and accepts no responsibility for any issues that may arise out of attempting such an implementation.*

If you're still interested, read on!

What's been accomplished is that my son, Allan Broskowitz, was able to install the DCS Application on a Kindle Fire 5th Generation tablet using Fire OS 5.6.0.1. Subsequently, I installed the DCS Application on a Kindle Fire 7th Generation tablet using Fire OS 5.4.0.1. We were able to accomplish this in two ways:

- By installing a copy of the Android version of the DCS Application that was previously upgraded to the Premium version.
- By installing the free copy of the Android version of the DCS Application and then upgrading it to the Premium version.

The DCS Application that was installed worked with both the WIU and also with the DCS Explorer.

The following process involves first downloading the Google Play Store application to the Kindle tablet and then using the Google Play Store application to download the DCS Application itself and, if necessary, to perform an in-app upgrade of the free, Basic version of the DCS Application to either the Standard version of the DCS Application or the premium version of the DCS Application.

To install the DCS Application on the Kindle tablet, proceed as follows:

- On the Kindle tablet's Home screen, tap on the Kindle Play Store application and download the free ES File Explorer Manager application.
- On the Kindle tablet, tap on Settings, then tap on Security and enable the option to download "Apps from Unknown Sources".

Next, on the Kindle tablet's Home screen, tap on the Kindle Silk web browser application and download each of the following four APK files from their associated web addresses. Note that the following web addresses are quite long and may prove difficult to enter correctly. It might be a good idea to first key them into a text document or E-mail, and then copy and paste them into the Silk web browser's address line.

If after downloading a file, you are offered an option to Open the downloaded file, do so. This will install the file.

The four APK files to download are as follows:

- Google Account Manager 5.1-1743759

    https://www.apkmirror.com/apk/google-inc/google-account-manager/google-account-manager-5-1-1743759-release/google-account-manager-5-1-1743759-android-apk-download/

- Google Services Framework 5.1-1743759

    https://www.apkmirror.com/apk/google-inc/google-services-framework/google-services-framework-5-1-1743759-release/google-services-framework-5-1-1743759-android-apk-download/

- Google Play Services 11.5.09 (230-164803921)

  https://www.apkmirror.com/apk/google-inc/google-play-services/google-play-services-11-5-09-release/google-play-services-11-5-09-230-164803921-android-apk-download/

  NOTE: If you have a Fire HD 8 or HD 10, 2017 (7th Generation) Kindle tablet, use the following APK below instead of the one above.

  https://www.apkmirror.com/apk/google-inc/google-play-services/google-play-services-11-5-09-release/google-play-services-11-5-09-240-164803921-android-apk-download/

- Google Play Store 8.3.41.U-all [0] [FP] 170066753

  https://www.apkmirror.com/apk/google-inc/google-play-store/google-play-store-8-3-41-release/google-play-store-8-3-41-u-all-0-fp-170066753-android-apk-download/

After downloading the APK files, if any of the files were not opened (installed) by the Kindle Silk web browser application, tap on the ES File Explorer Manager application on the Home screen to install any such files. Then:

- Tap on the Google Play Store application on the Kindle's Home screen.
- Log in to the Google Play Store and search for the DCS Application. A good search term to use is "mth dcs wifi".
- Download and install the DCS Application.

You can now tap on the DCS Application on the Kindle's Home screen and use it to operate your trains as if you were using it on a standard Android smartphone or tablet.

Index

67407412R00135

Made in the USA
Columbia, SC
26 July 2019